EQUALITY
and
DIVERSITY

Phenomenological
Investigations of Prejudice
and Discrimination

EQUALITY

and

DIVERSITY

MICHAEL D. BARBER

Humanity
Books

an imprint of Prometheus Books
59 John Glenn Drive, Amherst, New York 14228-2197

Published 2001 by Humanity Books, an imprint of Prometheus Books

Inquiries should be addressed to
Humanity Books
59 John Glenn Drive
Amherst, New York 14228–2197
VOICE: 716–691–0133, ext. 207
FAX: 716–564–2711
WWW.PROMETHEUSBOOKS.COM

05 04 03 02 01   5 4 3 2 1

Library of Congress Cataloging-in-Publication Data

Barber, Michael D., 1949–
    Equality and diversity : phenomenological investigations of prejudice and discrimination / Michael D. Barber.
        p. cm.
    Includes bibliographical references and index.
    ISBN 1-57392-651-5 (cloth : alk. paper)
    1. Prejudices—Philosophy. 2. Discrimination—Philosophy.
3. Phenomenological sociology. I. Title.

HM1091 .B37 2000
303.3'85'01—dc21   00–052988

Printed in the United States of America on acid-free paper

To the Leo Brown Community

CONTENTS

ACKNOWLEDGMENTS

I would like to thank Eduardo Mendieta for his critical comments on this book and Keith Ashfield and Eugene O'Connor for their continued encouragement. I am grateful, too, for discussions that I have had over the years with members of the Philosophy Department of St. Louis University, such as Scott Berman, Richard Blackwell, James Bohman, William Charron, Richard Dees, Robert Gibbs, John Kavanaugh, S.J., Jack Marler, Colleen McCluskey, Vincent Punzo, Eleonore Stump, George Terzis, and Ted Vitali. These discussions have helped my own thought mature. Thanks especially to Ted Vitali, Chair of the Philosophy Department, who has given me constant support, and to graduate students such as Leamon Bazil, Terrence Kelly, and Matthew Kunz. I appreciate discussions with other colleagues such as Stephen Crowell, Enrique Dussel, Lester Embree, William Hamrick, Kathryn Kuhn, and Luis Sanchez. I must also acknowledge Maurice Natanson, who gave me a deep appreciation for phenomenology and its possibilities. I am grateful to my friends in the Leo Brown Community, to E. Edward Kinerk and Charles Shelton for their continued interest. I could not have done this work without the love and friendship of my parents, Patricia and David, my brothers, Timothy and Terrance, and their families, my long-time friends Virginia Duckworth, Thomas Kelly, and Ollie Roundtree. Patricia O'Connor's help was also invaluable.

INTRODUCTION

Newspapers throughout the world report daily examples of prejudice against Jews, women, African-Americans, and other minority groups—examples in which those with prejudices classify members of such groups antagonistically and act and think toward them accordingly. When such prejudices shape institutions that treat the members of these groups unfairly or exclude them, one can speak of discrimination. Prejudice and discrimination abound in spite of the fact that legal and educational programs worldwide have attempted to redress past offenses and change present attitudes. In the face of these seemingly intractable social problems, several philosophers have examined prejudice from their varied philosophical frameworks. It is an impressive fact that three prominent philosophers who have contributed important works to this topic trace their philosophical roots to the tradition of phenomenology, initiated by Edmund Husserl. Jean-Paul Sartre devoted a major work to anti-Semitism, Simone de Beauvoir one to sexism, and Alfred Schutz one to racism. Besides focusing on these concerns in major works, each author examines other forms of prejudice, even within those major works, and it will be instructive to draw connections between their approaches to different prejudices. Is there perhaps a dynamism in phenomenology that might have led these thinkers to turn their attention to these pressing concerns? Moreover, what aspects, methods, or concepts particular to phenomenology help illuminate prejudice?

Taking a cue from this striking convergence of three thinkers within the same philosophical tradition upon the single question of prejudice, the first part of this book undertakes a study unique to the history of phenomenology. That is, it explores how the three major phenomenological figures brought their underlying philosophical paradigms to bear upon this problem of prejudice. Of course, each author selected from the treasure trove of Husserlian phenomenology different concepts, emphases, and methods. Thus it will be necessary to present first of all Husserl's own approach to phenomenology, viewed under the auspices of his own struggle against "prejudice," in the highly abstract meaning that that term held for him—a meaning different from but related to the meaning of the prejudice as commonsense bigotry. Then, in the case of each successor to Husserl, before discussing in-depth their specific works on discrimination, it will be important to present their general phenomenological viewpoints and to make clear the modifications they introduced into the tradition that Husserl began.

Even though at least forty years have passed since these three philosophers produced their works on prejudice, many of their insights are as valuable today as they were then, and, as will be shown, the critical, reflexive method of phenomenology was crucial in the production of these insights. On the other hand, by an exposure of the phenomenological roots of their varied approaches to prejudice, the meaning of phenomenology itself will become clearer and its relevance to contemporary issues more manifest.

There is value in considering these three analyses of discrimination in juxtaposition in the first section entitled "Phenomenological Perspectives," since the shortcomings and strengths of their various adaptations of phenomenological method will become all the more evident. In a sense, this interplay between viewpoints will involve a self-critique of phenomenology itself. Further, although one cannot claim that anti-Semitism, sexism, or racism are the "same" kind of discrimination, there is value in examining them in tandem, as Lewis Gordon has suggested, and the contrasts and similarities between them will surface more conspicuously when the three different discussions are laid out side by side.[1]

In addition, this consideration of the phenomenon of prejudice from three different perspectives will bring to the surface a dialectic between equality and alterity that will be important for the rest of the book. Each of the thinkers opposes prejudice in the name of equality, and yet each worries that the struggle for equality runs the risk of overlooking or even suppressing the distinctiveness of the very groups against whom there is prejudice. In this sense, these authors in their own way anticipate the later, present-day conflict between modernity and postmodernity, without, however, falling into its polarizations. While modernity tends to favor the Enlightenment's vision of the equality of all rational agents, postmodernity mistrusts the repressive, homogenizing effects of Enlightenment rationality, particularly insofar as it prides itself on being *only* rational.

Of course, there are limits to phenomenological approaches to prejudice that focus on the dynamics of consciousness involved in prejudicial activity. While Sartre, Beauvoir, and Schutz place discussions of consciousness within the context of intersubjective relationships and institutional arrangements perhaps more than other phenomenologists, they do not undertake detailed analyses, as sociologists and economists might, of the social-structural or economic factors that underpin most forms of prejudice and that would need to be studied in any full consideration of prejudice. Schutz himself is quite aware that the phenomenological take on social reality is limited, but it still captures aspects of that social reality that differing strategies of investigation will of necessity neglect. One need not cover every dimension of a problem in order to understand it quite well from one particular angle.

One of the main limitations of phenomenological method as it has been practiced is that it has tended to concentrate on epistemological or ontological questions rather than ethical ones. Such a concentration can be traced historically back to the founder of phenomenology, who published extensively on epistemology but never synthesized and published his views on ethics. It is true, however, that the Husserl Archive contains numerous manuscripts dedicated to value-theory and ethics and some of Husserl's lectures on the subject have been collected in a volume of the *Husserliana* series. In these manuscripts and lectures, Husserl continues in ethical theory the struggle against psychologism that is one trademark of his epistemology by distinguishing between feeling-acts and the values given in those acts and yet irreducible to them. On the object-side, Husserl develops an axiology, a formal logic, by which one might direct one's choices between values, and, on the subject-side, he elaborates a pure pragmatics in which rightness of will consists in willing as every other subject would will, that is, as an impartial spectator would will. Although Husserl's pragmatics is compatible with Kantian ethics and with the goal of self-formation characteristic of Husserl's later writings, Husserl also considered a kind of material value-ranking that would find its fullest articulation in the works of Max Scheler, one of the most famous phenomenologist-ethicians. On the one hand, the argument in this book, as shall be seen, favors on one plane a Kantian ethics that has made the linguistic-intersubjective turn, such as Karl-Otto Apel's, and so could subsume much of Husserl's pragmatics. On the other hand, this book supplements Apel's transcendental ethics with Emmanuel Levinas's phenomenology of alterity, that, as I have argued elsewhere, upholds the best of Scheler's a priori ranking of values while avoiding its weaknesses. In spite of the valuable insights scattered throughout Husserl's manuscripts and lectures, the fact that he never systematically presented his ethics indicates that it was never his major preoccupation.[2]

Husserl's phenomenological successors did not fare much better when it came to ethics. Although Beauvoir authored *The Ethics of Ambiguity* and Sartre his posthumously published *Notebooks for an Ethics*, they do not present a fully worked out systematic ethics that might justify their ethical outrage about sexism and anti-Semitism, in part because their existentialist leanings left them somewhat antipathetic to ethical theory. Schutz, because of his descriptive approach as well as his social scientific suspicion that ethical codes serve to shore up fragile in-group identities, kept himself at a distance from ethical theory, even though a strong ethical repugnance pervades his descriptions of the mechanisms of racial prejudice.

I will suggest, however, that Beauvoir's *The Ethics of Ambiguity* and Sartre's posthumous *Notebooks for an Ethics* point in the direction of the ethics that I will elaborate in the second, systematic part of the book—an ethics that synthesizes the ethics of Apel's transcendental pragmatics with Levinas's phenomenology of alterity. Nevertheless, this first part of the book neither examines versions of phenomenological ethics nor explores future prospects for a phenomenological ethics. Rather its purpose is to survey three phenomenological approaches to the problem of prejudice, to concentrate on specific works dedicated to forms of prejudice, and to bring to the surface the dialectic between equality and alterity that will become a central topic in the second part of the book.

The second part, "Systematics: Ethics and Affirmative Action," attempts to articulate a theoretical ethics comprehensive enough to address the relation between equality and alterity. On the one hand, it will argue that Karl-Otto Apel provides an adequate justification for a Kantian-type ethics that would support that equality between rational agents that those in the phenomenological tradition in part 1 insisted upon without sufficiently justifying. On the other hand, Emmanuel Levinas's phenomenology attends to the question of alterity by descibing the ethical dimensions of the encounter with the Other. While these two philosophers are taken to represent antagonistic trends in contemporary philosophy, such as that of German versus French philosophy or modernity versus postmodernity, this book will integrate their diverse but complementary projects within a common philosophical architectonic, a two-tiered ethical theory, modeled on Husserl's distinction between the transcendental and life-world (or pretranscendental) poles. Apel's transcendental pragmatics, which integrates within itself the hermeneutical life-world phenomenology of Heidegger and Gadamer, concentrates on questions of justification and validity on a transcendental plane akin to Husserl's, whereas Levinas locates his phenomenology of alterity at a pretheoretical level functioning on the same level as the life-world for Husserl.

In articulating this architectonic, it will be important to adjust and attune the different levels to each other. Since the architectonic is Husserlian in inspiration and since Levinas admits the Husserlian origins of his own philosophy, it will be necessary in chapter 5 to consider how transcendental pragmatics harmonizes with Husserlian phenomenology, particularly in developing aspects already present in Husserl's transcendental philosophy, and yet corrects it in other aspects. The presentation of transcendental pragmatic ethical theory and its justification will follow on this rapprochement with Husserlian phenomenology. While Apel's transcendental pole establishes a notion of equality on the basis of discourse itself, it also opens toward alterity, but it requires the supplementation and radicalization of Levinas's phenomenology of alterity at a pretheoretical, life-world level, as shall be shown in chapter 6. That chapter will show that Levinas's notion of the Third is the point where his phenomenology meets transcendental pragmatics and that his critique of reason enriches rather than contradicts transcendental pragmatics. A final section in chapter 6 will elucidate how this delicate reconciliation between these divergent standpoints, in which the distinctiveness of each and the capacity of each to complete and challenge the other is preserved, will of necessity be an uneasy one.

In the final two chapters, I will attempt to illustrate the significance and relevance of this two-tiered ethics, which reconciles transcendental pragmatics and the phenomenology of alterity, by bringing it to bear on the question of affirmative action—an issue to which the previous discussions of discrimination are still relevant and in which the ideals of equality and responsiveness to alterity clash head-on. Although affirmative action originally aimed at restoring to equality those who had suffered centuries of exclusion, ironically in these days many complain that it is an unethical policy which violates the standard of equality by unjustly discriminating against white males and thus creating a new excluded alterity. These final two chapters will argue that affirmative action is at the least an ethical policy, apart from considerations of its constitutional or legal appropriateness. The first of these last chapters will show how deontological concerns have led to a refashioned and limited definition of affirmative action, and it will offer an understanding of equality (treating people not equally or the same but "as equals") that has been transformed through exposure to the excluded Other and that would justify a compensatory approach to affirmative action. The final chapter will defend affirmative action as an adequate form of compensation by *opposing* positions that claim its inadequacy because it is over- or underinclusive, because it cannot be proven that discrimination is the cause of the exclusion of those supposedly deserving compensation, and because it turns the tables on white males by discriminating against them.

By attempting to provide an ethical warrant for affirmative action, this book will do more than show the relevance of the two-tiered ethics to a concrete moral and political issue. The entire discussion of affirmative action has often proceeded with unexamined or unjustified notions of human solidarity, equality, compensation, inclusion, social causality, diversity, and so on. Moreover, reflections upon affirmative action often take place within a broader philosophical context that they rarely make explicit. I attempt to remedy these deficiencies by proceeding as phenomenology always has, illuminating on transcendental and pretranscendental planes the taken-for-granted, unacknowledged presuppositions at play. Because of unexamined presuppositions, opponents of affirmative action find it unethical, without even being aware that there are alternative ways to understand the basic concepts and alternative frameworks with which to approach the question. By making explicit such alternatives and arguing for their plausibility, this book seeks to persuade its reader in favor of affirmative action. But it also takes its place in the history of political and social philosophy, one of whose great founders, Plato, saw so clearly that Thrasymachus's dictum that might meant right required the

Republic's long and searching reply since Thrasymachus presupposed much that he did not even recognize about human nature, epistemology, metaphysics, rationality, and even the character of philosophy itself. It is rare to see a synthesis of Levinas and Apel, and even rarer to see such a synthesis proving its relevance to a key practico-ethical topic in contemporary society.

NOTES

1. Lewis R. Gordon, *Bad Faith and Antiblack Racism* (Atlantic Highlands, N.J.: Humanities Press, 1995), pp. 124–29.

2. Edmund Husserl, *Vorlesungen uber Ethik und Wertlehre 1908–1914*, ed. Ullrich Melle, vol. 28 of *Husserliana* (Dordrecht, Boston, London: Kluwer Academic Publishers, 1988), pp. xliv, xlvii, 138, 143, 150–51, 404; Alois Roth, *Edmund Husserls ethische Untersuchungen*, vol. 7 of *Phaenomenologica* (The Hague: Martinus Nijhoff, 1960), pp. 15, 27, 29, 66, 72, 113, 116–20; Max Scheler, *Formalism in Ethics and Non-Formal Ethics of Value: A New Attempt toward the Foundation of an Ethical Personalism*, trans. Manfred S. Frings and Roger L. Funk (Evanston, Ill.: Northwestern University Press, 1973); Michael D. Barber, *Guardian of Dialogue: Max Scheler's Phenomenology, Sociology of Knowledge, and Philosophy of Love* (Lewisburg, Penn.: Bucknell University Press and London and Toronto: Associated University Presses, 1993), pp. 154–65.

Part 1
PHENOMENOLOGICAL PERSPECTIVES

1

EDMUND HUSSERL

Prejudice and the Spirt of Phenomenological Reflection

Jean-Paul Sartre, Simone de Beauvoir, and Alfred Schutz, whose writings on various forms of prejudice will be considered in the chapters that follow, all considered themselves to be phenomenologists in the tradition of Edmund Husserl, even though they each introduced significant changes in the practice of phenomenology. It would be incorrect, however, to view the relationship between Husserl and these successors as merely extrinsic, as though these successors just happened to be affected by Husserl's prominence in the early and mid-twentieth century or as though they merely borrowed an occasional concept or idea from him. The entire spirit of Husserl's phenomenology, of which his successors deeply imbibed, involved a struggle against prejudice—a more abstract kind of prejudice than anti-Semitism, sexism, or racism, to be sure. But it is no mere accident that these followers of Husserl, trained by reading Husserl to resist taking things for granted, should have aimed their sights, in part, at the major forms of bigotry prevailing in their—and our—day. Before showing this intimate linkage between the spirit of Husserl and his followers, it is important to explain this spirit, particularly under the rubric of its antagonism toward prejudice.

To understand what Husserl meant by prejudice, one needs to consider the lived situation from which reflection and philosophy take their start. In his *Erste Philosophie*, Part Two, *Theorie der phänomenologischen Reduktion*, Husserl portrayed this lived starting point and thereby anticipated later discussions in the *Crisis* regarding the life-world and what has come to be known as Husserl's non-Cartesian entrance into transcendental phenomenology.[1]

But there still remain hidden validities [*Geltungen*] and an endless scope for such validities. In truth, we stand in the solitude of an infinite life-context, in the infinity of one's own and one's intersubjective and historical life-context. In this solitude, validities extend *ad infinitum* and present themselves *ad infinitum* as one penetrates into the horizons of the present, past, and future. It is clear, that there can be no talk here of a free will developing and presenting this manifold completely now or in the future. I refer here only to the wide realm of that forgetfulness, for which the favor of an awakening, associative motive in wide segments of life might either be at hand or enduringly lacking.[2]

These infinite extensions of validities—and an alternative translation of the German word *Geltungen* could be "presumptions about reality"—are such that whatever one might consciously bring into focus always contains its own empty horizons of unclarity and obscurity. In the face of such infinite extensions, Husserl proposes the possibility of a universal *epoché*, a "decision," "a universal regulation of the will," to inhibit (*inhibieren*) or to put out of play (*ausser Kraft zu setzen*) these reality-presumptions. Husserl here interprets this *epoché*, this refusal to participate in unexamined presumptions, as a resolve of will, similar to, but more thorough than, the commitments one makes to the values that direct one's life. Husserl, in effect, locates the rigor of this phenomenological *epoché* in a resolution of the *will* precisely because he is so thoroughly aware of what Merleau-Ponty would later call one's "complicity" with the world, that is, one's involvement in reality-presumptions that cognition never exhaustively illuminates or dominates. The will encompasses universally, in advance, a manifold that cognition uncovers only piecemeal and always with horizons yet to be explored. Husserl restates this situatedness of reflection in his later *Crisis*:

> Thus the particular object of our active consciousness, and correlatively the active, conscious having of it, being directed toward it, and dealing with it—all this is forever surrounded by an atmosphere of mute, concealed, but co-functioning validities [*Geltungen*], a *vital horizon* into which the active ego can also direct itself voluntarily, reactivating old acquisitions, consciously grasping new apperceptive ideas, transforming them into intuitions. Because of this constantly flowing *horizonal character*, then, every straightforwardly performed validity in natural world-life always presupposes validities extending back, immediately or mediately, into a necessary subsoil of

obscure but occasionally available validities, all of which together, including the present acts, make up a single, indivisible, interrelated complex of life.[3]

Since these "validities" or "reality-presumptions" are "mute," "concealed," "co-functioning," inherited from the past, and never completely brought to light, one is tempted to consider them "pre-judgments," although such a word would imply a more deliberate and reflective hold on tham then one actually has. Similarly, one could not exactly dub them "prejudices," since that word carries too many negative connotations and implies an incorrectness that the more neutral term "reality-presumptions" does not since such presumptions could turn out to be correct. Husserl, though, seems to believe that such presumptions, like prejudices, are naively held, often socially transmitted, and capable of blocking one's insight into what is actually given in experience.

The above citations indicate that Husserl was much more aware of his immersion in inherited and unreflectively assumed presumptions than either his critics recognize or his own presentations of phenomenology often acknowledge, especially when they commence too quickly with phenomenological reduction without establishing its context and that context's presumptions. The great attention Husserl paid to phenomenological reduction, his repeated attempts to redefine it, and even its excessively rigoristic Cartesian versions may well reflect his underlying appreciation of how deeply imbued one is with the unexamined presumptions of one's background and environment and what effort is required to bring them to consciousness. Indeed, one can fault Husserl for his own unrecognized presuppositions only if one has already adopted, however implicitly, the very ideal of self-scrutiny that he himself espoused and articulated.[4]

Since some of these reality-presumptions might blind one to what is actually given, Husserl repeatedly enjoins philosophers to return "to the things themselves." The expression of this ideal in *Ideas I* occurs in a setting that illustrates a kind of reality-presumption, in fact a prejudice, that might block access to these things. In that setting, Husserl at first praises the radicalism of empiricistic naturalism for its "opposition to all 'idols,' to the powers of tradition and superstition, to crude and refined prejudices (*Vorurteile*) of every kind." The only problem is that the empiricists end up equating the return "to the things themselves" with sense-experience, without first examining the types of judgments to determine which judgments require grounding in sense-experience and which do not. In effect, the empiricists operate with a hidden essentialist conviction that all valid judgments must refer to empirical evidence, but an adequate intuition into the essence of judgment suggests that there are a variety of judgments depending on a variety of evidences. Husserl in effect brings to light a hidden essentialist presumption that empiricists themselves, frequently antipathetic to all essences, are reluctant to acknowledge. He then disputes the narrowness of this presumption, taken for granted as it is, only now by empiricists, who had prided themselves on the radicalism of their criticism. Husserl concludes that if "positivism" means the absolute unbiased grounding of all science, it is he who is the positivist insofar as he permits no authority, not even that of modern natural science that dictates empiricist methodology, to deprive him of the right of recognizing all kinds of intuition as equally valuable sources in the process of justifying knowledge.[5]

As Husserl's comment on positivism suggests, one can also succumb to unexamined presumptions if one concurs with authoritative pronouncements simply on the word of an authority. As a result, Husserl proposes as an ideal that a philosopher seek to acquire knowledge as that philosopher's own, aiming at a knowledge for which each alone can answer from the beginning. This inevitable solitude, an ideal correlative to the ideal of self-responsibility prominent in Descartes, must be seen as part of a struggle against an all too easy acquiescence in unscrutinized assumptions.

> Must not the demand for a philosophy aiming at the ultimate conceivable freedom from prejudice [*Vorurteilosigkeit*], shaping itself with actual autonomy according to ultimate evidences it has itself produced, and therefore absolutely self-responsible—must not this demand, instead of being excessive, be part of the fundamental sense of genuine philosophy?[6]

However unreachable such an ideal may be or however much Husserl seems to neglect how reflectively appropriated traditions or interventions from others can positively lead to insight, it does seem to be an inescapable trait of reflection and philosophical discourse that one must see for one's self and only assent to evidence insofar as it is convincing. The only alternative would be to lapse into uncriticized preconceptions.[7]

Husserl traces the origins of this philosophical ideal of the examined life back to the Greeks who introduced into the West the theoretical attitude of the philosophical person,

> the peculiar universality of his critical stance, his resolve not to accept unquestioningly any pregiven opinion or tradition so that he can inquire, in respect to the whole traditionally pregiven universe, after what is true in itself, an ideality.[8]

Once introduced, this ideal calls for a far-reaching transformation of the whole praxis of human existence and all cultural life. Whatever is traditionally valid is either discarded or its content is subjected to review, and philosophical justifications for it must be presented.[9]

Although Husserl spoke of inhibiting the presumptions of everyday life through phenomenological *epoché*, conceived as an act of will, this negative "refraining from" was always oriented in his formulations of the reduction and philosophical practice to a positive return to the things themselves, that is, to see whatever could not be seen as long as unexamined and mistaken presumptions skewed one's ability to see. Maurice Natanson offers such a positive portrait of reduction by moving away from a rigidly methodological interpretation of phenomenological reduction toward a more philosophical one. According to Natanson, reduction, "first a tool, becomes a means of enlarging and deepening the phenomenologist's range of experience." Reiterating Merleau-Ponty's mandate that one must break with one's familiar acceptance of the world, that is, one's presumptions about the way reality is, in order to see the world and grasp it as paradoxical, Natanson speaks of the " 'first-given' sense of the effulgence of subjectivity as its 'already-given' objects are newly displayed in the theatre of consciousness."[10]

At this point it is appropriate to consider several results that follow on a well-executed phenomenological reduction, which in varied ways permits one to see the things themselves freer of distorting biases than before. Moreover, the criticism of taken for granted presumptions achieved in phenomenological reduction becomes paradigmatic for the critique of such presumptions in other aspects of Husserl's thought: in eidetic analysis, his intepretation of the place of science, the levels of phenomenological analysis, regional ontologies, and the life-world. Phenomenological successors continued the trajectory of Husserl's thought by exploring the linguistic, bodily, social, and historical conditions of reflection itself and its assessment of presumptions.

First of all, there is little doubt that for Husserl the great discovery effected through phenomenological reduction was the disclosure of the field of human consciousness. As Alfred Schutz's review of Husserl's *Formal and Transcendental Logic* puts it, "To uncover the hidden achievements of constituting subjectivity in its theorizing is one of the preeminent tasks of phenomenology." In his revealing the field of consciousness, Husserl gives the impression that he has broken through centuries-old presuppositions about human consciousness, which, ever since it had been made focal by Descartes, had been construed as the more or less passive container in which unities of sensations represented a mysterious reality beyond themselves. The excitement Husserl communicates as he describes consciousness reminds one of Nietzsche's description of himself as he traversed, "as though with new eyes, the enormous, distant, and so well hidden land of morality . . . does this not mean virtually to discover this land for the first time?"[11]

Consciousness is directed toward an object, as, for instance, the act of perceiving a house *means* the house, but, in addition, each subjective process has its "horizon." Co-given with the object are its unseen sides, as yet indeterminate but determinable, and its background, not thematized but thematizable. Similarly the subjective act to which the object is presented is embedded in a flow of time, of the past acts which preceded this present act of perception and of the future possible acts, such as the acts of memory or imagination that might supplant the present act of perception. Such horizons reveal the dynamic character of consciousness, not as merely passive and receptive, but as always capable of refocusing its attention, exploring what had just been marginal, and making explicit what had been only implicit. As an instance of this dynamism, Husserl points out that the phenomenologist is not content to rest in any given object, but seeks to unfold the various acts of consciousness and their synthetic unity by which such an object is grasped. For example, the object "house" presupposes a series of anonymous, spatio-temporally located acts of perception that one accomplishes in circling a house in order to build up the idea of the house. The belief that one is standing before a house is either confirmed or disconfirmed as one passes through this series of perspectives on the house. The effects of this kind of constitutional analysis of how objects are built up resembles phenomenological reduction since both bring to light the hidden conscious activity often not seen because of one's focus on the object at hand. Indeed the centuries-old presumption, reigning throughout most of modernity, that consciousness is a passive container of sense-impressions making up objects, prevented the recognition of this hidden consciousness.[12]

This fluid, active consciousness building up unified objects through the course of experience is in fact constantly monitoring itself, operating with "hypotheses" that are either confirmed or disconfirmed as it passes through different perspectives on a perceptual object—and all this before one constructs hypotheses at a more theoretical or scientific level. Indeed the modalities of certainty, probability, and dubiousness discussed at the higher levels of logic trace their origins to the perceptual level in which the firmness of one's unarticulated "beliefs" about a present object undergo continual revision (either strengthening or weakening) as the course of experience unfolds. This wakeful consciousness, resisting fixation, continually in movement, ever pushing forward to new points of views and new perceptual possibilities, ever revisable—recovered by Husserl's own restless impatience with stagnant commonplaces and philosophical prejudices about consciousness—epitomizes the authentic human being which Sartre will later describe as "for itself." To reify one's own consciousness, to rest content with one's uncritically absorbed presuppositions, to stop questioning—these are all modes of opting to be "in itself" and to prefer a kind of inauthenticity for Sartre, as well as for Husserl. In a sense, the critical, self-reflective process of phenomenology uncovered that which is itself continually critical and self-reflective: human consciousness, whose self-reflective characteristics phenomenology exhibits at a higher reflective level.[13]

Just as consciousness explores new possibilities by moving to different spatio-temporal "takes" on an object, so phenomenology itself opens up new possibilities by the attitudinal "take" on experience that phenomenological reduction effects. Immersed in the everyday attitude of the natural attitude, one is not even aware that there are other possible attitudes to be taken and one's vision is narrowed to what is pragmatically pressing. The phenomenological reduction, suspending belief in the existence of objects, describing instead how those objects appear and rendering explicit hidden conscious activity in relation to those objects, enables the phenomenologist to see more than the denizen of the natural attitude usually imagines. Indeed, some kind of phenomenological reduction, some taking up the phenomenological attitude, is requisite if one is to even recognize the natural attitude as itself an "attitude," one of many possible ways of attending to the world and experience. Just as one perceptual viewpoint on an object points to the unfolding of a variety of alternative points of view, so the phenomenological attitude revealing itself and the natural attitude as alternatives suggests a plethora of alternative attitudes, such as those of theoretical science, of dreaming, of attending a dramatic performance, or of religious experience.[14]

In fact, for Husserl, phenomenology as the opening up of possibilities converges with its struggle to see unbiasedly. Free fancies, for Husserl, assume a privileged position over against perceptions insofar as they enable one to produce a continuous series of *possible* configurations. One can then inspect this series to determine which properties of the objects encountered in perception and experience perdure across a variety of instantiations and thus deserve to be considered as essential properties. This process of free variation, reminiscent of the perceptual passage through a series of perspectives in order to establish the identity of the perceived object, is certainly oriented for Husserl toward uncovering the essential features of the givens of experience. But it is also possible to envision that process as a critical process to fend off premature and inaccurate identifications of what is essential at the perceptual level and perhaps to identify what features are not essential. Indeed, as shall be shown later, Simone de Beauvoir employs a kind of free variation, a presentation of alternative possibilities, to offset unfounded essentialist claims about women.[15]

Just as this search for essential features, or "eidetic" analysis, can help to disclose uncriticized, horizontal rather than focal, essentialist presumptions at the perceptual level, Husserl's penchant for exploring unexamined horizons, epitomized in the reduction and its revelation of consciousness itself, leads to a broader critique of the presumptions of science. Although his most famous presentation of this critique occurs in the *Crisis*, a condensed version appears in *Ideas I*, #52. In that section, Husserl begins by showing how science, seeking to extend the predictabilities found in ordinary experience, elaborates the thing of physical *intellectio*, usually in terms of electrons, atoms, and so forth, and then contrasts this thing with the everday thing of plain sensory *imaginatio*. The thing of science serves then as an unknown world of things-in-themselves causally accounting for the thing of experience, even though originally science was nothing more than an explanatory account that began with the thing of experience and that finally enabled the scientist to develop more precise predictions. Eventually, Husserl claims, physics comes to explain not only the appearances of things, but the experiences of consciousness in which those appearances present themselves. Husserl complains that this historical development involves the positing of an unwarranted causal relationship between physical being and consciousness. Furthermore, the very consciousness which elaborated science in the first place and developed its concepts and explanations, beginning with imprecise everyday experience, becomes a dependent, secondary product, a mere effect of the atoms or nerve-firings that it has uncovered, if it is not totally explained away. As Husserl sums it up:

> In so doing, one attributes a mythical absolute reality to the being determined by physics, while completely failing to see what is truly absolute: pure consciousness as pure consciousness in its purity. Accordingly, no note is taken of the absurdity involved in absolutizing Nature as conceived by physics, in absolutizing this intentional correlate of logically determinative thinking.[16]

In "The Vienna Lecture," Husserl emphasizes that in spite of the fact that the human spirit has acheived a great triumph in science, scientific investigation often forgets the entire subjective realm and fails to take into account the scientist as the subject producing a scientific investigation. Husserl, whose phenomenological method has already been repeatedly characterized as a bringing out of obscurity a hidden, anonymous consciousness, argues in the end that science must abandon the natural scientific presumption that everything merely subjective must be excluded. Instead, there is a need to admit the consciousness of the scientists lying anonymously on the horizon of their own endeavor. Only then can science be truly responsible, leaving no horizons unexamined and no questions unasked and thus living up to the Greek ideal of rationality.

> The *ratio* presently under discussion is nothing other than the spirit's truly universal, responsible science, in which a completely new mode of scientific discipline is set in motion where all conceivable questions—questions of being and questions of norm, questions of what is called "existence"—find their place.[17]

The problem is not that science has been too rationalistic, but that it has not been rational enough insofar as it has allowed its *own* taken-for-granted presumptions about scientific method to consign the consciousness that produces science to oblivion.[18]

The neglecting of hidden subjectivity is not only a pitfall into which the natural sciences fall: even phenomenology itself is prone to such an oversight. Phenomenology at the beginning "penetrates the anonymous 'cogitative' life," and exposes the "noetic multiplicities of consciousness and their synthetic unity" by means of which intentional objects present themselves. Phenomenologists can restrict their attention to describing psychic life, the intentionalities and objects that present themselves in "inner experience," and they can attempt to establish the invariant, properly essential structures of a community of psychic life. This type of inquiry, known as a phenomenological psychology and carefully developed by Alfred Schutz in *The Phenomenology of the Social World*, is still "naive." It is "naive" in the sense that, in spite of its focus on intentional acts and their objects, it begins the way the positive sciences do, "settling on the pre-given soil of world-experience, a soil presupposed as obviously existing." Even though critical insofar as it self-reflexively strives to disentangle eidetic features, phenomenological psychology takes what is given in everyday experience as the ground for all its thematization. In the *Cartesian Meditations*, Husserl makes it clear that a further step is required, if one is to avoid acquiescing further in any unscrutinized reality-presumptions.

> We recall the radicalness of the Cartesian idea of philosophy, as the idea of the all-embracing science grounded to the utmost and apodictically. This idea demands an absolute universal criticism, which, for its part, by abstention from all positions that already give anything existent, must first create for itself a universe of absolute freedom from prejudice [*Vorurteilosigkeit*]. The universality of transcendental experience and description does this by inhibiting the universal "prejudice" [*Vorurteil*] of world-experience, which hiddenly pervades all naturalness (the belief in the world, which pervades naturalness thoroughly and continuously), and then—within the sphere that remains unaffected, the absolute sphere of egological being, as the sphere of meanings reduced to an unalloyed freedom from prejudice [*Vorurteilosigkiet*]—striving for a universal description.[19]

According to Kockelmans, it would not be accurate to envision phenomenological psychology only as falling short of transcendental phenomenology; rather such a psychology fulfills its own positive, limited task: to lay bare the *eidos* of the psychical. In contrast, transcendental phenomenology attempts to provide the ultimate explanation of the meaning and being of beings by returning to the final field in which all being comes to appearance and receives its meaning, even the psychical of phenomenological psychology: namely that of the transcendental consciousness.[20]

In a sense, as long as one remains at the level of a phenomenological psychology, examining the intentional structures of the social world, but taking the existence of that world and its individuals for granted, there remains a horizon that is unexamined—namely, the way in which the being of those things (and all things) is given only with reference to the field of consciousness. One can leave such a horizon in its latency and still carry out an adequate phenomenological psychology, but that would be tantamount to allowing the hidden subjectivity to which everything appears to remain hidden and to refusing to question a horizon that has not yet been thematized. In the *Cartesian Meditations*, Husserl comments on the ultimacy of the transcendental level since there would be no more tacit horizons and no more realms of investigation that might leave outside of their focus the conscious field in which they first come to appearance.

> Instead of eidetic transcendental phenomenology we then have an eidetic pure psychology, relating to the eidos psyche, whose eidetic horizon, to be sure, remains unexamined. If, however, it did become examined, the way to overcome this positivity would become open— that is, the way leading over into absolute phenomenology, the phenomenology of the transcendental ego, who indeed no longer has a horizon that could lead beyond the sphere of his transcendental being and thus relativize him.[21]

As Kockelmans points out, "phenomenological-psychological reduction is nothing other than the transcendental reduction that has not yet arrived at a complete understanding." In a sense, Husserl's own method of bringing to light hidden subjectivity, relentlessly pushing forward to question and explore any horizon, leaving no questions unasked, exposing what is presumed and taken for granted, made it impossible for him *not* to turn to the level of the transcendental ego.[22]

The uncovering of the ultimate hidden subjectivity, the field of transcendental phenomenology, is itself only a starting point for further explanations. Husserl conceives this transcendental phenomenology as engaging in a "radical clarification" of the sense and origin of the concepts such as "world," "Nature," "space," "time," "psychophysical being," "man," "psyche," "animate organism," "social community," "culture," and so forth. The carrying out of these investigations would have to lead to all the concepts which, as unexplored, are utilized by the positive sciences and often occluded from their sight. An example of such an investigation would be Alfred Schutz's *The Phenomenology of the Social World*, which attempts to depict the essential structures of the social world presupposed by the social sciences. However, Schutz, for rather complex reasons, believed that the uniqueness of the problem of intersubjectivity called for a methodic adjustment, namely, the utilization of a phenomenological psychology rather than constitution within the transcendental sphere.[23]

Although this presentation of Husserl's thought as an effort to irradiate unexamined presumptions has moved "upward" toward the level of transcendental phenomenology, in the *Crisis*, Husserl worked "downward," beginning with theoretical frameworks which suppose their own self-sufficiency.

> The supposedly completely self-sufficient logic which modern mathematical logicians think they are able to develop, even calling it a truly scientific philosophy, namely, as the universal, a priori, fundamental science for all objective sciences, is nothing but naivete.[24]

Such self-enclosed sciences, by neglecting their taken-for-granted horizon, the life-world, become paradoxically unscientific, in the sense of not rationally examining their own presuppositions.

> Its [Logic's] self-evidence lacks scientific grounding in the universal life-world a priori, which it always presupposes in the form of things taken for granted, which are never scientifically, universally formulated, never put in the general form proper to a science of essence. Only when this radical, fundamental science exists can such a logic itself become a science. Before this it hangs in mid-air, without support, and is, as it has been up to now, *so very naive that it is not even aware of the task which attaches to every objective logic*, every a priori science in the usual sense, namely, that of discovering how this logic itself is to be grounded, hence no longer "logically" but by being traced back to the universal pre-logical a priori through which everything logical, the total edifice of objective theory in all its methodological forms, demonstrates its legitimate sense and from which, then, all logic itself must receive its norms.[25]

The italics above, mine and not Husserl's, highlight the phenomenological endeavor to make explicit a hidden conscious activity, that of the life-world, of whose existence one ensconced at a theoretical level is often not aware.

Just as the *Crisis* involves a reflective breaking out of theory to reveal its pretheoretical subsoil, Merleau-Ponty, in his essay "The Philosopher and His Shadow," argues that Husserl's phenomenology had actually undergone such a shift in emphasis from *Ideas II* onward. Merleau-Ponty claims that for this later Husserl reflection no longer installs one in a closed, transparent milieu, but rather begins to lay bare beings which are not sustained by the centrifugal activity of consciousness, significations that consciousness does not spontaneously confer upon contents, and contents which participate obliquely in a meaning which does not bear the monogram or stamp of thetic consciousness. Merleau-Ponty recognizes the paradoxical character of rationality which, when pushed to its extremes, illuminates the prerational subsoil upon which rationality itself depends.

> Originally a project to gain intellectual possession of the world, constitution becomes increasingly, as Husserl's thought matures, the means of unveiling a back side of things that we have not constituted. This senseless effort to submit everything to the properties of "consciousness" (to the limpid play of its attitudes, intentions, and impositions of meaning) was necessary—the picture of a well-behaved world left to us by classical philosophy had to be pushed to the limit—in order to reveal all that was left over: these beings beneath our idealizations and objectifications which secretly nourish them and in which we have difficulty in recognizing noema.[26]

A dialectic emerges then, one of whose poles is the life-world terrain of language, body, history, and sociality which resists the gaze of reflection, announces itself as reflection's autonomous other, and provides the fertile ground for reflection's nourishment and renewal. At the other pole, transcendental reflection irradiates this otherness and constitutes it as an inmost feature of transcendental subjectivity; but such reflection never exhaustively explains its own subsoil, and each gain in insight turns up new horizons to be later pursued. The dialectic between life-world and transcendental level reveals reflection, discontent with its own immersion in unexamined presumptions and striving ceaselessly upward, and yet coming to realize that it itself stands in continual need of self-critique, rooted in an opacity on which it depends but which it never masters. Reflection, the very mechanism of uncovering presumptions and allowing the things themselves to be seen, has its own potential to be self-enclosed, immune to critique, and blindly presumptive. This dialectic will play itself out in chapters 5 and 6, which attempt to elucidate a two-tiered ethics, bringing into an uneasy synthesis Emmanuel Levinas's phenomenology on a life-world plane and Karl-Otto Apel's transcendental pragmatics—a discussion that sets the stage for an analysis of the more concrete issue of affirmative action.[27]

The unreflectively held philosophical presumptions, which Husserl struggled continually to expose, seem far removed from the "prejudices" operant in anti-Semitism, sexism, and racism. Yet, it will become evident that Husserl's successors, such as Jean-Paul Sartre, Simone de Beauvoir, and Alfred Schutz, partook of his spirit, as old as Plato and philosophy itself, which summons the philosopher "not to accept unquestioningly any pregiven opinion or tradition so that he can inquire, in respect to the whole traditionally pregiven universe, after what is true in itself." It is this spirit that led such philosophers to utilize many of Husserl's own findings, as we shall see, to move phenomenology in different directions, and to bring its resources to bear on more practical domains beyond formal philosophy.[28]

There is an indication that Husserl himself might have approved of such practical applications. In his "Vienna Lecture"—delivered by him in Vienna in 1935 because as a Jew he was not permitted to give lectures in Germany—Husserl describes in the first section the critical spirit of philosophy originating with the Greeks. This section serves as a prelude to the second section in which he argues that the natural sciences, for all their critical acumen, need to examine their own origins in human subjectivity, if they wish to be fully self-critical. Near the end of the first section, Husserl talks about how philosophy comports itself regarding traditions, either discrediting them or calling upon them to give an account. Hence, when philosophy meets religion, religion is forced either to develop philosophical justifications for itself or to refuse to engage in any philosophical inquiry.

> In the general process of idealization, which proceeds from philosophy, God is logicized, so to speak; indeed he becomes the bearer of the absolute *logos*. I would cite as something logical, incidentally, the fact that religion appeals theologically to the evidence of belief as a peculiar manner, and the deepest manner, of grounding true being. National gods, on the other hand, are [simply] there without question, as real facts in the surrounding world. Prior to philosophy no one poses questions critical of knowledge, questions of evidence.[29]

The term "national gods," in the setting of the Vienna Lecture, refers to Nazism, to the power of unjustifiable prejudice, to prejudice which stubbornly resists the critical force which philosophy introduces into culture. Such prejudice, in its many forms, has not died with the Nazis, but neither has its mortal enemy, philosophy.

NOTES

1. Edmund Husserl, *Erste Philosophie (1923/24)*, Part Two, *Theorie der phänomenologischen Reduktion*, ed. Rudolf Boehm, "The Editor's Introduction" (The Hague: Martinus Nijhoff, 1959), pp. xxvii, xxx–xxxi, xxxiii–xxxiv.

2. Ibid., p. 153.

3. Edmund Husserl, *The Crisis of European Sciences and Transcendental Phenomenology: An Introduction to Phenomenological Philosophy*, trans. David Carr (Evanston, Ill.: Northwestern University Press, 1970), p. 149; *Theorie der phänomenologischen Reduktion*, pp. 153–55, 163; Maurice Merleau-Ponty, *Phenomenology of Perception*, trans. Colin Smith (London and Atlantic Highlands, N.J.: Humanities Press, 1962), p. xiii.

4. Edmund Husserl, *Cartesian Meditations: An Introduction to Phenomenology*, trans. Dorion Cairns (The Hague, Boston, London: Martinus Nijhoff, 1960), pp. 34–35; Edmund Husserl, *Ideas Pertaining to a Pure Phenomenology and to a Phenomenological Philosophy*, Book 1: *General Introduction to Pure Phenomenology*, trans. F. Kersten (The Hague, Boston, London: Martinus Nijhoff, 1982), pp. 51–62.

5. Husserl, *Ideas*, pp. 35–39.

6. Husserl, *Cartesian Mediations*, p. 6.

7. Ibid., pp. 1–6.

8. Edmund Husserl, "The Vienna Lecture," in *The Crisis of European Sciences and Transcendental Phenomenology*, p. 286.

9. Ibid., pp. 287–89.

10. Maurice Natanson, "Descriptive Phenomenology," in *Essays in Memory of Aron Gurwitsch*, ed. Lester Embree (Washington, D.C.: Center for Advanced Research in Phenomenology and University Press of America, 1984), pp. 258–59; Merleau-Ponty, *Phenomenology of Perception*, p. xiv.

11. Alfred Schutz, Review of *Formale und transzendentale Logik*, *Deutsche Literaturzeitung* 54 (1933): 779; Friedrich Nietzsche, *On the Genealogy of Morals and Ecce Homo*, trans. Walter Kaufmann (New York: Random House, 1967), p. 21.

12. Husserl, *Cartesian Meditations*, pp. 33, 44–49.

13. Edmund Husserl, *Analysen zur passiven Synthesis, aus Vorlesung- und Forschungsmanuskripten 1918–1926*, ed. Margot Fleischer (The Hague: Martinus Nijhoff, 1966), pp. 25, 28, 29, 30, 31, 33, 37, 39, 66.

14. See Alfred Schutz's essay "On Multiple Realities," in *The Problem of Social Reality*, vol. 1 of *Collected Papers*, ed. Maurice Natanson (The Hague, Boston, London: Martinus Nijhoff, 1962), pp. 207–59.

15. Husserl, *Ideas*, 1:157–60.

16. Ibid., 1:122; for the whole argument in *Ideas*, see pp. 117–24.

17. Husserl, "The Vienna Lecture," p. 298.

18. Ibid., pp. 289–99.

19. Husserl, *Cartesian Meditations*, pp. 35–36.

20. Ibid., p. 47; Edmund Husserl, *Ideas Pertaining to a Pure Phenomenology and to a Phenomenological Philosophy*, Book 2: *Studies in the Phenomenology of Constitution*, trans. Richard Rojcewicz and Andre Schuwer (Dordrecht, Boston, London: Kluwer Academic Publishers, 1989), pp. 411–12, 427; Alfred Schutz, *The Phenomenology of the Social World*, trans. George Walsh and Frederick Lehnert (Evanston, Ill.: Northwestern University Press, 1967), pp. 43–44; Joseph J. Kockelmans, *Edmund Husserl's Phenomenology* (West Lafayette, Ind.: Purdue University Press, 1994), pp. 187, 242–43.

21. Husserl, *Cartesian Meditations*, p. 73.

22. Kockelmans, *Edmund Husserl's Phenomenology*, p. 239.

23. Husserl, *Cartesian Meditations*, pp. 154–55; Alfred Schutz, "The Problem of Transcendental Intersubjectivity in Husserl," in *Studies in Phenomenological Philosophy*, vol. 3 of *Collected Papers*, ed. Ilse Schutz (The Hague: Martinus Nijhoff, 1975), p. 51, see especially p. 82; Schutz, *The Phenomenology of the Social World*, pp. 43–44, 97–98.

24. Husserl, *The Crisis of European Sciences and Transcendental Phenomenology*, p. 141.

25. Ibid.

26. Maurice Merleau-Ponty, "The Philosopher and His Shadow," in *Signs*, trans. Richard C. McLeary (Evanston, Ill.: Northwestern University Press, 1964), p. 180, see also pp. 162, 165.

27. J. N. Mohanty, *The Possibility of Transcendental Philosophy* (Dordrecht, Boston: Martinus Nijhoff, 1985), p. 219.

28. Husserl, "Vienna Lecture," p. 286.

29. Ibid., pp. 288–89.

2

REASON AND THE CRITIQUE OF REASON IN SARTRE'S PHENOMENOLOGY OF ANTI-SEMITISM

1. JEAN-PAUL SARTRE'S PHENOMENOLOGY

Maurice Natanson in his early *Critique of Jean-Paul Sartre's Ontology* states in strong terms that Sartre departs from phenomenology, that he is not a phenomenologist, and that he does not claim to be one. Natanson acknowledges, however, in that same work that Sartre's method in *Being and Nothingness* was "quasi-phenomenological." Later, in *The Philosophy of Jean-Paul Sartre*, part of *The Library of Living Philosophers* series edited by Paul Schilpp, Natanson reiterates that many of Sartre's categories are "rooted in a phenomenology of prereflective consciousness which selected what it pleased from Husserl's bounty." In the same Schilpp volume, Sartre himself leaves no doubt about his own stance toward phenomenology when in response to a question as to whether he has ever abandoned phenomenology, he states, "Never. I continue to think in those terms. I have never thought as a Marxist, not even in the *Critique de la raison dialectique*."[1] These conflicting assessments suggest that Sartre, like most post-Husserlian phenomenologists, relied upon Husserl even while diverging from him in the process of creating his own niche in the enterprise of phenomenology.[2]

Indeed, several of Sartre's early works in phenomenological psychology, focusing on the imagination and the emotions, show themselves explicitly phenomenological in their systematic reflective efforts, and at times they even appeal for a deployment of the phenomenological reduction. In these early works, Sartre strives to dig beneath metaphysical and commonsense prejudices to return to "givens," such as the the image or the emotions and to illuminate their essential features. At the same time, he brings to light the hidden activity of consciousness, as, for instance, when he shows how the obsessions or emotional hysteria that seem to sap one's consciousness of any strength are actually its own product. Although Sartre later criticized his early work as a rationalist philosophy of consciousness, this work still gives evidence of a struggle to return to "the things themselves," such as consciousness and what is given to it. This very endeavor to return to given processes and structures that must be *discovered* by reflection indicates a resistance to an idealistic view of consciousness, transparent to itself and capable of spinning the world and itself out of its own resources—a view often falsely attributed to Sartre. To offset further any such omniscient idealism, Sartre insists that spontaneous unreflective consciousness lies at the basis of action and constitutes a certain existential level in the world, that a zone of semidarkness fringes consciousness, that bodily movements (e.g., nodding the head) accompany thinking, and that the comprehension of intellectual concepts depends upon prior images.[3]

Sartre's major phenomenological work prior to *Being and Nothingness, The Transcendence of the Ego,* launches an attack on the omnipotent ego that has often served as the origin of much idealism. In that work, when Sartre penetrates beneath the level of reflective consciousness to a level of prereflective spontaneity, he finds no "I" and concludes that the "I" itself is constituted by a later reflective consciousness. Thus, "The ego is not the owner of consciousness; it is the object of consciousness," and "the spontaneity of consciousness could not emanate from the *I*," but rather "the spontaneity *goes toward* the *I*."[4] Sartre assimilates this spontaneous, prereflective consciousness, aware of itself prior to reflective consciousness, to Husserl's transcendental consciousness:

> . . . transcendental consciousness is an impersonal spontaneity. It determines its existence at each instant, without our being able to conceive anything *before* it. Thus each instant of our conscious life reveals to us a creation *ex nihilo*.[5]

By constituting the ego as a kind of nearly substantial, congealed eternal truth, prereflective consciousness masks its own spontaneity from itself, hypnotizes itself before the ego it has produced, ignores its own construction and its own dynamism—until phenomenology unveils the bad faith into which it has fallen regarding itself. In addition, Sartre accuses the "psychology of states" of complicity in this process of reducing prereflective spontaneity to something inert. It is as though the reflective life of psychology by its very essence *poisons* spontaneous life. In spite of idealist-sounding talk about prereflective consciousness continually creating *ex nihilo*, Sartre asserts a world irreducible to consciousness insofar this transcendental field of prereflective consciousness is a pure nothing and insofar as all psychic objects, truths, and values are outside it. This becomes clear, for instance, when I stand before "Peter-having-to-be-helped" and recognize that the quality of "having to be helped" lies not in consciousness but in Peter. It is no wonder that Sartre ends this work by insinuating that his phenomenology has improved upon the phenomenology of the later Husserl whose idealist tendencies removed the phenomenologist from the things themselves. In Sartre's view, phenomenologists such as himself "have plunged man back into the world; they have given full measure to man's agonies and sufferings, and also to his rebellions."6

Being and Nothingness, subtitled *An Essay on Phenomenological Ontology*, continues this trajectory toward the things themselves by situating epistemology with reference to a more fundamental ontology. In the "Introduction," Sartre begins by asserting that there is a being of phenomena that surpasses the knowledge one has of it and provides the basis for such knowledge. And yet, this being is always relative to that being to whom all other appearances appear—consciousness, which in turn finds itself confronted with, that is, intentionally related to, a kind of being that is not itself. Sartre, however, moves beyond this dialectic between being and intentional consciousness on an epistemological plane to conclude that these epistemological relations are ontologically founded and that there are two absolutely separated regions of being: the being of the prereflective cogito and the being of phenomena, being for-itself and being-in-itself. These strategies in opposition to idealism—that is, focusing on the independence of being-in-itself and founding epistemology in a prior ontology—are further strengthened by the fact that they are situated at a level beneath that of epistemological judgment. Hence, it is the for-itself's ontological relationship to being-in-itself, that is, the capacity of consciousness to negate a ground in order that a figure might emerge, that forms the basis and condition for there being a negative judgment at all. Nonbeing is not introduced by a higher-level negative judgment. Sartre's antipathy to an omnipotent consciousness stands out also in his account of the givenness of the Other that constitutes an irreducible, relational fact that cannot be deduced either from a conceptual analysis of the Other-as-object or of one's own being-as-subject.[7]

Sartre spends a great deal of the rest of *Being and Nothingness* laying out the differences between being-in-itself and being-for-itself. On the one hand, being-in-itself is inherence in itself without any distance from itself, it is "glued to itself." It is opaque to itself because filled with itself. It is what it is and cannot be other than it is by, for example, choosing to be other than it is. It is solid, full positivity, absolute plenitude. Being-for-itself, on the other hand, arises in relation to being-in-itself, denying its undifferentiation, taking distance from it, and raising questions about it. Being-for-itself, an indivisible, indissoluble plenum of existence—but not a substance supporting qualities—not only introduces distinctions between itself and being-in-itself, it even turns on itself in a way that being-in-itself never could. It self-bifurcates, for example, in the sense that every positional consciousness of an object involves at the same time a non-positional consciousness of itself or in the sense that reflecting consciousness can take for its object this unreflective consciousness that precedes it and exceeds its grasp. The fact that consciousness, or the for-itself, can execute a nihilating withdrawal, a wrenching away from being or from its previous unreflective state springs from consciousness's character as continually unstable. It can order the totality of being around itself as its instruments and in the next moment re-order that totality differently. Whatever or however it has been in the past, even in the past instant, it can decide not to be, it can put its past out of play by inserting its nothingness between the past and the present. Whatever situations confront it, whatever motives appear to it, whatever values are proposed to it, the for-itself can constitute itself in relation to those situations or motives and then re-establish that relation in the next instant. "It is the obligation for the for-itself . . . to exist as a being which perpetually effects in itself a break in being."[8]

Sartre, thus, begins with phenomenological descriptions of the difference between consciousness and object that lead to an ontological divide that Sartre then confirms by further phenomenological descriptions, such as those elaborating the different features of for-itself and in-itself. This interplay between phenomenological description and ontology aims at elucidating a reality obscured by current, widespread prejudices.

One of the strongest of these prejudices is that being-in-itself can somehow or other causally determine for-itself. Since inert things cannot directly cause consciousness because its own assessing, interpreting, and choosing activity is always already involved in any encounter with such things, and if such things were to determine causally a for-itself, all such activity would have to be suspended or cancelled. But in removing this conscious, meaning-endowing activity, consciousness itself would be reduced to something passively pushed and pulled about like any thing in the world: it would become in-itself. Thus, Sartre maintains that, when it comes to these two separate regions of being, the being of phenomena can in no way act upon consciousness. Thus, the conscious questioner always has the permanent possibility of dissociating from the causal series which constitutes being and which can produce only being.[9]

Sartre reiterates this theme in various keys throughout the rest of *Being and Nothingness*. For instance, the precipice on which one is trapped does not cause one to fall since one can choose to take precautions. Or, what one has been in the past in no way determines one's future. The motives prompting action do not force it. It is always possible to turn to the habitual behaviors and values in which one has been raised or in which one is immersed and revise them. The freedom of for-itself, negated by any psychological determinism that would reduce for-itself to in-itself, requires as a therapeutic correlate existential psychoanalysis, in which the therapist helps the client uncover the choices and projects that have resulted in repression instead of, as Freudian theory does, attributing its origins to the pathological interaction of libidinal causal chains. Even the coefficients of adversity, e.g., the crag that resists one's scaling it, can acquire their character as impediments only in the face of one's freely adopted project. Since, in Sartre's view, the components of one's situation, i.e., one's place, one's past, one's environment, one's death, one's fellow human being, do not causally produce one's free reaction, Sartre concludes "that there is no situation in which the *given* would crush beneath its weight the freedom which constitutes it as such." This conclusion, however, leads Sartre to the seemingly exaggerated claims such as that not even torture dispossesses one of one's freedom and that even the slave in chains is free to break them. In spite of its difficulties, Sartre's conception of freedom as absolute highlights just how the categories of a mechanistic, causally deterministic science and the commonsense opinions it has influenced have unwittingly been applied to consciousness itself, even though these categories are only appropriate for explaining the behavior of things. The result is that consciousness has been concealed from itself through the conscious activity of science, and a phenomenology like Sartre's, critical of engrained prejudices, can unveil so well-hidden a subjectivity—after the pattern of Husserl's criticism of the physicist's causal elimination of consciousness in *Ideas I*.[10]

Sartre also targets this practice of burying free consciousness in his analysis of bad faith. In bad faith, rather than see one's chosen possibilities as sustained by a pure nihilating freedom, one apprehends them as engendered by an object outside of oneself, as if elements of one's situation caused one's free reactions to that situation. Of course, the very endeavor to blind oneself to an aspect of experience, such as one's freedom, implies that one has already recognized what one strives not to see: "one must think of it constantly in order to take care not to think of it." In addition to being a flight from responsibility for one's actions by projecting it onto factors outside of oneself, bad faith also entails a peculiar refusal of reflection, a decision to refrain from asking questions about one's own free conscious activity, just as the positivist stubbornly opposes any inquiry into the conscious activity establishing naturalism. In effect, the person of bad faith, by persistently resisting the mobility and liveliness of rationality, particularly its ever-readiness to turn flexibly wherever questions arise, even in regard to oneself, seems more and more to be characterized by the static immobility of the in-itself.[11]

In Sartre's thought, the Other, whose givenness at a prereflective level in the Look is detailed in extensive, rich phenomenological descriptions, can be neither encompassed by idealist constructions nor even "de-realized" through phenomenological reduction. Neither one's knowledge, nor a projection of oneself, nor some category unifying experience can account for the Other, since quite simply the Other is and does not derive from oneself. In fact, the Other is bound to oneself through a bond of being, not of knowledge. With the Other, a new dimension of existence opens upon beyond for-itself and in-itself, each of which still remains intact. To be sure, Sartre's description of the Look as alienating, spelling the death of one's possibilities, and reducing one to an object reflects the polarization between for-itself and in-itself. Just as the for-itself continually negates any tendency to congeal into being or be swallowed up by it, so the for-itself faced with another for-itself fears being consumed by it. In a passage echoing Hegel's dialectic, Sartre sums up his account of intersubjectivity, "Not only do I make myself not-be this other being by denying that he is me, I make myself not-be a being who is making himself not-be me."[12] In this oppositional pattern of relationship, in which one strains to reduce another or oneself to the status of an object in concrete relationships of love, masochism, indifference, desire, hate, or sadism, Sartre unveils how an all-but-suppressed consciousness continually surges up to undo the objectification. Sartre's recovery of such consciousness, as well submerged in relationships as it had been in bad faith or psychological determinism, reflects his phenomenological underpinnings as well as the surprising reversals of fortune in Hegel's Master-Slave dialectic. Finally, if in bad faith one can flee one's own subjectivity by attributing responsibility for one's actions to a created or inherited unchangeable *essence*, so it is possible in intersubjective relationships to subsume the Other under one's look by assigning to the Other a nature or universal essence that covers over the singularity and vibrancy of the Other's for-itself, which must wait for a later phenomenological uncovering.[13]

The phenomenology of *Being and Nothingness* underlies several of Sartre's important discussions of prejudice, such as *Anti-Semite and Jew*, *Black Orpheus*, and "The Respectful Prostitute." While Sartre may have modified this phenomenology in later works, he himself acknowledges that he never abandoned it. Hence, the later biographies of Baudelaire, Genet, and Flaubert center on the struggle of conscious freedom to fashion a self in the face of a conditioning, but not determining situation that includes the Look of others. While the later Sartre acknowledges that his early view of freedom had been exaggerated and that life had taught him the "power of circumstances (*la force des choses*)" he also admits at the same time that "a man can always make something out of what is made of him." Even in the *Critique of Dialectical Reason*, where the word phenomenology is never mentioned and certain revisions of *Being and Nothingness* are introduced, as shall be seen, reflection and free action liberate collectivities from the inertia of the practico-inert (itself a human product) and from dispersion in seriality. In such processes, collectivities become "fused groups," giving the law to themselves through a pledge of faith. Indeed, the very notion of dialectical reason encompassing the more narrow scientific analytic reason is itself a kind of transcendental phenomenological self-reflective reasoning that reasons about reason itself, as Husserl had done in his examination of positivism. Since the phenomenology of these later works is present but muted, it will be necessary to touch only briefly on how these later works enrich the understanding of discrimination articulated within the earlier works produced in the wake of *Being and Nothingness*.[14]

2. SARTREAN PHENOMENOLOGY, ANTI-SEMITISM, AND DISCRIMINATION

In 1944, a year after *Being and Nothingness* appeared, Sartre produced his first and perhaps most thorough piece devoted to bigotry, *Anti-Semite and Jew (Reflexions sur la question juive)*, which, published in 1946, contained pages that Frantz Fanon described as "the finest I have ever read." The first two parts of the text explore the position of the crude anti-Semite and the democratic anti-Semite who constitute a "situation" of anti-Semitism in the face of which the Jew can adopt the inauthentic or authentic responses that are explained in the third and fourth sections. The structure of the book, pivoting about the notion of "situation," follows the pattern of Hegel's Master-Slave dialectic in which the master paradoxically forfeits his authenticity through domination while the slave attains his through labor. But twentieth-century phenomenology informs *Anti-Semite and Jew* as much as Hegel's Master-Slave insofar as the book demonstrates the processes by which consciousness either flees itself or takes possession of itself, or, to put it in Sartrean terms, how for-itself seeks to sink into in-itself or to recuperate its own authenticity.[15]

The crude anti-Semite represents most clearly a bad-faith struggle on the part of for-itself to negate itself and to become in-itself—the futile, secret dream that in *Being and Nothingness* Sartre attributes to all human reality, intent, as it is, on becoming an unchanging God, that is, on becoming not what it is and becoming what it is not. The crude anti-Semite espouses mere opinions that, like tastes, are all equally valid and so beyond rational disputation. For instance, crude anti-Semites affirm unfounded opinions such as that all Jews are selfish and tactless, that they encourage servants to insubordination, that all furriers are Jews, or that Jews are favored unfairly on competitive state examinations (although it might be possible to wrest from the anti-Semite an admission to not having studied for such an examination). The patent invalidity of these affirmations belie the anti-Semite's confidence that anti-Semitism is causally elicited by an obvious, external, factor: Jewish despicability. Rather, this confidence that anti-

Semitism is determined from without actually conceals the anti-Semite's "free and total choice of oneself, a comprehensive attitude." By conceiving anti-Semitism as causally induced, crude anti-Semites appear to be a mere in-itself upon which other in-itself forces have impacted and left their mark, as if no for-itself or no subjectivity were involved at all. In this respect, the anti-Semite unwittingly mimics the reductionistic physicist who, according to Husserl, holds that the object of physics causes the very consciousness that makes that object's appearance possible. The result is, of course, that anti-Semitic preconceptions and choices are not even seen and so never subjected to critique—the anti-Semite ultimately fears reasoning itself. Anti-Semites further reinforce their lack of self-critique by touting society's concurrence with their opinions and by seeking refuge in the "herd" instead of facing themselves.[16]

In addition to this cognitive rigidity, anti-Semitism is rooted in attitudes promoting obstinate unchangeability. If Jews are the source of all evil in the world, as the anti-Semite believes, the simple *negative* removal of the Jews would eliminate all evil, and thus the anti-Semite is exempted from exercising that *positive* inventiveness and initiative required of those who are masters of their own destiny, weighted with agonizing and infinite responsibility. Similarly by treating the Jew as an inferior, anti-Semites catapult themselves among the elite; however this elitism, won simply by birth as a gentile, resembles a kind of aristocratic elitism that one does not merit by one's labor and that is given once for all and so needs no struggle to be preserved. Anti-Semites can demand order of others, but assault Jews since they are not themselves accountable. Finally, the anti-Semitic preference for being static is projected onto the Jew to whom the anti-Semite ascribes a metaphysical essence, "Jewishness," that drives the Jew to do evil and that the Jew cannot modify any more than fire can avoid burning.[17]

Whereas rational persons grope for truth, recognize the tentativeness of their reasoning, maintain themselves in openness to any intervening doubt—epitomizing the for-itself and consciousness as Husserl has described it—the anti-Semite undertakes a project of bad faith, deliberately deploying his consciousness to turn himself into an cognitive and attitudinal in-itself.

> We are now in a position to understand the anti-Semite. He is a man who is afraid. Not of the Jews, to be sure, but of himself, of his own consciousness, of his liberty, of his instincts, of his responsibilities, of solitariness, of change, of society, and of the world. . . . He chooses

[paradoxically!] the permanence and impenetrability of stone, the total irresponsibility of the warrior who obeys his leaders—and he has no leader. He chooses to acquire nothing, to deserve nothing; he assumes that everything is given him as his birthright—and he is not noble. He chooses finally a Good that is fixed once and for all, beyond question, out of reach; he dares not examine it for fear of being led to challenge it and having to seek it in another form. The Jew only serves him as a pretext; elsewhere his counterpart will make use of the Negro or the man of yellow skin. . . . The anti-Semite is a man who wishes to be pitiless stone, a furious torrent, a devastating thunder-bolt—anything except a man.[18]

Perhaps out of zeal to defend the Jew and other minorities against the conventional, nonrational prejudices of crude anti-Semites, the democratic anti-Semite attempts to uphold the abstract and universal subject of the rights that pertain to all human beings as citizens. According to Sartre, the democratic anti-Semite envisions the individual only an ensemble of the universal traits constitutive of human nature, denies that there even is a problem of Jewish exclusion, resents the clannishness of minority groups, encourages assimilation, and discourages overt expressions of Jewishness that, in the democrat's view, are likely to evoke anti-Semitism. But, as Sartre sees it, this emphasis separates "the Jew from his religion, from his family, from his ethnic community, in order to plunge him into the democratic crucible whence he will emerge naked and alone, an individual and solitary particle like all the other particles." In requiring that the Jew be a human being before being a Jew, the universal nature takes precedence over the individual for-itself, a metaphysical essence is imposed as much as it is by the crude anti-Semite, and finally the democratic look that entombs the Other's subjectivity masquerades under the aspiration to universalist emancipation. A phenomenology with eyes for the particular can penetrate beneath the prejudice of universalization that pretends to be only rational and not prejudicial at all. This pretense to universality divorced from any subjectivity turns out to be the best device to conceal what may be the most active and destructive subjectivity of all—the subjectivity of the democratic anti-Semite.[19]

The very structure of the book, which inserts a discussion of the "situation" in between these versions of anti-Semitism and the Jewish responses to it, highlights the spontaneous, uncaused subjectivity of the Jew in the face of this situation. If anti-Semitism could causally produce a demoralization in the Jew without the Jew in at least some inchoate way freely cooperating with this demoralization, then the Jew would be reduced to in-itself and the sharp line separating human reality from the in-itself would be blurred. Furthermore, if the active subjectivity cooperating with its own enslavement recedes from view, so also would its capability of choosing to be otherwise.[20]

However, when Sartre sets out to specify the "situation" of the Jew, that is, to determine the characteristics that confront and define Jews and that Jews can freely reject or appropriate, he denies any importance not only to hereditary and somatic characteristics, but also to factors such as religion and history that Jewish consciousness and activity would have played an active role in constituting. For Sartre, the common bond of Jews does not derive from anything that Jews have done, but from the fact that "they live in a community which takes them for Jews." At the very moment that Sartre denies that the situation exercises power over the free Jewish for-itself, he also denies that same Jewish for-itself any role in the establishment of its own Jewish identity. Fortunately, Sartre later repudiated this position as a superficial description prevalent in Christian circles, and he also conceded that he had read no Jewish author in preparation for *Anti-Semite and Jew*. These errors in Sartre's analysis, and his own subsequent retraction, indicate that even sympathetic gentile opponents of anti-Semitism can construct a portrayal of their Others, namely Jews, that is always liable to contestation by the irrepressible subjectivity of the Other, who can always look back at the look that reifies.[21]

Having defined authenticity as true and lucid consciousness of one's situation and assumption of the risks and responsibilities it implies, Sartre proceeds to point out what he takes to be inauthentic Jewish responses to the situation defined by anti-Semitism. The inauthentic Jew may adopt an almost continuous reflective attitude that can manifest itself in excessively self-conscious attempts to avoid being characterized as Jewish. Thus, for example, many Jews extensively deliberated as to whether they should enter the French resistance against the Nazis since such resistance was so in line with Jewish interests that they might not be able to embrace the resistance as they thought they should, namely as French and not Jewish. Furthermore, for Sartre, the subtle turning on oneself typical of Jewish self-irony preempts any critique from an external look. This self-aware distancing from self characterizes Jewish efforts to assimilate, to be recognized as a human being first, even though such attempts rarely succeed. Aware of the anti-Semitic look even in the privacy of the home, the Jew can try to weed out obvious "Jewish" behaviors in his wife or children through a kind of reflective standing over against one-self, as if the Jew had internalized the anti-Semite in order to flail masochistically himself and his family.[22]

A related inauthentic response involves heightening one's abstract, rationalist, or intellectual qualities. On the one hand, such Jewish rationalism wins Sartre's admiration since it often manifests itself as a creative, youthful, lively love of humanity; as a passion for a univer-sality opposed to all particularist conceptions; as an ascetical, purified disembodiment; as an insistence on proof and evidence to be given through rational intuitions. Such Jewish rationalism is antagonistic to the irrational powers of tradition, race, national destiny, and instinct that are the refuge of the anti-Semite. On the other hand, this ratio-nalism results in deleterious effects for the Jew in Sartre's view: a deprivation of vital values, lack of veneration for and instrumentaliza-tion of the body, discomfort with one's own body leading to shame or extreme modesty, an absence of the tact that is associated with irra-tional traditions of politeness, and finally a predeliction for money, the universal, abstract means of exchange that protects Jewish anonymity. Although Sartre in this sketch of the Jew seems to have tried to explain sympathetically stereotypes of the Jews that he has uncritically accepted as accurate, it is also evident that the Jew here portrayed by Sartre exhibits all the spontaneity, freedom, self-reflexive agility, and unprejudiced rationality that are the marks of Sartrean for-itself and the Husserlian consciousness. Paradoxically, for all its value, Jewish rationalism, according to Sartre, often issues in a suppression of Jewish particularity as did democratic anti-Semitism. Jewish ratio-nalism permits Jews to conform to societal (liberal, democratic) expectations, deny their Jewishness, and banish their true, individual for-itself beneath a putative universalization. Hence, for Sartre, while anti-Semites conceal their for-itself beneath the guise of reducing others and themselves to in-itself, inauthentic Jews can mask their own deterioration into an unfree, conformist in-itself beneath the veneer of a vivacious for-itself.[23]

While rationality is the medicine for the irrational, crude anti-Semite, it becomes an instrument of oppression disguised as emanci-pation in the hands of the democratic anti-Semite and the inauthentic Jew. Similarly, the very notion of equality that must be upheld against anti-Semitism can in turn be deployed to disavow one's distinctiveness and alterity. Sartre's analysis here seems to have arrived at a precipice from which Nietzsche and some postmodern skeptics have already leapt in despair over rationality's continual tendency to pulverize and level out differences. Only in chapter 6 will it become clearer that this mistrust of rationality, universalization, and the value of equality itself springs from a richer notion of rationality born out of a phenomenological desire to burrow beneath what is taken to be universal, to return to the things themselves, and to have eyes for what is particular or different.

Cognizant of rationality's pitfalls and, more importantly, its masquerades, which Nietzsche above all uncovered, Sartre places his final hope in that which resists idealist constructions, which is irreducible to his projections and categories, and which in no way derives from himself: the Other, whose subjectivity surges up in the eyes that gaze back at the gentile. Contrary to Margaret A. Simons's belief that the concept of the Other is not to be found in *Anti-Semite and Jew*, Sartre places his final hope in the ability of the authentic Jew to make "himself a Jew, in the face of all and against all." This comment anticipates his later observation in his preface to Frantz Fanon's *The Wretched of the Earth*, "We only become what we are by the radical and deepseated refusal of that which others have made of us."[24]

If gentiles in the course of *Anti-Semite and Jew* may have succumbed to any forgetfulness about their own responsibility for anti-Semitism, Sartre brings it to consciousness by insisting, in the end, that anti-Semitism is not a "Jewish problem" but a gentile one, just as the "Negro problem" in the United States is really a white one. Remedies must be sought in a concrete liberalism, in education, in a socialist revolution that will restore human solidarity, and in a militant league of both Jews and non-Jews banded against anti-Semitism.[25]

Sartre extends his phenomenological examination of in-itself, subjectivity, and intersubjectivity beyond anti-Semitism to other forms of discrimination, such as racism. In *Black Orpheus*, published in 1949, Sartre interprets Negritude, which Africana poets promoted as a glorying in the blackness despised by colonizers, as an affective attitude toward the world. Like Genet exulting in the imposed title of thief, the Negro took up the words of the colonizers, "gathered them from the mud in order to wear them with pride." Like the for-itself, Negritude is a becoming, "the surpassing of a fixed situation by a free consciousness." Although Sartre recognized that the Negritude movement, by appropriating oppressive terms, preempted further oppression, as did Jewish self-irony, and that this movement allowed Africans to stand before the colonizers as subjects, he later grew more critical. The proud demand for Negritude ended up confirming segregation insofar as it internalized the enemy's *Weltanschauung*, including the belief that there is a distinctive black character (conceived first of all by the colonizer, as one might expect, in terms of being lazy, thieving, etc.). As in *Anti-Semite and Jew*, the very instruments to which one turns for liberation can become part of one's subjugation.[26]

A more in-depth presentation of racism, repeating many of the themes of *Anti-Semite and Jew*, occurs in Sartre's drama *The Respectful Prostitute*, published in French in 1947. In this play, a prostitute in the southern United States is pressured into testifying against an African-American in order to protect a prominent white citizen who has killed another African-American and sexually molested her. The characters participating in various degrees in racist attitudes resemble the irrational, crude anti-Semite, who exchanges the freedom of for-itself for the security of in-itself. Hence these racist personages are presented as superstitious (e.g., blaming a bracelet for their problems or wondering if it is bad luck to see a "nigger" when waking up), traditional/religious (e.g., Lizzie, the woman, is afraid "to bear false witness"), authoritarian (Fred forbids Lizzie to talk about his mother), paternalistic (Senator Clark calls Lizzie "my child"), projecting their own wickedness onto the Other epitomized as evil (Fred tells Lizzie that she and the "nigger" are the Devil), determined by social pressure and hungry for social approval (the senator asks Lizzie "do you suppose that a whole town could be mistaken" in its racism?), inconsistent and unaccountable (Thomas, who shot the African-American and molested Lizzie, is a "leading citizen" and should not be punished, even though innocent African-Americans should be), prone to impute essences to their enemies (e.g., "niggers" dawdle, chisel, sign, buy pink and green suits; "communists" are unquestionably evil), and sadistically seeking to dominate the bodies of others through lynching or rape, as if one could manipulate their very subjectivity (Fred tells Lizzie that the lynching of an innocent African-American made him want her). These proclivities to debase one's own or another's for-itself to a mere thing, a mere in-itself, could be rectified by heightening one's own rationality and self-critique, by being more fully the for-itself from which one in bad faith flees. But Sartre shows himself no more sanguine about the emancipative power of reason here than he was in *Anti-Semite and Jew*, as is evident when Sartre has his main character, Fred, reflect on how racism subverts all rational standards and so all possibility of self-criticism. Thus, Fred observes, "There is no truth; there's only whites and blacks, that's all."[27]

As a result, Sartre seeks to supplement rationality with an alternative remedy for prejudice. At the end of the play, Lizzie, the prostitute, comes *face to face* with the "The Negro," whose lack of a personal name in the play suggests the metaphysical essence or universal imputed to him by a racist society. Even though she has testified falsely against him, he surprises her by respecting her, treating her with warmth, and even refusing to shoot white people. Upon meeting the Negro *face to face* and being confronted with his ethical goodness beneath the impersonal and derogatory category of "nigger," she finds herself placed most deeply in question. She desperately resorts to a rapid-fire series of reassuring conventions, "Don't touch me," "I don't like niggers," "a whole city can't be completely wrong." In this play, as in *Anti-Semite and Jew*, Sarte envisions a two-pronged cure for discrimination: augmented rationality and exposure to the look of the Other, contesting one's categorizations.[28]

While phenomenology generally restricts itself to a study of meaning-structures, Sartre ventures a discussion of the systematic, socio-political, and economic dimensions of racism in his *Critique of Dialectical Reason* and in *Situations 5*, published in 1960 and 1964, respectively. For instance, Sartre argues that the French annihilated the internal, feudal, agricultural structures of Algeria and replaced them with liberal capitalism. In order to maintain this system, they found themselves trying to keep the Arabs disunified, or serialized, to the point of even recruiting highly sectarian Islamic cultists to propagate divisive superstitions among the Arabs. Besides this strategy, it was necessary to justify the brutality through which the French had first of all imposed colonization, and so the colonizers ascribed a racist "essence" to the colonized, asserting that natives were lazy, dishonest, dirty, eternally uncontrolled children, and hence the colonists *had to* subjugate them and maintain them in servitude. As the colonizers reduced natives to a thing, they also reduced themselves to in-itself insofar as they claimed that their brutal act of colonization was "caused" by native helplessness, almost as though no free choices on their part were involved. After the initial colonization, racism came to form part of the practico-inert, serializing relations between colonizers and colonized and among the colonized themselves. When the Algerians rebelled against this entire system, the French again responded with violence and again justified themselves by claiming that Algerian violence "provoked" them. Further, as the anti-Semite did with Jew, the French attributed to Arabs a fixed essence that inevitably produced the violence that evoked counterrevolutionary violence. The end effect, though, was the dehumanization of the French themselves, as Sartre observes in *Situations 5*:

> The impossible dehumanization of the oppressed returns and be-
> comes the alienation of the oppressor: it is he, it is he himself who
> resuscitates by his least gesture the humanity that he wishes to
> destroy; and, as he denies it among the others, he finds it especially
> as a hostile force. To escape this, it is necessary to mineralize oneself,
> to give oneself the opaque consistency and impermeability of a rock,
> in short, to "dehumanize oneself" in turn.[29]

Of course, the French engaged in further bad faith evasions of their own responsibility by claiming that they were too far away to know what was really going on in Algeria or by constructing the false universal that Algerian counterviolence was exactly the same as French repression.[30]

While battling these rationalizations, or distortions of reason, with better reasoning and the reasoned recovery of the subjectivity one has hidden from oneself, Sartre, in this later treatment of systematic discrimination, reverts again to his other critical touchstone in the struggle against prejudice: exposure to the face of the Other. When tortured within an Algerian prison, Henri Alleg, "nude, trembling with cold, tied to a board, and clammy with dried vomit, reduces all these ploys to the pitiable truth: they are comedies played out by imbeciles."[31] The resurgent subjectivity of the Other puts an entire violent system on trial.[32]

Saint Genet presents Sartre with another arena for deploying the weaponry of his phenomenology in the war against discrimination. Even though in that work Sartre modifies his earlier grandiose conception of human freedom by admitting that there are people who are what they are "by birth and without hope of change," Sartre nevertheless appreciates Genet's homosexuality as a free defiance of what is. Genet rebuffs the moralistic classifications that conventional society would impose upon him and thus confronts their look with his own insolent look—to society's great astonishment. Otherness here affords the possibility of societal critique and renovation since the ways in which people are not "normal" are taken by Sartre as key to autonomy and freedom. In fact, abjection, like phenomenological *epoché*, bestows a kind of cognitive autonomy by permitting one to see clearly the world over against oneself. Those whom society has confined to the background—adolescents, women, homosexuals—exercise a "corrosive action on being." Clearly the idea of the Other whom no cultural system or cognitive framework can subsume without remainder rises to prominence in this work long before that idea would become central in Levinas's philosophy.[33]

In spite of Sartre's obvious commitment to combat these varieties of discrimination with the weapons of phenomenology, there is a significant body of literature that makes a convincing case regarding the shadows of his own unexamined prejudices, particularly regarding women. Various feminist scholars point out how Sartre presents all his female fictional characters (such as Lizzie above) as passive, reactive characters whose lives support the desires of male characters who, in their turn, often speak of women in a derogatory way. Moreover, his descriptions of desire for women resemble that desire that one might have for inanimate objects, and he depicts the process of knowing as "deflowering," "penetration," "conquest," and "appropriation." In addition, his existential framework appears to resurrect a classical form of voluntarism which, some authors argue, could be used insidiously to blame women for the sexism they have internalized, just as he seems to impute responsibility to Jews for cooperating with anti-Semitism insofar as they may have internalized any of its beliefs. In spite of his abolition of determined natures or essences for for-itself, Sartre so assimilates distinctly female qualities with the in-itself that he implies an in-itself nature for women that is invested with utterly negative value. Indeed in his discussion of slimes and holes in *Being and Nothingness*, Sartre associates holes with the idea of woman's sex as a "voracious mouth." Hazel Barnes concurs with these criticisms, and she adds that Sartre himself admitted to vestiges of an engrained male chauvinism that he found difficult to eradicate. Barnes concludes, though, that such sexism is at variance with the central philosophy of *Being and Nothingness* that remains potentially valuable as a support to feminism insofar as it in general denies that biology constitutes destiny.[34]

3. CRITIQUE

As was the case for many second-generation phenomenologists, Sartre shaped his phenomenology in reaction to what he perceived as the excessive idealist tendencies of the late Husserl. Thus Sartre strove to unseat Husserl's omnipotent, transcendental ego by returning to the spontaneous, prereflective consciousness that constitutes the transcendental "I" and that introduces negation into the world long before one formulates negative judgments at a predicative level. In the "Introduction" to *Being and Nothingness*, Sartre begins with a brief phenomenological account of the epistemological experience involved when consciousness confronts the being of phenomena over against itself. In an effort to preclude any idealism that might ensue from such an *epistemological* starting point, Sartre, like Heidegger, moves swiftly to point out the *ontological* foundations of this epistemological experience, completely in accord with the subtitle of his *magnum opus, An Essay on Phenomenological Ontology*. From that point, Sartre proceeds to delineate two absolutely separated regions of being: for-itself and in-itself, and then confirms this ontological dichotomy by extensive phenomenological descriptions of how differently being-for-itself and being-in-itself are experienced. Later, rich phenomenological descriptions of the Look reveal the Other, underivable from the consciousness to whom that Other is given, and a new ontological dimension, being-for-others. Sartre, in effect, has attempted to spell out a theory before all theory, a theory which lays out the ontological relationships "which must render all experience possible."[35]

Sartre's starting point, the epistemological experience between consciousness and its object, which he immediately amplifies into an ontology with rigidly distinct regions of being, presupposes, however, a more originary starting point, namely the unreflective stage preceding the clear distinctions that Sartrean reflection introduces. Merleau-Ponty, who follows the later Husserl in trying to think behind theory itself, describes this moment when one is not set over against the world as a subject, but is plunged into the midst of the world, where it is not easy to separate clearly what belongs to the subject and what to the object. Furthermore, Sartre's ontological bifurcation does not do justice to one's lived experience of the body which is neither an inert in-itself, as Descartes thought, nor the lucid consciousness of for-itself, but rather possesses a bodily "knowing" or "intentionality" all its own, as is illustrated by the body's ability to maneuver in its spatial environs or to perform actions (e.g., typing) without engaging in any symbolic or objectifying function. For all Sartre's efforts to escape Husserl's idealism, his own brief phenomenological descriptions, attenuated by his haste to arrive at ontology, fail to do justice to the complexity and ambiguity of lived experience, which he forces into conformity with his ontological categories.[36]

Another difficulty is that Sartre's subject-object starting point pre-scinds from the social relations of the life-world, articulated so thoroughly by Alfred Schutz, who followed the later Husserl's path in returning to the life-world as the matrix of all theory. Even though it is true that Sartre advanced phenomenological discussions of the Other by his discussion of intersubjectivity later in *Being and Nothingness*, still his analysis suffers insofar as it depends not so much on phenomenological description as on the earlier developed ontological polarization between for-itself and in-itself, as will be shown below.

Merleau-Ponty and Schutz not only reflect more expansively on the starting point for reflection and theory than Sartre does, they also reflect on their own reflecting, that is, they set forth more carefully than Sartre their own methodologies. Thus, Merleau-Ponty thinks of himself as engaging in a "radical reflection" that reflects on reflection itself as reflection-on-an-unreflective-experience. Similarly, Schutz acknowledges that he is engaging in a constitutive phenomenology of the natural attitude from within the natural attitude, that is, a phenomenological psychology describing the social world as it is given to its actors before the intervention of formal phenomenological reduction would require a bracketing of its existence. In contrast, since Sartre does not reflect as carefully or methodologically on his own reflection, it is not surprising that he begins with the subject-object relation—a starting point that presupposes without recognizing its own extensive reflective abstraction from an already encompassing unreflective setting. It is as if Sartre's zeal to get on with an ontology does not allow him the leisure to reflect on his own method or to elucidate more thoroughly the circumstances from which his ontology commences. Sartre's theory before all theory itself rests on too much unrecognized theory.[37]

Because Sartre neglects his own phenomenological origins and often replaces good description with rational reconstruction, as several commentators have observed, he misunderstands the nature of freedom and subsequently prejudice. For instance, the claim that if anti-Semitism initially demoralizes Jews, it is because somehow Jews in some inchoate way permit it to have that effect on them seems to impute too much vigilance to consciousness. Rather, one often absorbs prejudices from one's environment immediately, without free, conscious assent, as if one were somewhere in between in-itself and for-itself, and only subsequently recognizes and assesses such prejudices. In this context, Sartre's intent to keep separate the in-itself and the for-itself here seems to outpace what phenomenological description permits.[38]

Of course, as is well known, Sartre underwent something of a revolution in his own theoretical viewpoint, as he struggled to integrate his earlier existential standpoint with Marxism, which he described in his *Search for a Method* as "the one philosophy of our time which we cannot go beyond." In that book, he concurs with Marxist and psychoanalytic accounts of social, economic, historical, and psychological conditioning, but he does not abandon entirely his earlier writings and succumb to mechanistic determinism since freedom acts back on its own conditions. Similarly his *Critique of Dialectical Reason*, published at the same time as *Search for a Method*, examines how "all men are slaves in so far as their life unfolds in the practico-inert field and in so far as this field is always conditioned by scarcity." However, via progressive, incremental reflection, groups resist the inertia they unreflectively live, exercise freedom and creativity, form fused groups, revise social structures, and, unfortunately, may in the end capitulate to the inertia of inflexible institutionalization, until a future moment of freedom will begin the cycle again. These later revisions of Sartre's proceed by incorporating his earlier existentialism within a wider socio-historical context and modifying it accordingly, but not by reviewing his practice of phenomenology, as this chapter suggests he ought to have done.[39]

In scattered comments throughout his later works, Sartre acknowledged that he had founded *Being and Nothingness* (and presumably the texts immediately following its publication) upon an excessively rationalist philosophy of consciousness, that life had taught him the force of things, and that people can be damaged from birth "without hope of change." In the latest of his works, *The Family Idiot*, he admits that parents reduce children to quasi-objects by executing their judgments for them so extensively that it becomes impossible ever to root out all that pertains to the bourgeois identity one has received. Thus, the later Sartre seems to have abandoned his categorical concept of freedom and to come around to what Frederick Olafson called "dispositional freedom." Merleau-Ponty described this kind of freedom when he noted that one *lives* one's class or social existence long before one comes to recognize it through piecemeal acts of reflection and decides to affirm or deny it. Merleau-Ponty's comment suggests that Sartre's reversion to the pretheoretical level would have done well to focus not on the subject-object encounter but on the lifeworld in which one inherits socially transmitted and reinforced typifications, which one only gradually and reflectively abandons or appropriates. Indeed, a work such as *The Respectful Prostitute* indicates how deeply ingrained such typifications are and how recalcitrant they are to reflective revision. In spite of Sartre's later modifications and retractions, it cannot be denied that his account of freedom's subterfuges and its possibilities has contributed greatly to the phenomenological project of bringing consciousness out of hiding.[40]

Some of Sartre's insights in *Being and Nothingness* that are most fruitful for the problem of prejudice cluster about his phenomenology of the Other who looks back at those looking at him or her and who can contest and refuse the essences or universals that are the onlooker's instruments of domination. This Other, given at a prereflective level prior to knowledge or concepts, resists and places in question even reigning systems of rationality that are so adept at concealing their own power motivations. Perhaps the hostile Hobbist character of this look may be appropriate for victims of prejudice such as Jews, blacks, and homosexuals, whose difference and distinctiveness have been obliterated or ignored for so long. Nevertheless, there are limitations in this reciprocally predatory and polarized picture of human relationships, as Sartre himself seems to have understood in *Notebooks for an Ethics*. Such limitations can be traced back to the original for-itself/in-itself separation in which for-itself conceives in-itself "as closing in upon the for-itself," threatening to engulf it, and thus must resist by negating or nihilating the in-itself. Once Sartre has presented this polarization, it is perfectly consistent that this defensively defined for-itself, when confronted by the look of another for-itself, should transfer its behavior toward in-itself to the newly appearing for-itself and thus should strive "to be what it is in the form of a refusal of the Other." It is no wonder that in human relationships as Sartre describes them, "Not only do I make myself not-be this other being by denying that he is me, I make myself not-be a being who is making himself not-be me."[41]

Sartre's phenomenology of the Other, to whom one is related by a relationship of being, beneath knowledge and irreducible to one's knowledge of the Other, merits praise, but do human relationships involve nothing more than each seeking to master the Other? Levinas's phenomenology suggests the same independence and autonomy of the Other, but his Other summons one to be ethical and invites solidarity. Levinas's account of intersubjectivity, to be presented in depth later, seems more accurate, but it is also more suited for healing the politics of a war of all against all that rules in contemporary political processes and that leads some to understand all societal procedures, including for example, affirmative action, to be discussed later, as nothing other than one group seeking to impose its will upon another. Sartre's view might only reinforce this stridency and competitiveness; indeed it itself may be a philosophical symptom of underlying political and economic relationships lacking any sense of solidarity, as he himself suggested. Levinasian alterity would be more likely, it would seem, to invite the for-itself to exchange its self-protectiveness for generosity and thus to surpass itself infinitely as befits for-itself in Sartre's phenomenology.[42]

But Sartrean alterity, which objects to rationalizations and counterfeit universals, including the false equality trumpeted by the democratic anti-Semite, involves no repudiation of rationality but rather its critique, as the title of this chapter suggests. There is no doubt that Sartre's problem with the crude anti-Semite and the racists portrayed in *The Respectful Prostitute* is that they refuse to face up to their own preconceptions and subject them to rational scrutiny. Their taking refuge in whatever is widely socially acceptable, their immersion in superstition and tradition, their intellectual inconsistency and lack of accountability, and their reliance on the irrational forces of national destiny and instinct inevitably issue in the kind of violent outcomes that would never result were rational self-awareness to govern their behavior. At the same time, Sartre has his hesitations about the emancipative power of rationality *by itself*. For he is well aware that the democratic anti-Semite as well as the inauthentic Jew's embrace of rationalism, universality, and abstraction even in the name of undercutting crude anti-Semitism's irrationalism can camouflage the suppression of differences. Exposure to the Other's contestation makes it possible for one to be rationally critical even of one's rationality.[43]

Sartrte's writings on prejudice display the restless, dynamic movement of the for-itself. That for-itself is ever turning on itself, self-bifurcating, wrenching itself away from a previous unreflexive state, breaking with what it had just thought, undermining stability, and questioning what has been taken for granted. In fact, one can interpret the for-itself as well as the Husserlian account of consciousness as prototypes of how rationality itself functions. In other writings, too, Sartre seems to be fashioning a theory of rationality which the for-itself exemplifies. For instance, in his posthumously published *Truth and Existence*, Sartre presents the relativistic abandonment of philosophical discourse as equivalent to the demise of the for-itself, since to judge is to will, to risk oneself, to commit one's life to the revelation of truth, to expose oneself generously to the other's critique, in contrast to acquiescing passively in opinions assimilated from one's heredity, environment, and education, without feeling any need to validate what one holds. In addition, Sartre suggests a similar model of rationality in *The Communists and Peace*, when he notes how the bourgeoisie infects a whole intellectual culture with individualism. In bourgeois culture, one samples probabalism, tolerance, skepticism, objectivism and reaches the relativistic conclusion that all opinions are equally respectable and so sit lifelessly side by side without every provoking mutual exchange, engagement, or revision. Persons end up ensconced in themselves, atomized, serialized, incapable of growing or moving beyond themselves; relativism reduces a person to inert in-itself. For Sartre, these epistemological relations reflect underlying capitalist property relations that promote the reciprocal exteriority, impenetrability, and self-enclosure that are the marks of the in-itself. Finally, as another instance, Freud's progress in *The Freud Scenario* through the practice of hypnotism to an explanatory model utilizing sexual abuse to, finally, the Oedipus drama exemplifies the dynamism of rationality and its prototypical counterpart, the for-itself, as they surpass one partial viewpoint after another.[44]

Sartre's more practical writings on discrimination presuppose the higher-level reflections in *Being and Nothingness* on the character of for-itself. In turn, if the for-itself-rationality discussed in *Being and Nothingness* is not to short-circuit its own dynamic movement, some reflection, not as clearly present in Sartre as in Merleau-Ponty or Schutz, would be required on this very discourse of *Being and Nothingness* that articulates the for-itself. Similarly, for Husserl, raising the question of the transcendental ego was inevitable since anyone reflecting would be impelled by one's own reflection to give an account of one's own conscious reflective processes and structures and finally to give an account of the reflective process in which one gives an account of those conscious reflective processes. The reflective process initiated in opposition to the blind prejudices of racism and anti-Semitism are situated at the concrete level of a trajectory that would climax in reasoning about the character of rationality itself, unless for some arbitrary reason one decided to break off the questioning process. There are traces of such a high level of self-reflexivity in Sartre's own works, for example, when he reasons about the character of reason as dialectical and analytic in the *Critique of Dialectical Reason*, when he speculates that reason is not purely utilitarian (strategic?), or when he distinguishes science from art and ethics or practical thought from scientific thought.[45]

Nevertheless, these are only embryonic references to a transcendental perspective, which, like that of Karl-Otto Apel to be developed in chapter 5, might furnish a theory of ethics, practical rationality, and equality in the light of which the immorality of prejudice, of which Sartre is obviously convinced, can be justified. Furthermore, when it comes to determining which first principle might prevail in a Sartrean ethical theory, there are only hints. At the end of *Being and Nothingness*, Sartre suggests that a Kantian-type ethics might follow from his belief that freedom is the unique source of value. In his essay "Existentialism Is a Humanism," he continues in this direction by arguing that people reveal themselves as lawmakers every time they make a choice, but in the end his existentialism prohibits any wholehearted embrace of what he takes to be Kant's rule-centered ethics. Unfortunately, Sartre here fails to realize the distinction that Kantians, and most recently Jürgen Habermas, have drawn between a transcendental (or quasi-transcendental) discourse through which one could establish and justify a first principle and a discourse of application that does not function deductively from such a first principle but that rather calls for existential, creative, intuitive as well as argumentative abilities to apply it to unique situations.[46]

Thomas Anderson praises Sartre's later ethics, found principally in his 1964 Rome Lecture, an unpublished, uncirculated manuscript kept at the Bibliothèque Nationale in Paris. This later ethics, in Anderson's view, is founded on basic human needs and sounds very much like a natural law ethics and which, unlike an ethics based on freedom, would avoid arbitrariness. Anderson, though, overlooks how formal Kantian ethics also proscribes any arbitrariness. Furthermore, it seems strange to imagine Sartre espousing natural law theory since he shows himself so opposed to an ethics based upon Being throughout his published works and particularly in *Saint Genet*, in which he considers Genet's preference for imaginative beauty over being as creative as his preference for evil over good, defined in terms of conforming to nature.[47]

It is in Sartre's *Notebooks for an Ethics*, however, that one glimpses his sketch of a new first principle of ethics that resembles the formal, transcendental, discourse ethics elaborated by Apel and Habermas. These notebooks, written by Sartre between the spring of 1947 and the autumn of 1948 and posthumously published, do not constitute a scholarly tract on ethics, but rather "the outlines of a book on ethics," as

David Pellauer has observed. Sartre's reflections in these notebooks, while not carefully systematized, are in the vein of ethical foundationalism, even though he does not clarify his own position vis-à-vis the great ethicians in the history of philosophy. Throughout the notebooks he addresses assorted questions, such as freedom and history, Marxism, violence, lying, prayer, the meaning of a gift, love, and alienation.[48]

When Sartre turns to the question of violence, he morally condemns it because it involves the interruption of discourse, the refusal of the temporal and discursive structures of existence, a withdrawal from the discursive community, and an immunization of onself against outside influence. Even an *ad hominem* argument constitutes a form of violence, insofar as it violates a norm, intrinsic to discourse itself, that calls upon discussants to respect mutually each other's freedom, their for-itself, and to take seriously each other's arguments. Whereas violence in *Being and Nothingness* might have contradicted the character of the for-itself by treating the person as a thing, in *Notebooks for an Ethics* violence distorts what appears to be a transcendental structure of discourse itself, the very structure presumably operant in any discussion of ethics and in any theoretical discourse, even the discourse in which the skeptic disputes the knowability or validity of any ethical norms. In this regard, it is interesting that a recent proponent of Sartrean theory, Lewis Gordon, acknowledges that *Being and Nothingness* depicts relationships in bad faith, but then appeals to Sartre's relationship with his reader, that is, to the conditions of his own discourse, as exemplifiying a kind of authentic intersubjectivity akin to Martin Buber's. By transposing the source of ethics from a philosophy commencing with an isolated consciouness and freedom to the practice of intersubjective discourse, Sartre—at least in Gordon's reading of him—seems to be following the route that critical theory took from Adorno to Habermas. On the basis of this incipient intersubjective, discursive ethics, one could make the case that discrimination contravenes the for-itself of its victims by doing violence to their dignity as free, unconstrained discourse partners who deserve to be taken seriously and respectfully.[49]

An ethical theory at the *transcendental* level, such as that suggested in *Notebooks for an Ethics*, could correspond nicely with the intersubjective turn that Sartre inaugurated at the *pretheoretical* level in his discussion of the Look. If Anderson is correct that Sartre's faith in the perceptions and moral evaluations of the oppressed seems excessive and if one ought not accept whatever the Other says at face

value as valid since there is always room for apology and disagreement, as Levinas argues, then the transcendental level can provide one
who faces the Other at the pretheoretical level with theoretical principles for assessing the Other's claims. At the same time, since it is
always possible for one's reasoning to conceal buried motives aimed at
domination, the Look of the Other, the face that pre-exists rationality
and constantly contests it, can actually enhance its authenticity. Later,
I will develop an ethical theory on two tiers that will reconcile the pretranscendental level at which Levinas works with Apel's transendental
level, while preserving a distinctive role for each. It is in the dialectic
between these two tiers that the quests for respect for alterity and
equality, so polarized in an issue such as affirmative action, can be
mediated. It is to Sartre's credit to have anticipated this dialectic in his
phenomenological study of anti-Semitism.[50]

NOTES

1. "An Interview with Jean-Paul Sartre," in *The Philosophy of Jean-Paul Sartre*, ed. Paul Arthur Schilpp, *The Library of Living Philosophers*, vol. 16 (Lasalle, Ill.: Open Court, 1981), p. 24.

2. Maurice Natanson, *A Critique of Jean-Paul Sartre's Ontology* (Lincoln: University of Nebraska Press, 1951), pp. 69, 73; "The Problem of Others in *Being and Nothingness*," in *The Philosophy of Jean-Paul Sartre*, p. 341.

3. Jean-Paul Sartre, *The Emotions: Outline of a Theory*, trans. Bernard Frechtman (New York: Philosophical Library, 1948), pp. 5–12, 18, 47, 50–59, 78; Jean-Paul Sartre, *Imagination: A Psychological Critique*, trans. Forrest Williams (Ann Arbor: University of Michigan Press, 1962), pp. 101, 130, 132–35, 140; Jean-Paul Sartre, *The Psychology of Imagination*, trans. Bernard Frechtman (New York: Philosophical Library, 1948), pp. 5–6, 15, 20, 29, 118–19, 125–26, 146, 163–64, 201, 206, 222, 224; Jean-Paul Sartre, *Between Existentialism and Marxism*, trans. John Mathews (New York: Pantheon Books, 1974), p. 41.

4. Jean-Paul Sartre, *The Transcendence of the Ego: An Existentialist Theory of Consciousness*, trans. Forrest Williams and Robert Kirkpatrick (New York: The Noonday Press, 1957), pp. 97–98. (Italics in original.)

5. Ibid., pp. 98–99. (Italics in original.)

6. Ibid., pp. 39, 42, 45, 50, 53, 59, 60, 66–67, 76, 80–81, 82, 87, 90, 97–98, 100–101, 103, 104–105.

7. Jean-Paul Sartre, *Being and Nothingness: An Essay on Phenomenological Ontology*, trans. Hazel Barnes (New York: Washington Square Press, 1953), pp. 9, 10, 17–21, 23, 26, 36–44, 345.

8. Ibid., p. 126; cf. also 12–13, 15–16, 27–29, 43–44, 47–49, 58–59, 64,

67–72, 75–80, 121–26, 133, 139; cf. *The Transcendence of the Ego*, pp. 45, 58 where Sartre argues that the unreflected consciousness takes ontological priority over the reflected-on because the unreflected-on consciousness does not need to be reflected upon in order to exist.

9. Sartre, *Being and Nothingness*, pp. 15–16, 26, 58, 66–78, 570, 627–29, 702–703, 731.

10. Ibid., pp. 66–78, 617, 627–28, 672, 700–703, 728, 731, 768.

11. Ibid., pp. 82–83; cf. Marie-Denise Boros Azzi, "Representation of Character in Sartre's Drama, Fiction, and Biography," in *The Philosophy of Jean-Paul Sartre*, p. 465.

12. Ibid., p. 379; Sartre later admitted that this excessively Hobbist characterization of human relationships has more to do with historical, socio-economic conditions than with the ontology of human relationships. See Jean-Paul Sartre, *Cahiers pour une morale* (Paris: Gallimard, 1983), p. 430; English translation, *Notebooks for an Ethics*, trans. David Pellauer (Chicago: University of Chicago Press, 1992), p. 415. Cf. Alfred Schutz, "Sartre's Theory of the Alter Ego," in *The Problem of Social Reality*, vol. 1 of *Collective Papers*, ed. Maurice Natanson (The Hague: Martinus Nijhoff, 1962), pp. 197–203.

13. Sartre, *Being and Nothingness*, pp. 81, 340–72, 379, 394, 471–534.

14. Thomas R. Flynn, *Sartre and Marxist Existentialism: The Test Case of Collective Responsibility* (Chicago and London: University of Chicago Press, 1984), pp. xii–xiii, 206; "An Interview with Jean-Paul Sartre," p. 24; Jean-Paul Sartre, *Saint Genet, Actor and Martyr*, trans. Bernard Frechtman (New York: George Braziller, 1963), pp. 8–9, 125, 358, 372, 489; Jean-Paul Sartre, *Baudelaire*, trans. Martin Turnell (New York: New Directions, 1950), pp. 40, 69, 99, 169, 189, 191; Jean-Paul Sartre, *The Family Idiot: Gustave Flaubert, 1821–1857*, trans. Carol Cosman, 5 volumes (Chicago and London: University of Chicago Press, 1981–1993), 1:37, 39, 121, 258–59, 457, 530; 2:418–19; 3:135, 268, 442, 608; 4:49, 103, 105; 5:150, 160, 206, 223, 394; Sartre, *Between Existentialism and Marxism*, pp. 33, 35; Jean-Paul Sartre, *Critique of Dialectical Reason*, vol. 1: *Theory of Practical Ensembles*, trans. Alan Sheridan-Smith (London: NLB, 1976), pp. 316, 373–74, 404, 585, 671, 673, 678, 783, 788; William Leon McBride, "Sartre and Marxism," in *The Philosophy of Jean-Paul Sartre*, p. 610.

15. Flynn, *Sartre and Marxist Existentialism*, 51; Frantz Fanon, *Black Skin, White Masks*, trans. Charles Lam Markmann (New York: Grove Weidenfeld, 1967), p. 181.

16. Sartre, *Being and Nothingness*, 139–40; Jean-Paul Sartre, *Anti-Semite and Jew*, trans. George J. Becker (New York: Schocken Books, 1976), pp. 7, 13–17, 19, 22, 25, 31, 40, 51.

17. Sartre, *Anti-Semite and Jew*, pp. 27, 31–32, 37–39, 40, 44.

18. Ibid., pp. 53–54, cf. also 18–19.

19. Ibid., pp. 55–58. The subtlety of this analysis suggests that Thomas Flynn may be correct in asserting that the real target in *Anti-Semite and Jew* is the liberal democrat. See his *Sartre and Marxist Existentialism*, p. 54.

20. Sartre, *Anti-Semite and Jew*, pp. 59–60.

21. Ibid. pp. 67–89; Jean-Paul Sartre and Benny Levy, *L'Espoir maintenant: Les Entretiens de 1980* (Lagrasse, France: Verdier, 1991), pp. 71–74; see Robert Bernasconi, "Sartre's Gaze Returned: The Transformation of the Phenomenology of Racism," *Graduate Faculty Philosophy Journal* 18 (1995): 202–205.

22. Sartre, *Anti-Semite and Jew*, pp. 90, 94–109.

23. Ibid., pp. 109–29.

24. Ibid., p. 137; Margaret A. Simons, "Beauvoir and Sartre: The Philosophical Relationship," in *Yale French Studies*, no. 72: *Simone de Beauvoir: Witness to a Century*, ed. Helene V. Wenzel (New Haven, Conn.: Yale University Press, 1986), p. 173; Frantz Fanon, *The Wretched of the Earth*, preface by Jean-Paul Sartre, trans. Constance Farington (New York: Grove Press, Inc., 1963), p. 17.

25. Sartre, *Anti-Semite and Jew*, pp. 135–36, 152–53.

26. Jean-Paul Sartre, *Black Orpheus*, trans. S. W. Allen (Paris: Presence Africaine, 1963), pp. 41, 57, 63; *Saint Genet*, p. 57; *The Family Idiot*, 2:174–77.

27. Jean-Paul Sartre, *The Respectful Prostitute* in *No Exit and Three Other Plays* (New York: Vintage, 1955), pp. 249–74. For a contemporary attempt to analyze racism via the Sartrean notion of bad faith, see Lewis R. Gordon, *Bad Faith and Antiblack Racism* (Amherst, N.Y.: Humanity Books, 1995).

28. Ibid., pp. 274–81.

29. Jean-Paul Sartre, "Portrait du Colonisé," in *Situations*, vol. 5: *Colonialisme et Neo-colonialisme* (Paris: Gallimard, 1964), p. 55.

30. Sartre, *Critique of Dialectical Reason*, 1:300–303, 653, 714, 720, 723, 725, 733; *Situations*, 5:32, 39, 44, 47, 54, 55, 60; Jean-Paul Sartre, *Plaidoyer pour les intellectuels* (Paris: Editions Gallimard, 1972), pp. 49, 55; English translation, "A Plea for Intellectuals," in *Between Existentialism and Marxism*, pp. 250, 252–53; on the evasion of responsibility that comes through clinging to ignorance, cf. Jean-Paul Sartre, *Truth and Existence*, trans. Adrian van den Hoven (Chicago and London: University of Chicago Press, 1992), pp. 33, 38, 52, 53. Sartre calls it a refusal to have responsibilities except for ourselves, an act of bad faith, as if the ignorance we freely choose determines us.

31. Sartre, *Situations*, 5:77.

32. Ibid., pp. 77, 87–88.

33. Sartre, *Saint Genet*, pp. 8–9, 30, 125, 358, 372, 489.

34. Jeffner Allen, "An Introduction to Patriarchal Existentialism: A Proposal for a Way Out of Existential Patriarchy," in *The Thinking Muse: Feminism and Modern French Philosophy*, ed. Jeffner Allen and Iris Marion Young (Bloomington and Indianapolis: Indiana University Press, 1989), pp. 75, 77; Julien S. Murphy, "The Look in Sartre and Rich," *The Thinking Muse*, p. 103; Judith Butler, "Sex and Gender in Simone de Beauvoir's *Second Sex*," *Yale French Studies*, no. 72 (1986): 40; Margery L. Collins and Christine Pierce, "Holes and Slime: Sexism in Sartre's Psychoanalysis," *The Philosophical Forum* 5, nos. 1–2 (fall/winter

1973–1974): 117–21; Michèle Le Doeuff, "Simone de Beauvoir and Existentialism," *Feminist Studies* 6, no. 2 (summer 1980): 280, 281, 282, 286, 288; Hazel Barnes, "Sartre and Sexism," *Philosophy and Literature* 14, no. 2 (1990): 340–42.

35. Sartre, *Being and Nothingness*, pp. 36, 44, 244, 318; *The Transcendence of the Ego*, pp. 45, 59, 81, 83, 97–98; *The Emotions*, pp. 50ff.; *Imagination, A Psychological Critique*, p. 101.

36. Merleau-Ponty, *The Phenomenology of Perception*, pp. 87, 121, 131, 136–47, 212–14, 453; Maurice Merleau-Ponty, *The Visible and the Invisible*, ed. Claude Lefort, trans. Alphonso Lingis (Evanston, Ill.: Northwestern University Press, 1968), pp. 37–38, 65, 69, 87, 100–101.

37. Merleau-Ponty, *The Phenomenology of Perception*, pp. xiii–xiv, 62–63, 165, 439; *The Visible and the Invisible*, 33–34, 38, 87; Alfred Schutz, *The Phenomenology of the Social World*, trans. George Walsh and Frederick Lehnert (Evanston, Ill.: Northwestern University Press, 1967), pp. 43–44, 97; Maurice Natanson, "The Problem of Others in *Being and Nothingness*," in *The Philosophy of Jean-Paul Sartre*, pp. 331, 337, 341.

38. Merleau-Ponty, *The Phenomenology of Perception*, p. 443; Natanson, *A Critique of Jean-Paul Sartre's Ontology*, p. 105; Edward Casey, "Sartre on Imagination," in *The Philosophy of Jean-Paul Sartre*, p. 161; Thomas C. Anderson, *Sartre's Two Ethics: From Authenticity to Integral Humanity* (Chicago and LaSalle, Ill.: Open Court, 1993), p. 12; Butler, "Sex and Gender in Simone de Beauvoir's *Second Sex*," p. 40; Le Doeuff, "Simone de Beauvoir and Existentialism," pp. 280, 286, 288.

39. Jean-Paul Sartre, *Search for a Method*, trans. Hazel E. Barnes (New York: Alfred A. Knopf, 1963), pp. xxxiv, 30, 47, 57, 63–64, 71, 75, 93, 99, 135, 151, 173, 180; Jean-Paul Sartre, *Critique of Dialectic Reason*, vol. 1: *Theory of Practical Ensembles*, pp. 331, 373–74.

40. Sartre, *Between Marxism and Existentialism*, pp. 33, 41; *Saint Genet*, p. 31; *The Family Idiot*, 4:49; 5:150; *Being and Nothingness*, pp. 672, 703; Frederick Olafson, "Freedom and Choice," in *Phenomenology and Existentialism*, ed. Robert C. Solomon (Boston and London: University Press of America, Inc., 1980), p. 483. In fact, as early as *Being and Nothingness* Sartre speaks of our immersion in values by noting, "Our being is immediately 'in situation'; that is, it arises in enterprises and knows itself first in so far as it is reflected in those enterprises" (p. 77).

41. Sartre, *Being and Nothingness*, pp. 133, 345, 350–52, 377–400; *Notebooks for an Ethics*, p. 415.

42. Regarding Sartre's later criticism of his earlier depiction of intersubjectivity, cf. note 12 above.

43. A kind of dialectic must be established here since a rational assessment of whether the Other's critique of one's rationality is itself rationally acceptable. As shall be seen later, such a dialectic can be examplified in the affirmative action debate in which the notion of equality can be expanded but without lapsing into a rejection of the moral principle of equality.

44. Sartre, *Truth and Existence*, pp. 12, 42, 66; Jean-Paul Sartre, *The Communists and Peace, with a Reply to Claude Lefort*, trans. Martha H. Fletcher with the assistance of John R. Kleinschmidt (New York: George Braziller, 1968), p. 126; *The Family Idiot*, 3:135; 4:105; 5:205; Jean-Paul Sartre, *The Freud Scenario*, ed. J.-B. Pontalis, trans. Quintin Hoare (Chicago: University of Chicago Press, 1985), pp. 322, 348, 374.

45. Edmund Husserl, *Cartesian Meditations*, pp. 37, 68; Sartre, *Critique of Dialectical Reason*, 1:56–59, 75; *The Family Idiot*, 3:274; 4:190; Ph. Gavi, J. P. Sartre, P. Victor, *On a raison de se revolter, Discussions* (Paris: Editions Gallimard, 1974), p. 279.

46. Sartre, *Being and Nothingness*, p. 797; Jean-Paul Sartre, *Essays in Existentialism*, ed. Wade Baskin (New York: The Citadel Press, 1965), pp. 38, 55–56; Jürgen Habermas, *Justifications and Applications: Remarks on Discourse Ethics*, trans. Ciaran Cronin (Cambridge, Mass., and London: MIT Press, 1993), pp. 28, 33, 37, 40, 50, 65, 75, 79; Sartre, *Saint Genet*, pp. 156, 358, 370, 498, 558, 598; Klaus Günther, *The Sense of Appropriateness: Application Discourses in Morality and Law*, trans. John Farrell (Albany: State University of New York Press, 1993).

47. Anderson, *Sartre's Two Ethics*, pp. 122, 154, 157.

48. David Pellauer, "Translator's Introduction" in *Notebooks for an Ethics*, pp. ix–x, xiii, xix.

49. Sartre, *Notebooks for an Ethics*, pp. 172–214; *Plaidoyer pour les intellectuels*, pp. 32–38; *Between Marxism and Existentialism*, pp. 238–44. It is interesting to note how in *The Family Idiot* such a discourse ethics is implicitly at work when Sartre observes how Flaubert's damaged past kept him from discourse, how animals rage at being excluded from discourse, how truth is a communal enterprise, how silence is part of a conversation, and how in one's first discourse with parents one is not treated as a for-itself but rather suffers from imposed judgments, *The Family Idiot*, 1:37, 137, 151; 2:17; 4:49. Cf. Gordon, *Bad Faith and Anti-Black Racism*, pp. 161–62.

50. Anderson, *Sartre's Two Ethics*, p. 136.

3
SIMONE DE BEAUVOIR
Phenomenology, Ambiguity, Sexism

1. A DIVERSIFIED APPROPRIATION OF PHENOMENOLOGY

Simone de Beauvoir, who claimed in her autobiographical *The Prime of Life* that upon reading Husserl she never felt herself closer to the truth, adopted the phenomenological method enthusiastically. This chapter, which will offer a phenomenological reading of *The Second Sex*, joins company with several other critics, such as Debra Bergoffen, Karen Vintges, Eleanore Holveck, and Kristina Arp, who assert the importance of Husserlian phenomenology's influence upon Beauvoir's thought. The linking of Beauvoir's work to phenomenology also redresses what Jo Ann Pilardi has pointed out as a lack of attention paid to Beauvoir by those within the existential-phenomenological tradition.[1]

It is well known, though, that Beauvoir asserted that her greatest philosophical debt was to Sartre, to whom she assimilated herself by, for instance, affirming that she adhered completely all her life to *Being and Nothingness*; by frequently speaking of Sartre and herself in the first person plural "we"; and by stating that Sartre was the philosopher on whom she depended since she was not one—although she did admit to originality in literature. For these and other autobiographical revelations indicating that she focused excessively on Sartre's thinking at the expense of her own, she has come under fire from feminist critics.[2]

Nevertheless, several Beauvoir scholars have pointed out how Beauvoir disagreed with Sartre and actually influenced him. Margaret Simons, for instance, contends that Beauvoir objected to the early Sartre's exaggerated voluntarism, as comments in *The Prime of Life* confirm, and moved him toward a more conditioned notion of freedom. Judith Butler concurs with Simons, asserting that Beauvoir takes Sartre at his non-Cartesian best and aids him in a process of exorcising the ghost of Cartesianism by the time of his later works. Sonia Kruks advances further evidence of Beauvoir's originality by showing how institutions play a prominent role in *The Second Sex* long before Sartre made them focal in his *Critique of Dialectic Reason.* Kate and Edward Fullbrook, as well as Simons, have developed the idea that Beauvoir focused on the Other in her literary and autobiographical works, particularly *She Came to Stay* (1943), before Sartre was thematizing these issues in his philosophy. The Fullbrooks, however, do not attend sufficiently to *The Transcendence of the Ego* (1937), where Sartre raises questions of whether the Other can be known without being objectivated.[3]

Most recently, Margaret Simons, on the basis of a 1927 diary of Beauvoir's held at the Bibliothèque Nationale, has gone even further in concluding that Beauvoir, already in 1927, was raising questions about nothingness, despair, self-deception (without the explicit category of bad faith), and the search for self, and that she "described these experiences at the center of the existential phenomenology that she would later share with Sartre." As a result, Beauvoir's later autobiographical disclaimer about being a philosopher must be seen as a deception and the question of her possible influence upon Sartre needs to be reopened. Hazel Barnes, in contrast to Simons, believes that Beauvoir did not define the major themes of *Being and Nothingness* and that Simons has been "misled by purely verbal resonances and vague ideas" to find in the 1927 diary the source of the philosophy to which Sartre, and he alone, would give expression in his major work.[4]

If Beauvoir's appropriation of phenomenology resembles Sartre's, it is no doubt because they collaborated in developing the existential phenomenology they shared, as Simons herself suggests. Besides highlighting these resemblances, it is beyond the scope of this work to determine who influenced whom. In fact, I will argue that Beauvoir's phenomenology, taking its origin from Husserl, bears a likeness to those of Merleau-Ponty and Levinas, whose later works she anticipates by decades, and not just Sartre's.

Beauvoir herself insists in her autobiographical writings that, although she was influenced by other philosophers, she chose her own philosophical route and never adopted any idea without first analyzing it and accepting it on her own, in the tradition of self-responsible philosophizing that extends from Husserl back to Descartes and even to the Greeks. Hence, I hope to show that although she relied upon key notions that found expression in *Being and Nothingness*, such as the for-itself/in-itself distinction, situation, and bad faith, in *The Second Sex* she employs Husserlian phenomenology in other ways, particularly in regard to eidetic methodology and the concept of ambiguity.[5]

Any perusal of Beauvoir's early philosophical treatise, *Pyrrhus et Cinéas* (1944) would indicate how fundamentally important Husserlian notions of intentionality and temporality were to Beauvoir's thought since she depicts the human being as "constitutively oriented toward what is other than itself" and not inert, not folded in upon itself, but ever free "to transcend every transcendence." In *The Ethics of Ambiguity*, she acknowledges that just as Husserlian reduction suspends all affirmation concerning external reality without contesting its presence, so existentialist conversion does not repress plans or values, but refuses to set them up as absolutes. Just as Husserl goes behind objects to uncover the conscious processes before which those objects appear without being negated by consciousness, so Beavoir and Sartre, in her view, return to the other side of the options before which freedom stands poised, with those options still standing as its possibilities. In a similar way, as shall be seen, Levinas, also using the language of "reduction," reverts to the hither side of the contents exchanged between interlocutors (the said) to the saying relationship that subtends the plane of the said, whatever verdict one might eventually pass on the contents of the said.[6]

In a 1945 review of Merleau-Ponty's *Phenomenology of Perception* in *Les Temps Modernes*, Beauvoir endorses phenomenology's emphasis on the inescapable intertwinement of subject and object and on the world as a horizon beyond the perspectival views one takes up toward it. But in that review she also contrasts Merleau-Ponty and Sartre, without deciding between them, on the issue of the subject, who according to Merleau-Ponty, rather than exercising a negating power against being, communicates with the world "older than thought" and thus is never pure *pour soi*. In addition, she reiterates without critique Merleau-Ponty's account of the lived body and his injunction that we abandon ourselves to the world so that it can think itself in us, and she concludes by commending Merleau-Ponty for his "very rich suggestions" on the question of sexuality and language. In an essay published ten years later in *Les Temps Modernes*, "Merleau-Ponty and Pseudo-Sartreanism," she criticizes Merleau-Ponty's critique of Sartre by, paradoxically, showing that Sartre's position is actually much closer to Merleau-Ponty's than Merleau-Ponty recognizes.[7]

Not only does Beauvoir proceed eclectically, drawing inspiration from Husserl and playing Sartre and Merleau-Ponty off each other dialectically, her writings reflect more on the ethical dimensions of intersubjectivity than did those published at that time by either Sartre or Merleau-Ponty. In *Pyrrhus et Cinéas*, for instance, she dwells on the dissonances in understanding between persons and examines extensively the machinations of paternalism—a theme also prominent in *The Ethics of Ambiguity*. Furthermore, in this later work Beauvoir advances the notion of ambiguity to counter those who, succumbing to seriousness about their own ethical ends, inflict violence without giving a second thought to the ambiguity involved in their sacrificing individuals to their moral goals. When Beauvoir refers to the fact that young Nazis denied any ambiguity about their own purposes and consequently trained themselves to ignore others' suffering by plucking out the eyes of live cats, it is as if she locates a significant source of ambiguity in the ethical appeal of the Other calling into question and muddying up one's pursuit of ethical projects. On a more positive note in *Pyrrhus et Cinéas*, she finds in the very structure of discourse, "an appeal to the liberty of the other." Instead of enclosing oneself within the circle of one's consorts, prudently avoiding questions and living in surety, the free person is one who exposes oneself to others, "throws oneself into the world without calculation, without stakes."[8]

Debra Bergoffen has identified in *The Ethics of Ambiguity* a specific type of intentionality that aims at disclosing being generously and that includes willing and acting on behalf of the freedom of others as opposed to an intentionality that insists on the "my-ness" of the being disclosed by me. While the first type of intentionality is generous, the second is anxious and assertive; the first founds an ethic of generosity, the second an ethic of the project. In *America Day by Day*, which I have argued elsewhere is much more than a travelogue, Beauvoir gives clear expression to the "ethic of the project," with all its Sartrean overtones, in her description of American cities:

> This is what moves me about the skyscrapers: they proclaim that man is not a being who stagnates but one who is full of energy, expansion, conquest. And in the extravagant profusion of drugstores, there's a poetry as exciting as in a baroque church: man has caught the raw thing in the trap of his desires; he asserts the power of his imagination over matter. New York and Chicago reflect the existence of this demiurge of imperious dreams. . . .[9]

In the same work, Beauvoir repeatedly exemplifies an ethic of generosity much like that recommended by Levinas when she allows herself to be affected by the suffering of African-Americans under the burden of systematic discrimination. Similarly, she criticizes American "college girls" for refusing to dismantle their interior defenses, clinging to Puritan backgrounds or desires to dominate men, and being unable to make an erotic animal gift (*un don animal*) of themselves to another. While Beauvoir makes an interesting connection here between eroticism and generosity, a connection reiterated in *The Second Sex*, Bergoffen is right to point out that Beauvoir in her essay "Must We Burn Sade?" also recognized that one could express through erotic activity fears, hostility, a longing for sovereignty over others, the pursuit of pleasure without regard to equality or reciprocity—as Sade's own life illustrates.[10]

In what follows, I will examine how phenomenological practices pervade the entirety of *The Second Sex*, and I will focus on two of Beauvoir's most significant, phenomenologically based contributions in that work: her critical use of eidetic method and her attentiveness to lived experience issuing in a recovery of ambiguity. Finally, as I did with the previous chapter, I will conclude by raising critical questions in the areas of intersubjectivity, rationality, and ethics.

2. PHENOMENOLOGY AND *THE SECOND SEX*

After stating in her introduction to *The Second Sex* that woman has become man's inessential Other—a concept which she attributes to Levinas although she objects to his "assertion of masculine privilege"—Beauvoir goes on in the section entitled "Destiny" to consider how the theoretical frameworks of biology, psychoanalysis, and historical materialism have "tried to legitimate the established order."[11] This section opens with the statement that those prone to oversimplification believe that woman is only a womb, an ovary, thereby reducing her to a detached organ—an *in-itself* without consciousness. Beauvoir proceeds to combat various false understandings of the biological data that have been used to support the subjugation of women, such as the belief that the ovule is static while the spermatozoa active. In fact, the ovule is essentially active in its nucleus and, given the fact that in the act of fusion the individuality of both gametes is lost, it is false "to say that the egg greedily swallows the sperm, and equally so to say that the sperm victoriously commandeers the female cell's reserves." Similarly, one can also misinterpret the facts by, for instance, emphasizing that among ants, bees, termites, spiders, and mantises the female enslaves and sometimes devours the male—without considering that in these cases both sexes are totally subordinate to processes of preserving their species. Beauvoir's attack on these faulty biological justifications involves the phenomenological effort to dismantle prejudicial readings of the biological facts in order that one might see the things themselves afresh, i.e., as they are. In such a project, she finds herself in league with the best trends in modern biological science, which, for instance, in the area of procreation, has dispelled numerous superstitions.[12]

Delving further into different species' behaviors, Beauvoir grants that mammalian species have achieved an increase in freedom and individuation in contrast to insects, but in her view it almost seems as if the human species avenges itself against the human for-itself by subjecting woman to an arduous nine-month enslavement in pregnancy. However, Beauvoir rebels against any biologism that might envision woman as a thing dominated by the species, as if for-itself could be reduced to an in-itself physical organ, instrumentalized by the species. To overcome such biologism, she situates biology's findings, even those yet to come, within their broader context: these findings constitute the *situation*, but not the *destiny* of woman, since "the facts of biology take on the values that the existent bestows upon them." If an individual or culture were to contend that the biological make-up of woman, such as the encumbrances of menstruation and pregnancy, determine her destiny, they would bypass and even hide the existential free choice by which women (or a culture) decide upon the meaning of these elements presented by the situation. Beauvoir's resistance to biological reductionism reminds one of Husserl's critique of such reductionism when he pointed out the paradox of conscious activity, whether of the individual, culture, or community of scientists, explaining itself away and freely deciding that free choices will make no difference. The bad faith, by which a biology allied with misogynist culture hides its own responsibility for justifying such oppression as if it were the inevitable result of female biology, calls out for a phenomenologically inspired refusal to allow subjectivity to remain hidden, whether that subjectivity be that of the proponents of biologism or their uncritical followers.[13]

Although Beauvoir often views these features of female biology in a negative light, she presents these biological differences between the sexes as intersecting with cultural interpretations, which could endow these differences with more positive meanings, and hence pregnancy could be understood as a matter of creativity and giving life. Because her project involves resisting misogynist deployments of biological information, Beauvoir tends to emphasize the freedom of for-itself over against its situation. If, however, one wishes to address how one's consciousness is conditioned by the bodily processes in which it is embodied and from which it emerges, e.g., that one who has experienced pregnancy might tend, without reflection, to be more alert to certain aspects of experience, one might stress an approach closer to Merleau-Ponty's.[14]

A multidimensional approach, similar to that adopted toward biology, characterizes Beauvoir's critique of psychoanalysis. In the first place, Freud imbibed the prejudices of a male-dominated culture in understanding female libido derivatively, that is, via the castration complex that presents woman as a mutilated man. Once again, however, it is not the lack of a penis that causes female inferiority, but a culture which breeds in females feelings of inferiority and then hides its own role in producing such feelings by the bad faith maneuver of ascribing the origin of this sense of inferiority to the female anatomy. Beauvoir uncovers bad faith at work not only in psychoanalytic explanation of female inferiority by the castration complex, but also in the psychoanalytic project itself. By describing psychological aberrances as the product of libidinal mechanisms that have not yet carved out their proper channels and by focusing on past trauma, psychoanalysis neglects precisely what existential analysis would emphasize: the patient's *existential choices* of projects that have not promoted wholesome development. For existential analysis, once one has recognized such choices, which one can freely unmake, alternative future possibilities open up. Existential psychoanalysis thus affords its patients hope. In Freudian psychoanalysis, however, one assigns to psychodynamic mechanisms responsibility for a pathology that really rests with one's *choice* of a repressive lifestyle and thereby conceals one's subjectivity from oneself. Likewise, historical materialism engages in bad faith by contending that the discovery of tools led to the seizure of property, its privatization, and the subsequent enslavement of others since it ignores the existential choice to base one's worth on what one owns—a choice that, once illuminated, dispels deterministic fatalism.[15]

Beauvoir completes her study of the facts of biology, psychology, and historical materialism by a quick excursus through history which confirms her earlier insight that "it is not the inferiority of women that has caused their historical insignificance: it is rather their historical insignificance that has doomed them to inferiority." Continuing this endeavor not to allow the (cultural) subjectivity responsible for the oppression of women to engage in any bad faith blaming of its victim, Beauvoir links her analyses of sexism with the U.S. black liberation movement—upon which Nelson Algren suggested that she model *The Second Sex*. Hence, just as Gunnar Myrdal in *The American Dilemma* had affirmed that there is no Negro problem but only a white problem and just as Sartre had pointed out that that anti-Semitism is a gentile problem, Beauvoir asserts that sexism, the "woman problem," is really a male problem.[16]

The third major section of the first volume of *The Second Sex* addresses "myths," the projection of male hopes and fears upon woman as nature, virgin, beauty, danger, sorceress, mother, and wife. Such projections involve an attempt to constitute unilaterally the Other, but insofar as one passes from one projection to another and insofar as any one projection is often accompanied by its opposite (e.g., one would want a wife who is virgin and seductress too), these projections betray a certain male uncertainty about who women really are. This uncertainty corresponds to the free for-itself of women, which enables them to defy the inventions projected upon them and which even the projecting males seem to recognize implicitly by their hesitancy. In spite of such one-sided, mythic projections, Beauvoir hints at the possibility of a reciprocal relationship when she cites a scene from Malraux's *La condition humaine* in which Kyo asks May to love him as he is instead of sending back to him a fawning reflection of himself. This theme of reciprocity between equal for-itselves, missing from *Being and Nothingness*, shapes Beauvoir's subsequent discussion of five authors' treatment of women. At one extreme stands Montherlant, who enjoys urinating on caterpillars to feel himself godlike and who insists upon his sovereign male consciousness, unwilling to depend upon or receive from females or to expose itself to the "menace" of reciprocity. At the other is Stendhal, whose women bring to men in reciprocal recognition the same truth they receive from them. In Beauvoir's view, myths, each often claiming to hold the sole truth about women, are in fact irrational, resistant to contestation, and subversive of relationships insofar as they reduce a partner to a ready-made classification, a function, an inflexible thing, an *en-soi*, to whom one can relate only in the spirit of seriousness, that is, without surprise or playfulness.[17]

Book Two of *The Second Sex* considers the development of the woman from childhood to old age. Paradoxically, Beauvoir, defying the individualism typically ascribed to existentialism, shows herself fully aware of the destructive character of the young girl's *social conditioning*, which, for instance, denies her participation in the sports in which she might vent those conquering, competitive attitudes essential to the formation of an autonomous freedom. Such conditioning urges the young girl to become a passive sex object instead of an active subject, to indulge in narcissism and romantic dreaming in inverse proportion to her ability to affect the world, and to submit to societal norms for her adult role even as her for-itself may be rebelling by resorting to humor, gross language, lesbianism, or even crimes, such as kleptomania. Faced with suffering a humiliating sexual initiation at male hands, the powerless young woman may nonetheless exhibit masochistic behaviors, whose apparent willingness to abdicate masquerades an underlying assertion of self. Marriage, since it converts into rights and duties an exchange that ought to be founded on spontaneous elan, from the start crushes the woman's for-itself, and she is subsequently compelled to set up a universe of permanence and stability so that her husband and children can exercise their free self-transcendence outside the household. Like the person of *ressentiment* in Nietzsche's slave morality and Sartre's crude anti-Semite, the wife often strives for no positive good, but only for the negative goal of repelling dirt by housework. Although the wife often tries to persuade herself in bad faith that she is happy with marriage, the institution, in Beauvoir's view, usually ends up mutilating women by dooming them to repetition, routine, and evenings at home characterized by lack of communication and ennui—all in utter contradiction to the free, unfettered consciousness disclosed by phenomenology. Motherhood fares no better, since, after resisting the reification of pregnancy, mothers find themselves in a struggle against the freedom of sons and daughters as intricate as the struggle for recognition in Hegel's *Phenomenology of Spirit*. Just as Beauvoir treats lesbianism as an alternative to brutal sexual initiation by males, so prostitutes and hetairas escape domination in marriage, but only at the price of being treated as instruments. Finally, after the aged woman has lost the struggle to remain timeless and has failed to justify herself through children and grandchildren, she resigns herself to the desert of the future—she is prey to solitude, regret, and boredom. "With the needle or the crochet-hook, woman sadly weaves the very nothingness of her days."[18]

In spite of the constraints imposed during the "normal" development of women, the for-itself is not vanquished since, as Beauvoir points out near the end of Book Two, it still is able to devise "justifications," that is, to give meaning to its oppressive situation. Thus, narcissistic women attempt to achieve the impossible perfection of in-itself/for-itself, by, for example, arriving at a beauty both self-achieved and unchangeable. Unfortunately, though, they become enslaved to their admirers, just as women in love seek to transcend narcissistic self-enclosure by a self-donation that is rarely reciprocated. Mystics seek the transcendence of love but in pursuit of God, whose love seems not quite personal insofar as it is impossible for God to betray them or leave them unrequited. While the project of mysticism often lapses into masochism, it paradoxically is also able to generate such undaunted characters as Therese of Avila or Joan of Arc.[19]

To conclude this lengthy book, Beauvoir addresses the issue of authentic feminine liberation. Sympathetic to Marxism and phenomenology, she argues that such liberation requires economic independence, even as she reiterates that economics must be seen against the horizon of its wider existential context, in relation to which she had situated biology, psychology, and historical materialism at the opening of her treatise. Moreover, autonomous freedom continually progressing beyond its present given status cannot rest content with liberation understood only as appropriating itself, embracing its humanity, and achieving self-confidence. Rather, in Beauvoir's view, it must transcend even this stage of its own liberation by forgetting itself in generous, non-narcissistic, creative devotion to a project of giving meaning to the world through art, literature, or philosophy, that is, to founding "the world anew on a human liberty." While this emphasis on generosity, anticipating the writings of Levinas, surpasses the ethics of the project characterizing most of Sartre's published works at that time, Beauvoir here seems to fuse the ethic of the project and ethic of generosity that Bergoffen has distinguished. To conclude, Beauvoir appeals to the ideal of reciprocal relationships between equal subjects, and thus her book becomes itself a work transcending the customs and modes of thought which promote nonmutual relationships and hobble human liberation. *The Second Sex* is thus an achievement by for-itself aimed at liberating for-itself. Beauvoir cautions, though, that such equality does not spell the end of love, happiness, poetry, dreams, or the difference between man and woman—for to do away with these would be to crush the unique subjects this entire text seeks to unchain.[20]

One reading *The Second Sex* cannot help but see in it resemblances with Sartrean and Husserlian phenomenology: the view of philosophy as an exercise in responsibility, the criticizing of unexamined presumptions; the situating of the sciences in a broader philosophical context; the subordinating of the thing to consciousness; the revealing of hidden subjectivity; and the understanding of consciousness as dynamic, restless, and critical. However, throughout *The Second Sex* Beauvoir shows her greatest creativity in the use of phenomenological procedures in her discussions of essence and ambiguity.

3. ESSENCE AND AMBIGUITY

As stated above, Husserl conceived the phenomenological reduction and eidetic free variation not only as methods aimed at finding essences, but also as means for critically scrutinizing what habitual thinking has taken to be essential in contrast to what is found when one returns to the things themselves. In the *spirit* of phenomenological reduction (rather than its deliberate, methodic implementation), Beauvoir undertakes a sustained critique of such habitual ways of thinking.[21]

For Beauvoir, it is due to commonsense's ready-made, routinized preconceptions and evaluations that, for instance, men substitute false idols for relations with flesh-and-blood women, that wives are unable to comprehend in the least their husbands' worldly achievements, and that middle-aged women overlook male mystifications until the disappointed expectations of old age and the resultant irony and spicy cynicism accompanying it lift the veil. In order to cast doubt upon the commonsense preconception that there is a "maternal instinct," that maternity crowns a woman's life, and that the child is sure of being happy in its mother's arms, Beauvoir brings forward counterexamples such as Madame Tolstoy's loathing for her own children, Katherine Mansfield's portrayal of a mother's resentment for her young son, the frequent mistreatment that young girls inflict on the dolls serving as their "children," and the ambivalent feelings of countless mothers toward their own offspring. For Beauvoir, those who criticize women for not taking advantage of new openings in factories, offices, or universities, as men would, actually partake in unexamined, everyday universalizations insofar as they fail to take account of surviving, age-old prejudicial traditions that constitute the unique situation of women and that rob women of confidence today as they have for centuries. Beauvoir exposes as out of touch the commonsense universalization that independent women are as capable of satisfying physical desires through sexual adventures as men by pointing out how promiscuous women would face more moral criticism than men would, how counterintuitive the idea of a brothel of men for women patrons would be, how physically dangerous it would be for women to "pick up" men on the street, how the very aggressiveness requisite for such rendezvous would alienate most men, who resent women taking initiatives, and how contrary such casual sexual relations are to the nature of female eroticism. By highlighting such discrepancies between men and women, Beauvoir lays bare the taken-for-granted operational universalizations that effectively conceal the asymmetries between male and female situations.[22]

Besides criticizing everyday conceptualizations and universalizations, Beauvoir resists and rebuts the theoretical or pseudotheoretical reductionisms that would suppress underlying diversity in their own way by reducing *all* liberation to economic liberation; *all* emotional life to sexual drives; *all* human behavior to sexual behavior; and *all* mysticism to hormonal, nervous, or anatomical determinants. In addition, Beauvoir shows herself reluctant to extend her own insights into mixed motivations beyond their legitimacy, as when she denies, for instance, that *all* women are narcissistic (in spite of her incisive grasp of female narcissism) or that *all* grandmothers resent grandchildren because they are the children of their daughters-in-law or that *all* passivity in sexual love is masochistic. Even the institution of marriage, which *all* are expected to endorse and which moral thinking usually justifies, is not so straightforward an institution, insofar as it transposes into a system of rights and duties spontaneous eros, which would be better expressed through a pact based on liberty and sincerity and more congruent with free for-itself.[23]

But just as phenomenology corrects false essences by free variation, that is, by running through alternative possibilities that might show that a feature taken for essential is not or one that has not been so taken is, Beauvoir, in a less formalized rendition of free variation, "de-essentializes" premature essentialist-type claims by conjuring up overlooked variegations. For instance, to counter the view that male fecundation is essential to all reproduction, Beauvoir's first chapter on biology presents the facts that asexual multiplication can go on indefinitely without degeneration, that in many species parthenogenesis can render males superfluous, and that the perpetuation of various species does not necessitate sexual differentiation. Beauvoir offsets the view that male sexual development is essentially superior by showing how haphazardly the originally indifferent gonadal material is determined and how supposedly male/female characteristics are distributed among both sexes. To undermine the opinion regarding the inevitability of the burdensomeness of reproduction, she mentions fish and bird species in which the egg is expelled from the female's body before the embryo develops.[24]

Moreover, Beauvoir's strategy of explaining the diversity of problems women encounter at distinctive phases of their life undermines any univocal notion of "women's problems" and corresponds more with the continual unfolding of a never fixed for-itself. Furthermore, given interpretive freedom and the diversity of basic attitudes toward the world among women, there is no *one* way in which women experience pregnancy, breast-feeding, or mothering; and prostitutes and hetairas in conjunction with others of their kind construct "counter-universes" to whatever the "standard" woman's universe might be, if there could be such a thing. Finally, rigid categories to the effect that masculine-acting women are lesbians and feminine-acting women heterosexual fail miserably. Unfortunately, women themselves at times succumb to inflexible conceptual schemata, as is evident in the Manichean housewife who divides the world into neat classifications of good and evil, cleanliness and dust, or the woman theoretician who "will be forced to repudiate whatever she has in her that is 'different.'" There is something homogenizing about such unreflexive schematizations, typical of the natural attitude, and Beauvoir, like Husserl, seems committed to recovering the pluralism of possibilities.[25]

Given Beauvoir's critical usage of a modified method of free variation and her proclivity to dwell on diversity, it is not surprising that she does not believe in any "essence" of femininity or masculinity. While children trust as much that there are essences for men and women as that the sun is distinct from the moon, Beauvoir at every key introduction, transition, and conclusion in *The Second Sex* rejects such essences. In the Introduction, she argues that since every concrete human being is always a single, separate individual, one must abandon ideas such as the eternal feminine, the black soul, or the Jewish character. The biological and social sciences confirm this central tenet in existentialism since, rejecting unchangeably fixed entities, they claim that characteristics are at least in part situation-dependent. At the end of Book One, Beauvoir criticizes men who, by considering women to be "mysterious" by essence, exempt themselves from trying to understand women, excuse women's capricious behavior, and ignore the actual "mysterious" aspect that both men and women share insofar as they are *pour soi*, always capable of reversing whatever immobility is imposed upon them from without. In brief, like the crude anti-Semite's assignation of a Jewish "essence," the attribution of sexual essence involves nothing more than a bad faith flight from freedom in oneself and the Other. In the Introduction to Book Two, not found in the English translation, Beauvoir states:

> When I use the words "woman" or "female," I do not refer obviously to some archetype, to some immutable essence; after the majority of my affirmations it is necessary to understand "within the present state of education and customs." One is not enunciating eternal truths, but describing the common base from which every singular female existence commences.[26]

Again, in the chapter culminating her account of the development of womanhood from childhood to old age, she reiterates that none of woman's traits reflects a perverted "essence" and that efforts to show that either male or female essences are superior beg the question.[27]

At the conclusion of the book, after denying once again any Eternal Masculine or Feminine, Beauvoir recognizes that the critique she develops of essential differences could easily lead to the false conclusions that there are no differences and that males and females are all essentially the same. Like Sartre in his handling of the democratic anti-Semite, Beauvoir perceives the danger that equality might suppress alterity, but she insists that denial of essential differences need not reduce to sameness *individual* males and females, whose differences a critical phenomenology can always bring into focus.[28]

At this juncture, it is worth mentioning that Beauvoir indirectly suggests, like Sartre, that increased *self*-criticism is not the only available resource for challenging false universalizations, including the universal ideal of "equality" that, by progressing beyond cruder discriminations, can seem to carry an air of innocence about it. The possible contribution that the Other might make to disabusing one of false universals stands out *by its absence* when one considers, as does Beauvoir, the case of Montherlant. Montherlant dreams of a sovereign, autonomous subjectivity, intent on "taking without being taken," complacent in giving pleasure but never receptive since receptivity implies dependence, as Sade also thought. Imitating God's despotic solitude, Montherlant urinates on caterpillars, exterminating some and sparing others, without feeling any threat in return, and he equates women with beasts to be subdued, comparing them to a horse trained not to urinate or break wind when the man is in the saddle. For Montherlant, as remote as possible from an unconstrained discourse between unfettered participants, there is only one consciousness in the world, his own, and, as such, he epitomizes all that is wrong when one clings to conceptualizations without testing them against the Other they circumscribe.[29]

In spite of Beauvoir's agnosticism about essences, occasionally she slips into an uncritical essentializing herself, for instance, when she speaks of the peculiar *nature* of female eroticism which is not satisfied by casual sexual liaisons, or when she pretends that the highly dubious Christology underpinning bizarre mystical behaviors is the *true* one, or when she claims that "for a man, the transition from childish sexuality to maturity is relatively simple." When it comes to homosexuality, on the one hand, Beauvoir appears somewhat enlightened in dissenting from false universal claims, such as that all masculine women are lesbians, that feminine women are not lesbians, or that homosexuality is a matter of arrested development. At one point, she even places all women in solidarity with lesbians, since they all resist the loss of their autonomy to men. On the other hand, she seems to lapse into common prejudices when she emphasizes how lesbianism springs from *negative* origins such as a fear of the possibly brutal sexual initiation at men's hands or a lack or excess of maternal affection, instead of accentuating how it often involves a *positive* choice in the face of a situation affected by psychological and/or physiological factors.[30]

According to Beauvoir, while woman's situation may have deprived her of opportunities for grandiose objectives, it has also kept her from viewing herself as if she were blameless, that is, from "behind the mask of human dignity," and hence enabled her to pay more heed to her own interior experiences, to her "undisciplined thoughts, her emotions, her spontaneous reactions," which she can thus express "more frankly." Whether it is true or not that women have an introspective advantage over men, Beauvoir shows herself uniquely attentive to the phenomenon of ambiguity, emphasized by Merleau-Ponty. Beauvoir admits that she acquired this attentiveness to ambiguity only through time and struggle and often in opposition to Sartre's overly rationalized outlook. To be sure, Sartre is by no means oblivious of ambiguity. For instance, the critique of rationality in *Anti-Semite and Jew* displays an admirable analysis of the complexity of reason as an instrument befouled by the pathologies it seeks to overcome and capable of concealing that very taintedness. Furthermore, Sartre's discussion of bad faith and his recovery of hidden subjectivity in desire, sadism, or masochism in *Being and Nothingness* also capture the ambivalence of a subjectivity presiding over its own effacement and so never really effaceable. Beauvoir, like Sartre, captures the ambiguous, paradoxical, and ironic character of human situations and the elusiveness of human consciousness when, for instance, she portrays the ambiguous situation of the young girl who does and does not accept the destiny assigned her by society and nature. This young girl rebels through mechanisms such as laughter about sexual language, the use of obscene language, strange eating habits, self-mutilation, or even kleptomania (to take without being taken—just as the man will do to her). However, these very actions, while expressing defiance of conventions, do not effectively transcend the natural or social order or transvalue values but leave them intact and thus end up covertly affirming the very order against which they revolt. These pseudorebellions veil a subjectivity all too willing to conform in spite of its desires for freedom.[31]

In addition to capturing the ambiguity inherent in situations, Beauvoir proves herself even more adept when it comes to detecting *within the consciousnesses of women themselves* feelings so conflictual that it is frequently impossible for women even to admit their coexistence within the same consciousness. For instance, the newly married woman looks upon her husband as a demigod endowed with virile prestige and destined to replace her father as protector, teacher, and guide, and yet at the same time she often shares with him a "shameful," "grotesque," or "objectionable" experience of sensual indulgence to which he subjects her, leaving her with a strange blend of love and hatred for him. Similarly, the newly pregnant woman experiences feelings of revolt, resignation, satisfaction, or enthusiasm; she is proud that she is about to give birth and yet resentful of being tossed and driven as if she were the plaything of obscure forces, as if she were trapped in her body at the very moment when she is about to transcend herself. Likewise, when the child is born, the mother can both cherish it and yet resent it, as Linda does in Katherine Mansfield's short story "At the Bay." In spite of such ambiguities, the married woman, feeling love and hatred for her husband, is commanded by society to love her husband and to be happy, and so she begins her marriage in bad faith, readily persuading herself that she feels a great love for her husband. In like manner, the pregnant woman will convince herself of the illusion that she is now of herself a value and keep her misgivings about pregnancy silent. Finally, the mother represses feelings of hostility toward her children because women are supposed to be possessed of a "maternal instinct." Hence we learn from Sophie Tolstoy's journals that upon giving birth she

> tries in vain to express the conventional joy, but we are struck by her sadness and her fear of new responsibilities, though she avows a strong maternal feeling and says she loves her husband because the child is his. But it is clear that she thus parades her love for her husband only because she actually did not love him. This dislike was in reality reflected upon the child conceived in loathsome embraces.[32]

The bad faith which here dictates that one crush all discordant sentiments ultimately takes its toll. "To compensate for the disappointment that at first she will not admit even to herself," the married woman may commence to desire her husband insatiably, and yet the negative aspects resurface in violent or argumentative outbursts that reveal hostility against his domination. Or, if the sexual disgust persists, the married woman may transpose her marriage to an imaginative plane, growing increasingly jealous or possessive. Rather than admit that the illusions with which she entered and maintains the marriage are crumbling, she might, as is the wont of "the woman in love," invent rivals, who warrant further proprietary measures, which in turn express that amalgam of love and hatred that characterized her love from the start. The pregnant woman might resort to uncontrolled vomiting, or she could experience constipation, diarrhea, expulsive efforts, or even spontaneous miscarriage to eliminate the pregnancy toward which she feels an unacknowledged resentment. Finally, abusiveness, manipulation, and sadism can all characterize the treatment of a child by the mother both unwilling to own the enmity she feels for her own child and yet willing to mask her cruel actions by justifying them as "necessary for the child's formation."[33]

These examples all indicate that women so internalize oppressive social expectations about what they *should be* and shape their self-concepts accordingly that they are unable to admit who they *are* and what they feel—with severely deleterious results for all involved. Although such self-concepts usually are only retrospectively considered to be freely chosen since one at a later moment discovers oneself free enough to discard them, they effectively determine whether or not the ambiguities that ought to set the stage for any higher level decisions are even recognized at all. Here categorizations (of how one ought to be) do not so much freeze a fluid for-itself or deny its changeability as regiment a manifold of multivalent, equivocal feeling tones within univocal, consistent channels in such a way that incongruous feeling tones can barely cross the threshold of consciousness, if at all. Here one reifies for-itself consciousness by depriving it of the liveliness springing from its nebulous, discrepant aspects. Since these troubling feelings register a protest against the diminishments suffered in marital and maternal relationships, to silence them inflicts a self-mutilating violence at a primordial level. One excises the very feelings that acquaint one with one's mutilation, and thus one is so mutilated that one cannot even recognize that one is being or has been mutilated. Domineering husbands or sexist social structures need not exert themselves much when women inflict such damage upon themselves, often without being aware of the processes at work. The frequent *moral* character of many of these prohibitions, purifying away the dissonant fringes of consciousness, justifies this violence against the self and makes it appear to be virtue not violence, in spite of the fact that such repression issues in frenetic efforts to subjugate a spouse, terminate a pregnancy, or abuse a child. Beauvoir's attention to such affective subtleties, the coexistence of such incompatible feelings within a conflicted consciousness, represents a recovery of "the things themselves" beneath prejudices and with a perspicaciousness in the affective domain rarely exhibited by other phenomenologists.

Just as Nietzsche uncovered the terrain of the well hidden land of morality as the reward of a long, brave, industrious, and subterranean seriousness of which not everyone is capable, so a phenomenological resolve akin to Beauvoir's is required if one is to open up the field of consciousness and illuminate its dark corners. Only in recognizing what Nietzsche called the "plain, harsh, ugly, repellent, unchristian, immoral" truths about oneself can one take oneself authentically in hand, choose one's future, and avoid a train of future deceptions, hypocrisies, and cruelties.[34]

Ambiguity provides an interpretive key to much of *The Second Sex*. In addition to the already mentioned ambivalences, namely, that female desire for males fuses love with disgust, that masochism expresses self-assertion through abdication, that female self-abasement serves as a means to control, or that generosity between the sexes gives rise to exigencies, Beauvoir inundates the reader with further examples of mixed feelings and motivations. For example, male images of the woman's vagina as containing a serpent reflects male fears of female freedom in the fusion of the sexual act that was supposed to eliminate all individuality. Likewise, reverence for mothers veils antagonism, mothers experience sexual feelings toward the children entrusted to their supposedly altruistic care, anti-abortion politics may reflect and hide male sadism, and gifts extend one's tyranny over others. In eros, ambiguity prevails because it is rationally impenetrable and perturbing, because it requires of couples that they respect each other and yet become flesh for each other, and because it admixes generosity and possessiveness. Fearing such confusion, young girls resist puberty, the first experience which muddles the clear and distinct categories of childhood, and, as a result, it is not surprising that Beauvoir in her own autobiography should gratefully attest to the fact that eros played a key role in freeing her from her own excessive juvenile rationalism.[35]

Ambivalence is typical of institutions such as matrimony, which paradoxically heightens the taste for adultery, deadens spontaneity, and secures rights for women while reducing them to vassals. In accord with this taking of stock of institutions long before Sartre considered them in the *Critique of Dialectic Reason*, Beauvoir also reflects on how increased industrialization, which liberates women from family burdens, nonetheless enslaves them to hard work for low wages. Courses of action result in ambiguous, unintended consequences when women's refusal to be placed upon a pedestal leads to a suprisingly better integration within society, when men seek to possess women and find themselves possessed, when anticipations of the wedding night stifle generosity in sex or heighten disillusionment the morning after, when conformity to a husband's wishes renders a wife boring, when the woman in love follows a trajectory from narcissism to devotion to frustration, and when this woman's putting her life in another's hands produces a worse punishment than a hideous crime. This fluidity and indeterminacy of action, whose temporal unfolding is unpredictable, perhaps explains why Beauvoir in *The Ethics of Ambiguity* emphasizes the importance of exercising freedom in the face of risks from which a set of moral rules cannot relieve one.[36]

The framework of existentialism underpinning Beauvoir's analysis itself functions as a principal source of ambiguity. By refuting the false claim that female anatomy provides the key to female *destiny* and by envisioning it more as part of the *situation* toward which women may take up a free stance, Beauvoir in fact opens the door to more choice, to a pluralism of possibilities, and thus to more uncertainty and ambiguity. For-itself, as always capable of eluding any causes which might univocally determine its reactions—as these causes can do with things—is itself always ambiguous and unpredictable. Of course, such a freedom can refuse the condition implied in being human, that is, by fleeing the risks that confront a free being immersed in the world via a body with carnal origins and social ties. Montherlant, for instance, sought such an escape by withdrawing from any engagement with mature women and by seeking out instead unthreatening liaisons with passive, infantile, stupid, and vegetal women. Nevertheless, as Sartre has shown, the for-itself is haunted by its own facticity by which it possesses the inescapable *nature* that it must choose since the very choice not to choose is itself a choice. The choice not to be engaged in the world, to shrink from its ambiguities, is a way of engaging the world through a posture of withdrawing and thus inserting oneself very onesidedly into the world, forsaking other options, and being left with the uncertainty as to whether one's own choice was correct, an uncertainty that besets any choice that one would make. Beauvoir comments upon this ambiguity ingredient in any situation freedom confronts.

> The individual who acts considers himself, like others, as responsible for both evil and good, he knows that it is for him to define ends, to bring them to success; he becomes aware, in action, of the ambiguousness of all solutions; justice and injustice, gains and losses, are inextricably mixed. But anyone who is passive is out of the game and declines to pose ethical problems even in thought: the good should be realized, and it if is not, there must be some wrongdoing for which those to blame must be punished. Like the child, woman conceives good and evil in simple images, as co-existing, discrete entities; this Manichaeism of hers sets her mind at rest by doing away with the anxiety of making difficult choices. To decide between an evil and a lesser evil, between a present good and a greater good to come, to have to define for herself what is defeat and what is victory—all this involves terrible risks. For the Manichaeist, the good wheat is clearly distinct from the tares, and one has merely to remove the tares; dust stands self-condemned and cleanliness is complete absence of dirt; to clean house is to remove dirt and rubbish.[37]

Although the separation of situation and freedom introduces the ambiguity of possibilities, the inevitability of choice rebinds freedom to engagement with the situation and the world—but instead of being a neat world, it is one fraught with perplexity. But such perplexity does not result in paralysis for Beauvoir since one would still be responsible even if one were to choose to be paralyzed. Rather, the ambiguity of the situation heightens for Beauvoir the sense of risk, daring, and adventure with which any freedom is already fully familiar insofar as it knows that it itself is its only foundation. Indeed, *The Second Sex* educates the for-itself to its own responsibility by showing that if in the end it succumbs to cultural prejudices imposed from without it will be because it has freely chosen to succumb.

4. CRITIQUE

Phenomenological influences are evident throughout *The Second Sex* insofar as Beauvoir seeks to recover a subjectivity submerged by the sciences (particularly in the first three chapters) and by common sense. By casting light upon the scientist's concealed subjectivity, that is, by situating biology and psychology with reference the existent (scientist) engaging in them and bestowing value upon their findings, Beauvoir brings to mind Husserl's own endeavor in the *Crisis* to locate the sciences within the broader human life-world in which they arise and to see them as part of the practice of a subject implicit and discoverable within all cognitive undertakings. In the spirit of phenomenology, Beauvoir strives to return to the things themselves and to abstain from prejudices, particularly those which present distorted images of women, whether they derive from the sciences, such as biological reductionism or the castration complex in psychology, or from the commonsense life-world. In this latter regard, Beauvoir's incisive attention to life-world roles or self-conceptions ("self-typifications" in Schutz's terminology) converges with many of the concerns and concepts treated in depth by Schutz's phenomenology of the social life-world. In her critique of false universalizations and essences and her careful observation of the ambiguous, disparate strands of feminine consciousness, Beauvoir represents the best of the critical tendencies of phenomenological procedures such as free variation or reduction. Although her work is clearly under the sway of phenomenology, surprisingly she rarely reflects explicitly upon phenomenological method.

Insofar as her earlier work makes use of the phenomenological ontology given expression in Sartre's works, her work reflects that ontology's limits: the lack of a methodological subtlety that tends to polarize the freedom and its conditions and that could have been ameliorated had she taken account of the life-world origins of reflexivity and freedom. However, the later Beauvoir of *The Prime of Life* (published as *La Force de l'âge* in 1960) admits that her earlier works suffered from a view of consciousness too detached from the social world.

> An individual, I thought, only receives a human dimension by recognizing the existence of others. Yet in, my essay [*Pyrrhus et Cinéas*, her early and perhaps most explicitly phenomenological work], coexistence appears as a sort of accident that each individual should somehow surmount; he should begin by hammering out his "project" in solitary state, and only then ask the mass of mankind to endorse its validity. In truth, society has been all about me from the day of my birth; it is in the bosom of that society, and in my own close relationship with it, that all my personal decisions must be formed.[38]

It is also evident, however, from these later autobiographical writings that she was already criticizing Sartre's early rationalistic account of freedom, out of touch with the power of social conditioning that her concrete analyses in *The Second Sex* elucidate. One wonders if a phenomenology of the social life-world, such as Schutz's, might better represent the mature Beauvoir's phenomenological starting-point, out of which develop reflexivity and freedom, some of whose aspects the for-itself/in-itself dialectic greatly illuminates.[39]

Furthermore, Beauvoir's account of intersubjectivity within *The Second Sex* reflects the dialectics of the master-slave in Hegel and of the for-itself /in-itself, which, as mentioned above, is transferred to the relationship between for-itselves. As a result of these dialectical bases, Beauvoir depicts human relationships as taking place between for-itselves, each wary of being reduced to an in-itself by the other, and as falling under the rubric of what Levinas later describes as "allergy." Such allergic relationships are evident in Beauvoir's accounts of the confining myths which men impose upon women; of the subjugation of woman as a child, in sexual initiation, marriage, parenthood, old age; of the resistance women offer men's categorizations; of the self-destructive resistance the young girl opposes to the exigencies of adulthood; of the hostile feelings toward others that women experience in marriage and pregnancy; and of the antipathy between mother and son and especially daughter. Though there is much about human relationships that this ontological fundament overlooks, it can serve nonetheless as a useful underpinning for a literature of protest—at that moment when women stand up in suspicious defiance of what men have done and are doing to them. Perhaps it is best to read Beauvoir herself as one of those insurgent females whom she herself honors in *The Second Sex*:

> Much more interesting are the insurgent females who have challenged this unjust society; a literature of protest can engender sincere and powerful works; out of the well of her revolt George Eliot drew a vision of Victorian England that was at once detailed and dramatic; still, as Virginia Woolf has made us see, Jane Austen, the Brontë sisters, George Eliot, have had to expend so much energy negatively in order to free themselves from outward restraints that they arrive somewhat out of breath at the stage from which masculine writers of great scope take their departure; they do not have enough strength left to profit by their victory and break all the ropes that hold them back. We do not find in them, for example, the irony, the ease of a Stendhal, nor his calm sincerity.[40]

Just as Sartre later admitted that his antagonistic view of intersubjectivity was shaped by the historical and socio-economic conditions under which it was written, so also it would not be surprising if the first great proponent of feminist theory, who first glimpsed the age-old bondage and inequities under which women have labored, might take up a view of intersubjectivity marked by the conflictual.[41]

What is interesting, though, is how Beauvoir, like Sartre in *Anti-Semite and Jew*, makes use of the paradigm of antagonistic relationships of *Being and Nothingness* within an explicitly *ethical* context, in pursuit of the liberation of women, and men, from a yoke under which they both labor. Thus the frequently used term *le regard* in *The Second Sex*, while drawn from the pessimistic, ethically neutral descriptions of alterity in *Being and Nothingness*, serves an ethical purpose, pointing to an oppressed Other, who on a prereflective level offers one resistance and places one in question. Such resistance and questioning are quintessential ethical activities in *Totality and Infinity*, where the "knowing whose essence is critique . . . leads to the Other." This critical potential the Other affords appears pointedly in Beauvoir's account of how the symmetries men assume about women's situation (e.g., their ability to satisfy sexual desires easily, their ability to assume without difficulty recently opened-up job opportunities) conceals asymmetries that only one who is familiar with the Other, that is, one who has been molded by face-to-face challenges, could appreciate. In addition, Montherlant's refusal of any exposure to the Other's contestation heightens his myopic self-enclosure and solipsism.[42]

As this attention to alterity anticipates Levinas's, so also one can detect throughout *The Second Sex* the lineaments of a reciprocal relationship between equals that functions, for Beauvoir's phenomenology as well as for Karl-Otto Apel's transcendental pragmatics, as a guiding norm in whose light nonreciprocal relations are recognized as distorted. In the contrasts she draws between Stendhal's presentation of women with Montherlant's and in her recollection of Malraux's story of Kyo's love for May, who he hopes will love him as he is instead of returning a "fawning reflection," Beauvoir clearly assesses relationships in terms of whether they can be characterized by a *mutual* generosity, vulnerability, recognition, and autonomy, in which each for-itself is upheld. It is rare to find such a positive portrayal of intersubjectivity in works published by Sartre during his lifetime, although a similar, positive ideal of human relationships does emerge in his posthumous ethics, *Cahiers pour une morale.*[43]

The tensions in *The Second Sex*'s presentation of intersubjectivity, between the struggle to exert or escape mastery, on the one hand, and generous self-donation culminating in a respectful reciprocity, on the other, between the extremes of Montherlant and Stendhal, corroborates Bergoffen's distinction between the ethics of the project and the ethics of generosity. Erotic relationships can give birth to generosity, as is exhibited in Malraux's and Stendhal's characters, or they can serve as a site for a detached observer to exercise domination over another by refusing to give oneself over, as is instanced in the cases of Sade and Montherlant. While the erotic in general, the erotic body, and the ethics of the erotic are often expressed with a muted voice in Beauvoir's works, her linkage of a concern for alterity and reciprocity with eros is thoroughly compatible with the decentering of the inviolable and invulnerable self described in Levinas's phenomenology of eros and in the examination of the ethical dimensions of eros by Alphonso Lingis in a Levinasian key.[44]

In moving toward the goal of reciprocity between equal freedoms, Beauvoir believes that one must admit first of all the existent asymmetries between men and women since men have developed unilaterally behaviors, structures, myths, and categories that relegate women to inferiority and that are maintained irrationally, in the face of contradictory facts. Then, to ensure the accuracy of men's beliefs about women and, even more importantly, the possibility of symmetrical relationships as well, Beauvoir invites men to practice undemanding generosity as a condition for equality, and she characterizes such generosity as humanity's highest achievement.

> It is the existence of other men that tears each man out of his imma-
> nence and enables him to fulfill the truth of his being, to complete
> himself through transcendence, through escape toward some objec-
> tive, through enterprise. But this liberty not my own, while assuring
> mine, also conflicts with it: each separate conscious being aspires to
> set himself up alone as sovereign subject.... It is possible to rise
> above this conflict if each individual freely recognizes the other, each
> regarding himself and the other simultaneously as object and as sub-
> ject in a reciprocal manner. But friendship and generosity, which
> alone permit in actuality this recognition of free beings, are not facile
> virtues; they are assuredly man's highest achievement, and through
> that achievement he is to be found in his true nature.[45]

But while, for the sake of reciprocal, symmetric relationships, Beauvoir asks of men a generosity, a Levinasian asymmetric displacement of self at the service of the Other, inverting the kinds of relationships depicted in *Being and Nothingness*, she also touts generosity as the key to women's self-transcendence. A mother, for example, needs a rare combination of generosity and detachment to experience her children as enriching her, without exercising the role of tyrant in their lives. Similarly, a stubborn narcissistic woman will be limited in love as well as in art through her inability to give herself. Beauvoir stresses this importance of the giving away of oneself by bringing up its importance for art at the conclusion of her final chapter on liberation. As long as women aim at aggrandizing themselves in their acting, painting, or writing, for instance, or at making their art the servant of their ego instead of the other way around, they will not give themselves over to contemplating the world and expressing themselves creatively.[46]

It is surprising to see Beauvoir, with good reason wary of the male capacity to take advantage of female self-surrender, recommend at the end, at the climax, of *The Second Sex* a self-forgetful immersion in art. But she goes one step further when she suggests that even the cause of women itself, to which her entire book has been dedicated, can become such a preoccupation that it impedes "the disinterested attitude toward the universe that opens the widest horizons." The for-itself that continually keeps itself free from being reduced to in-itself and from any masochism pretending to be self-donation, comes to a point where it can express its own authenticity, the apex of its own restless dynamism, by no longer clinging even to itself, unencumbered as much as possible with anxiety for itself, but daringly giving itself away. Levinas, too, traces this trajectory in which the "I" "at the apogee of its being, expanded into happiness, in egoism, positing itself as *ego*," appears "beating its own record, preoccupied with another being." Such self-donation is not something men should demand as part of a covert project of subjugation, but would rather be something to be chosen freely by women as one of their own innermost possibilities of self-transcendence.[47]

While these conclusions on intersubjectivity parallel Levinas's, the methodology by which Beauvoir arrives at them lacks the sophistication and self-reflexivity of Levinas's, which shall be discussed later. As with Sartre, however, this deficiency in methodological self-reflection indicates no deliberate rejection of rationality on Beauvoir's part. On the contrary, her phenomenology does not permit her to lapse deliberately into irrationality, but instead impels her to adopt a self-reflective critical stance toward natural attitude and scientific prejudices, to establish the contexts and limits for sciences such as biology and psychology, to recover the subjectivity latent in various forms of bad faith, and to retrieve the things themselves covered over by prejudice or moral conventions. Likewise, even Beauvoir's disinclination to accept uncritically universalizations or dubious essences—itself a instance of dedication to rational standards—cannot be construed as merely negative. When Beauvoir rejects false universalizations that reify women, as if they were a causally effected in-itself, she does so on the basis of an essence that she believes to be veridical, namely, woman's character as free for-itself. Paradoxically, it is on a phenomenologically established essential footing—such as for-itself, in-itself, bad faith, situation, incarnation, ambiguity, temporality—that Beauvoir finds definitions of the essence of woman repugnant. Just as Apel in his transcendental pragmatics will later expose the commitments to truth underpinning skeptical and relativistic strategies, so Beauvoir's positive phenomenologically based commitments underlie her negative assault on sexist belief-systems. These reconstructions of Beauvoir's approach to rationality attempt to make explicit what is often only implicit within her own thought. Whatever suspicion there may be about rationality in her thought generally springs from certain Nietzschean motivations that, however they may shake one's confidence in reason, themselves depend on a process of rational retrieval, that is, a "long, brave, industrious, and subterranean seriousness of which not everyone is capable."[48]

Just as Beauvoir's rational examination of the ambiguities of consciousness and its self-deceptions could lead to doubts about rationality, it can also generate a certain diffidence about ethical norms. The economic and power motivations underlying moral norms, disclosed by Marx and Nietzsche and visible in inconsistencies in practice, raise the question as to whether moral norms are nothing other than a facade allowing one to pursue one's interests without interference. For instance, since men forbid abortion for women and yet resort to abortion for their consorts when convenient, it could appear that male sadism rather than a passion for moral values underlies strong anti-abortion stances. Similarly, like Marx, Beauvoir wonders whether the abstract rights of women (e.g., the right to vote or to private property), defended in bourgeois society, pacify protesters and thus effectively hide and preserve unchanging economic inequities. In addition, those whose deplorable economic conditions drive them to prostitution, to make their living by serving male lusts, find themselves castigated as "perverse" by the hypocritical men who make use of them but who will not lift a finger to better their economic situation.[49]

Moral norms are questionable not only because the ambiguous motivations of their adherents give rise to them, but also because they must be applied to situations fraught with indeterminacy. Thus Beauvoir insists that "ethics does not furnish recipes" for action in the *The Ethics of Ambiguity.* There are many times, she suggests, when, in spite of the Kantian outrage one might feel at a single murder, a situation may call for what may seem like murder or violence (which terms have variable meanings depending on the situation) to avoid more murders or greater violence. For Beauvoir, morality resides in the painfulness of an indefinite questioning, and the person of good will differs from the tyrant in that she lives as an authentic, mutable foritself, continually asking "Am I really working for the liberation of men? Isn't this end contested by the sacrifices through which I aim at it?" The tensions between universalizations and the free for-itself reassert themselves in the ethical opposition between universal norm and concrete situation.[50]

Just as false universals did not undermine Beauvoir's reliance on phenomenological "essences," so her hesitations about ethics do not a priori rule out the possibility that separate existents can bind themselves to each other and forge laws valid for all. *The Ethics of Ambiguity,* a tract in support of ethics, as Lewis Gordon has observed, advocates that the moral laws that ought to be legislated for all are Kantian in character in opposition to utilitarian justifications of violence. In addition, she claims that to will oneself free is to will others free and that the only genuine seriousness involves liberation of self and others through means respectful of the ends intended. Indeed, on the basis of the distinction between free for-itself and inert in-itself, Beauvoir often appeals to the reader's intuition throughout *The Second Sex* that it would be contradictory to reduce a for-itself to a thing. While Beauvoir might espouse the principle that one ought not act in such a contradictory fashion and while such a principle would be thoroughly compatible with Kant's second formulation of the Categorical Imperative, she would no doubt want to preserve a broad, indeterminate domain in which free, critical agents might apply this principle according to their best lights.[51]

Beyond appealing to the reader's conceptual intuitions and to an ideal of behavioral consistency, Beauvoir never explicitly justifies a Kantian first principle of ethics. However, the seeds of such a justification can be found in the *intersubjective* ideal, that of reciprocity between equal for-itselves, that serves as a guiding thread throughout *The Second Sex*. This ideal, of course, would be congruent with Sartre's reference to ideal discursive relationships in *Cahiers pour une morale* which, for instance, proscribe *ad hominem* arguments because they inflict violence by dismissing and reifying a discourse partner. Like Karl-Otto Apel, one could argue not only that this ideal is useful for identifying concrete wrongs, but also that it governs the very discourse in which one identifies such wrongs or even the discourse in which one might dispute that ideal. Such an ideal functions in a transcendental fashion, since even if someone were to offer philosophical arguments against the ideal of reciprocity between equals, that very philosophical argument itself would involve a give and take, a mutual exchange of speaker and hearer roles, that would exhibit reciprocity between equal discourse partners. Although Beauvoir surpasses Sartre in her positive presentation of such an ideal, neither she nor Sartre develop a full account of such ideal relationships nor exploit their potential for providing transcendental grounding for a Kantian ethics. Of course, such a justification of first principles would not substitute for application discourses respectful of the diverse contexts of free participants and reliant upon Aristotelian *phronesis*. Furthermore, partners to such an application discourse would need to expose themselves continually to the gaze of the Other—not *Being and Nothingness*'s Hobbesian wolf who only threatens, but the Levinasian claimant who, as Beauvoir has noted, "tears each man out of his immanence and enables him to fulfill the truth of his being."[52]

Finally, while the transcendental structure of discourse might provide a justification for a Kantian moral principle, one would also need to differentiate the type of reasoning that is involved when one resorts to such justification. Scientific rationality, for example, warrants its claims by exhibiting empirical evidence; but ethical rationality brings forward first principles and defends them, at least in Apel's case, on the basis of the performative contradiction into which those who oppose them fall. Furthermore, ethical rationality appeals not to facts, but to the transcendental structure of discourse on whose basis all facts themselves are established. Ethical rationality, as Kant explained it, is not determined by the objects it observes. Hence, it is not constrained to conform to the way the world is as is natural science, but rather it commands human actions that might transform the way world is. Hence, ethical rationality is so little bound by empirical facts that it could command that one be a perfectly sincere friend, even though empirically one has never encountered such a friend. Furthermore, the factual truth that economic and power motives often press moral norms into their service and conceal such motives, would not invalidate a moral command that one *ought not* subordinate one's moral principle to such motives or, for that matter, other moral commands. Ambiguities in motivation could only discredit moral norms if those norms were deduced from factual states of affairs, but if these norms depend both on a kind of rationality distinctive from empirical science and on the exigency that one act consistently with the structure of discursive rationality within which all facts are established, they are not imperiled by facts about the pervasiveness of mixed motives.[53]

Although Beauvoir never develops a conception of practical rationality similar to Kant's, such an understanding of rationality would strengthen her position since it would concur with the anti-naturalistic tendencies that abound in her thought. After all, biological or psychological facts about female anatomy do not dictate how free for-itself consciousness ought to act—sex does not determine gender. Similarly, the ambivalence of motives, which Beauvoir most adeptly points out, in no way enjoins paralysis, but only constitutes the situation before which human freedom needs to assert itself, only now with greater daring and adventure than it had when it failed to acknowledge its dividedness. Finally, *The Second Sex* is itself an exercise in practical rationality—even if Beavoir never makes it explicit—since it demands that the way the world has been for centuries give way to the way it ought to be.[54]

NOTES

1. Simone de Beauvoir, *The Prime of Life*, trans. Peter Green (Cleveland and New York: The World Publishing Company, 1962), p. 162; Simone de Beauvoir, *Force of Circumstance*, vol. 1: *After the War*, trans. Richard Howard (New York: Paragon House, 1992), pp. 45–46; vol. 2: *Hard Times*, trans. Richard Howard (New York: Paragon House, 1992), pp. 366–67; Debra Bergoffen, *The Philosophy of Simone de Beauvoir: Gendered Phenomenologies, Erotic Generosities* (Albany: State University of New York Press, 1997), pp. 21, 36, and in particular see her discussion of the intentionalities at work in *The Ethics of Ambiguity*, pp. 76–89; Karen Vintges, "*The Second Sex* and Philosophy," in *Feminist Interpretations of Simone de Beauvoir*, ed. Margaret A. Simons (University Park: Pennsylvania State University Press, 1995), p. 46; Kristina Arp, "Beauvoir's Concept of Bodily Alienation," *Feminist Interpretations of Simone de Beauvoir*, p. 165; Eleanore Holveck, "Can a Woman Be a Philosopher? Reflections of a Beauvoirian Housemaid," *Feminist Interpretations of Simone de Beauvoir*, p. 73; Jo-Ann Pilardi, "The Changing Critical Fortunes of *The Second Sex*," in *History and Theory, Studies in the Philosophy of History* 32 (1993): 52; see *supra*, chapter 1, pp. 3–4.

2. Simone de Beauvoir, *The Prime of Life*, pp. 41, 118; Jo-Ann Pilardi, "Philosophy Becomes Autobiography: The Development of the Self in the Writings of Simone de Beauvoir," *Writing the Politics of Difference*, ed. Hugh J. Silverman (Albany: State University of New York Press, 1991), pp. 157–58; Margaret A. Simons, "Beauvoir and Sartre, The Philosophical Relationship," *Simone de Beauvoir: Witness to a Century, Yale French Studies*, no. 72 (New Haven, Conn.: Yale University Press, 1986), p. 168; Sonia Kruks, "Simone de Beauvoir: Teaching Sartre about Freedom," in *Sartre Alive*, ed. Ronald Aronson and Adrian van den Hoven (Detroit: Wayne State University Press, 1991), p. 286; Michèle Le Doeuff points to the Hegelian influence on Beauvoir's earlier works, but this need not offset the presence of Husserlian phenomenology in a later work like *The Second Sex*, cf. Michèle Le Doeuff, "Simone de Beauvoir: Falling into (Ambiguous) Line," *Feminist Interpretations of Simone de Beauvoir*, p. 61; Deirdre Bair, *Simone de Beauvoir: A Biography* (New York: Summit Books, 1990), pp. 174, 188, 195, 319, 478–79, 486.

3. Beauvoir, *The Prime of Life*, p. 346; Simons, "Beauvoir and Sartre: The Philosophical Relationship," pp. 165, 166, 169, 171–72, 177; Kruks, "Simone de Beauvoir: Teaching Sartre about Freedom," pp. 286–87, 288–90, 291; Pilardi, "Philosophy Becomes Autobiography: The Development of the Self in the Writings of Simone de Beauvoir," p. 155; Judith Butler, "Sex and Gender in Simone de Beauvoir's *Second Sex*," in *Simone de Beauvoir: Witness to a Century*, pp. 38, 48; Kate Fullbrook and Edward Fullbrook, *Simone de Beauvoir and Jean-Paul Sartre: The Remaking of a Twentieth Century Legend* (New York: Basic Books, 1994), pp. 107, 109, 110–11; see Jean-Paul Sartre, *The Transcendence of*

the Ego: An Existentialist Theory of Consciousness, trans. Forrest Williams and Robert Kirkpatrick (New York: The Noonday Press, 1957), pp. 82, 84, 93, 96, 98. It would be extremely valuable to follow up on Simons's and the Full-brooks suggestion that Beauvoir's discovery of the Other precedes Sartre's, especially in a book such as this in which Levinas's phenomenology of alterity will play a central role. However, such a study would be more extensive than what is allowable here. See in addition Simone de Beauvoir, *She Came to Stay* (Cleveland and New York: The World Publishing Company, 1954), pp. 68, 113, 126, 172, 211, 234, 301, 388–89; on the earlier indications of Sartre's concern with the Other, see Hazel Barnes, "Response to Margaret Simons," *Conflicts and Convergences: Selected Studies in Phenomenology and Existential Philosophy*, vol. 24, ed. Linda Martin Alcoff and Merold Westphal (Chicago: DePaul University, 1999), p. 32.

4. Margaret A. Simons, "An Appeal to Reopen the Question of Influence," *Conflicts and Convergences*, pp. 17–24; Barnes, "Response to Margaret Simons," pp. 29–34.

5. Beauvoir, *Force of Circumstance*, 2:366–67.

6. Simone de Beauvoir, *Pyrrhus et Cinéas* in *Pour une morale de l'ambiguïté suivi de Pyrrhus et Cinéas* (Paris: Gallimard, 1944), pp. 243, 245, 256, 258, 370; Simone de Beauvoir, *The Ethics of Ambiguity*, trans. Bernard Frechtman (New York: The Citadel Press, 1948); Emmanuel Levinas, *Otherwise Than Being or Beyond Essence*, trans. Alphonso Lingis (The Hague, Boston, London: Martinus Nijhoff, 1981), p. 45.

7. Simone de Beauvoir, "Review of *La phénoménologie de la perception*," *Les Temps Modernes* 1 (1945): 363–67; Simone de Beauvoir, "Merleau-Ponty and Pseudo-Sartreanism," *International Studies in Philosophy* 21 (1989): 3–48. In the initial section of the latter essay, Beauvoir insists that Sartre sees meanings as existing objectively in reference to freedom, but this is not equivalent to such meanings constituting the subject, as Merleau-Ponty argues. In some of the later citations near the end of that first section, Beauvoir touches on how language and environment constitute the subject, but these citations are drawn from *Saint Genet* and *Henry Martin*, works by Sartre in the 1950s after Beauvoir had moved him from the exaggerated notions of freedom in *Being and Nothingness* and more in the direction of Merleau-Ponty.

8. Beauvoir, *Pyrrhus et Cinéas*, pp. 282, 285, 312–23, 348–52, 358, 364–65; *The Ethics of Ambiguity*, pp. 64–67, 99–100, 134, 153.

9. Simone de Beauvoir, *America Day by Day*, trans. Carol Cosman (Berkeley, Los Angeles, London: University of California Press, 1999), p. 382; Beauvoir, *The Ethics of Ambiguity*, pp. 78, 86; Bergoffen, *The Philosophy of Simone de Beauvoir*, pp. 75–82, 103, 110; see Michael Barber, "Phenomenology and the Ethical Bases of Pluralism: Arendt's and Beauvoir's Treatment of Race in America," in *The Existential Phenomenology of Simone de Beauvoir*, forthcoming from Kluwer Academic Press.

10. Beauvoir, *America Day by Day*, pp. 202–203, 232–50, 272–77, 333–34;

"un don animal" appears in *L'Amérique au jour le jour* (Paris: Gallimard, 1947), p. 322; Simone de Beauvoir, "Must We Burn Sade?" in *The Marquis de Sade*, trans. Annette Michelson, ed. Paul Dinnage (London: John Calder, 1962), pp. 17, 28, 32–33, 38, 66; Bergoffen, *The Philosophy of Simone de Beauvoir*, pp. 36–42.

11. Simone de Beauvoir, *Le deuxième sexe*, vol. 1: *Les faits et les mythes* (Paris: Gallimard, 1976), pp. 37–38; *The Second Sex*, trans. H. M. Parshley (New York: Vintage Books, 1989), p. 5. Henceforth, French pages will be listed first followed by a slash and the English translation pages. At times, Parshley's translation takes the political force out of Beauvoir's French, as for example, when it translates "*Sur ce point encore, certains biologistes ont pretendu legitimer l'order établi*" with "Here again certain biologists have attempted to account for the existing state of affairs."

12. Ibid., pp. 15–16, 44–45, 54 /xxi, 11–12, 14, 18.

13. Ibid., pp. 35, 42, 56, 70–71, 73–77/3, 9, 20, 32, 34–37.

14. There is an extensive and important discussion in the secondary literature as to whether Beauvoir downplays or even reads negatively the physiological experiences of reproduction and thereby undercuts the possibility of feminine "differences" from men; cf. especially Beauvoir, *Le deuxième sexe*, 1:70–71/32. Critics, such as Julie Ward and Judith Butler, however, contend that economic and social conditions are involved in socially constructing a woman's experiences of her body which is never given apart from cultural interpretations; see Julie Ward, "Beauvoir's Two Senses of 'Body' in *The Second Sex*," in *Feminist Interpretations of Simone de Beauvoir*, p. 233; Pilardi, "The Changing Critical Fortunes of *The Second Sex*," p. 67; Celine T. Leon, "Beauvoir's Woman: Eunuch or Male?" in *Feminist Interpretations of Simone de Beauvoir*, p. 153; Barbara Klaw, "Sexuality in Beauvoir's *Les Mandarins*," in *Feminist Interpretations of Simone de Beauvoir*, p. 213; Butler, "Sex and Gender in Simone de Beauvoir's *Second Sex*, pp. 45–46; Judith Butler, "Sexual Ideology and Phenomenological Deception: A Feminist Critique of Merleau-Ponty's Phenomenology of Perception," in *The Thinking Muse: Feminism and Modern French Philosophy*, ed. Jeffner Allen and Iris Marion Young (Bloomington and Indianapolis: Indiana University Press, 1989), pp. 90–91. Lucius Outlaw envisions a similar interaction between biogenetic and cultural features in the process of raciation in *On Race and Philosophy* (New York and London: Routledge, 1996), pp. 84–85.

15. Beauvoir, *Le deuxième sexe*, 1:80–106/39–60.

16. Ibid., pp. 221, 225/128, 132; Blair, *Simone de Beauvoir: A Biography*, p. 388. For a work that unifies Beauvoir's concern for racial and women's equality, see Margaret Simons, *Beauvoir and The Second Sex: Feminism, Race, and the Origins of Existentialism* (Lanham, Md.: Rowman & Littlefield Publishers, Inc., 1999).

17. Beauvoir, *Le deuxième sexe*, 1:237–319, 321–38, 379–91, 395–405/139–98, 199–212, 240–49, 253–61.

18. Beauvoir, *Le deuxième sexe*, vol. 2: *L'expérience vecue* (Paris: Galli-

mard, 1976), pp. 92, 94, 98–100, 103–107, 121–40, 150–90, 195–98, 200, 226, 254–55, 259, 266–68, 279–80, 292, 343, 352, 360–61, 377–83, 468–77/330, 332, 335–36, 339–42, 350–69, 374–402, 407–409, 410, 429, 444, 447–48, 451, 456, 462, 492–93, 497, 504–505, 516–21, 584–92. Beauvoir's discussion of institutions such as marriage and social conditioning pass beyond the Sartrean framework, as commentators have noted: see Kruks, "Simone de Beauvoir: Teaching Sartre about Freedom," pp. 286, 290–91; Simons, "Beauvoir and Sartre: The Philosophical Relationship," p. 169; Butler, "Sex and Gender in Simone de Beauvoir's *Second Sex*," pp. 43, 46, 48.

19. Beauvoir, *Le deuxième sexe*, 2:529, 543/632, 640.

20. Ibid., pp. 597–600, 625–40, 661–62/679–82, 702–14, 730–31.

21. *Supra*, chapter 1, pp. 2–7; Husserl, *Ideas, General Introduction to Pure Phenomenology*, pp. 35–37; Husserl, *Cartesian Meditations*, pp. 35, 69.

22. Alfred Schutz, "Some Leading Concepts of Phenomenology," *The Problem of Social Reality*, vol. 1 of *Collected Papers*, ed. Maurice Natanson (The Hague: Martinus Nijhoff, 1962), p. 100; Beauvoir, *Le deuxième sexe*, 1:83, 231, 405; 2:32–33, 313, 383–86, 520, 586–87, 592, 600, 605–15/42, 136, 261, 282, 474, 521–23, 626, 673, 678, 682, 686–94.

23. Beauvoir, *Le deuxième sexe*, 2:186–87, 369, 475, 525, 560, 613, 644/399, 511, 590, 629, 652, 692, 717.

24. Ibid., 1:36–37, 39–40, 42–43, 49, 58, 61/4–5, 7, 9, 15, 22, 24.

25. Ibid., 2:192, 361, 363, 365, 366, 372, 440, 452, 496, 633/404, 504–505, 506, 507, 509, 562, 571, 607, 708.

26. Ibid., 2:9. The translation here is mine.

27. Ibid., 1:12, 24, 398–400; 2:20, 507, 521/xx, xxix, 255–57, 272, 615, 627.

28. Ibid., 2:661/731; see Margaret A. Simons, "*The Second Sex*: From Marxism to Radical Feminism," in *Feminist Interpretations of Simone de Beauvoir*, p. 255.

29. Beauvoir, *Le deuxième sexe*, 1:322–38/200–12; "Must We Burn Sade?" pp. 32–33, 38, 66.

30. Beauvoir, *Le deuxième sexe*, 2:147, 192–217, 590, 615/371, 404–24, 676, 694; Toril Moi also comments on Beauvoir's "far too sanguine view of masculinity," in "Ambiguity and Alienation in *The Second Sex*," in *Feminism and Postmodernism*, ed. Margaret Ferguson and Jennifer Wicke (Durham, N.C., and London: Duke University Press, 1994), p. 98.

31. Beauvoir, *Le deuxième sexe*, 2:121–28, 519/352–56, 625; Simone de Beauvoir, *Memoirs of a Dutiful Daughter*, trans. James Kirkup (New York: Harper & Row, 1959), pp. 17–20, 35–38, 192–93; *The Prime of Life*, pp. 17–22, 45–46, 56, 119, 259, 286–92, 435, 457, 474, 479; *Force of Circumstance*, 1:242–43, 270–76; 2: 41; Simone de Beauvoir, *All Said and Done*, trans. Patrick O'Brian (New York: Warner Books, 1974), pp. 11, 25–26, 126; on Beauvoir's disagreement with Sartre, see *The Prime of Life*, pp. 119, 346.

32. Beauvoir, *Le deuxième sexe*, 2:367/569, see also 2:290–94, 343–63, 365–76, 573/461–63, 492–506, 508–15, 662–63.

33. Ibid., 2:290–94, 343–63, 365–76, 573/461–63, 492–506, 508–15, 662–63.

34. Friedrich Nietzsche, *On the Genealogy of Morals and Ecce Homo*, trans. Walter Kaufmann (New York: Random House, 1967), pp. 21, 25.

35. Beauvoir, *Le deuxième sexe*, 1:92, 243, 257, 277, 262, 287, 300, 355, 397, 402; 2:20, 60–61, 116–17, 177–78, 190, 209, 333, 371, 563/49, 144, 153, 156, 166–67, 174, 184, 225, 254, 258, 272, 304, 348–49, 392, 402, 417, 486, 510, 651; *The Prime of Life*, 19–22, 56, 286, 474.

36. Beauvoir, *Le deuxième sexe*, 1:164, 165, 196–97, 272, 305; 2:254–55, 558, 576, 579/100, 101, 114, 164, 184, 444, 651, 665, 667; *The Ethics of Ambiguity*, pp. 123, 129, 133.

37. Beauvoir, *Le deuxième sexe*, 2:495–96/607. See also: 1:77, 101, 322, 328/37, 57, 200, 205; Sartre, *Being and Nothingness*, pp. 618–19.

38. Beauvoir, *The Prime of Life*, p. 435.

39. Ibid., p. 346; Beauvoir, *Force of Circumstance*, 1:199, 242.

40. Beauvoir, *Le deuxième sexe*, 2:634/709.

41. *Supra*, chapter 2, p. 12; Sartre, *Cahiers pour une morale*, p. 430/415.

42. Beauvoir, *Le deuxième sexe*, 2:65, 103, 120, 159, 162/308, 339, 351, 381, 382; Emmanuel Levinas, *Totality and Infinity: An Essay in Exteriority*, trans. Alphonso Lingis (The Hague, Boston, London: Martinus Nijhoff, 1979), p. 85.

43. Beauvoir, *Le deuxième sexe*, 1:237–38, 321–38, 379–91; 2:134–35, 302, 554, 579, 613/139–40, 185, 200–12, 240–49, 361, 471, 640, 667, 691; Sartre, *Cahiers pour une morale*, pp. 146, 177, 206, 218, 224, 248, 271, 273, 295, 297–98, 301, 311, 494, 522–24/138, 169, 198, 208, 214, 238, 261, 262, 283–84, 285, 289, 301, 478, 506–508.

44. Bergoffen, *The Philosophy of Simone de Beauvoir: Gendered Phenomenologies, Erotic Generosities*, pp. 67, 114, 122–23, 129, 137, 155–61, 163 173, 178, 185; Levinas, *Totality and Infinity*, pp. 256–66; Alphonso Lingis, *The Community of Those Who Have Nothing in Common* (Bloomington and Indianapolis: Indiana University Press, 1994), pp. 62–66; Alphonso Lingis, *Sensation: Intelligibility in Sensibility* (Atlantic Highlands, N.J.: Humanities Press, 1996), pp. 59–65.

45. Beauvoir, *Le deuxième sexe*, 1:237–38/140 and also 1:241–42, 395/142–43, 253.

46. Ibid., 2:186, 474, 538, 625–31/399, 589, 636, 702–707

47. Ibid., 2:635/709–10; Levinas, *Totality and Infinity*, p. 63.

48. An excellent example of Beauvoir's suspicion of rationality is to be found in her analysis of how a man acts as "an absolute superior and a dispenser of undeniable truths" in his relationship with his wife. He veils his violence beneath a veneer of logic, and, of course, would never appear violent but only logical to himself. Beauvoir, *Le deuxième sexe*, 2:295–96/463–64; Nietzsche, *On the Genealogy of Morals*, p. 21; *infra*, chapter 5, 5–12.

49. Beauvoir, *Le deuxième sexe*, 1:151, 227; 2:333, 342, 432, 443, 504/93, 133, 486, 492, 557, 564, 613.

50. Beauvoir, *The Ethics of Ambiguity*, pp. 114, 133–34, 138.

51. Ibid., pp. 18, 60, 73, 111; Gordon, *Bad Faith and Anti-Black Racism*, p. 200, n. 9.

52. Immanuel Kant, *Critique of Practical Reason*, trans. Lewis White Beck (Indianapolis and New York: The Bobbs-Merrill Company, Inc., 1956), pp. 17–18, 57; Immanuel Kant, *Grounding for the Metaphysics of Morals*, trans. James W. Ellington (Indianapolis and Cambridge: Hackett Publishing Company, 1981), pp. 19–20; Beauvoir, *Le deuxième sexe*, 1:237–38/140.

53. *Infra*, chapter 5, 12–17.

54. Bergoffen's thesis that ethical intentionality is "disclosive of being" threatens to confuse the distinction between the factual and the ethical central to practical rationality in Kantian ethics and implicit in *The Second Sex*; see Bergoffen, *The Philosophy of Simone de Beauvoir*, pp. 76–82.

4

ALFRED SCHUTZ, PHENOMENOLOGY, AND RACIAL DISCRIMINATION

1. ALFRED SCHUTZ'S PHENOMENOLOGY

While committed to Husserl's phenomenological project, Alfred Schutz found himself forced to adapt the usual phenomenological methods when it came to the social world. Thus, in good phenomenological style, he allowed the eidetic object of his investigations, in this case the social world, to dictate his methodology, even his phenomenological methodology, instead of the other way around. When Husserl confronted the problem of intersubjectivity, he gave an account of how the Other, whose existence the transcendental reduction had bracketed, comes to appearance in conscious experience. Husserl developed this account through a process of transcendental constitution in his Fifth Cartesian Meditation. Schutz's careful critique of this meditation points out how the second *epoché* which Husserl executes as a prelude to constituting the Other cannot effectively separate what is "properly of the ego" from what refers to others because even what is properly of the ego must make reference to its institution in the social "natural world" of everyday life, supposedly bracketed. Similarly, the congruent behaviors which verify that an Other is there and the commonality of objects in nature cannot escape reference to that natural world in which they were first experienced. As a result, Schutz concludes that

> Husserl's attempt to account for the constitution of transcendental intersubjectivity in terms of operations of the consciousness of the transcendental ego has not succeeded. It is to be surmised that inter-

subjectivity is not a problem of constitution which can be solved within the transcendental sphere, but is rather a datum (*Gegebenheit*) of the life-world. It is the fundamental ontological category of human existence in the world and therefore of all philosophical anthropology. As long as man is born of woman, intersubjectivity and the we-relationship will be the foundation for all other categories of human existence.[1]

The strength of Schutz's conviction in the second half of this quotation accounts for the methodological changes called for in the first half. It is because Schutz took so seriously human sociality and its pervasive presence that he felt impelled to dispense for the most part with the formally implemented phenomenological reduction and to set about instead describing sociality as a datum of the life-world in *The Phenomenology of the Social World*.

After briefly explaining at the end of chapter 1 of *The Phenomenology of the Social World* that his procedure will involve doing the kind of nontranscendental, phenomenological psychology that Husserl sketched in his "Nachwort zu meinen *Ideen*," Schutz spends the second chapter under the phenomenological reduction focusing on how consciousness constitutes meaning before he relinquishes the reduction in chapter 3. Such a temporary sojourn within the transcendental domain is necessary because Schutz emphasizes in his methodological note at the end of chapter 1 that his entire phenomenology, as one would expect, will focus on "the inner appearance" "of that which is peculiar to the psychic." The book will be "phenomenological" in the further sense that it seeks a science of essence, that is, it aims at the "invariant, unique, a priori structure of the mind, in particular of a society composed of living minds"—that is, the social world, the world of the natural attitude. At the opening of chapter 3 and for the rest of the book, Schutz accepts this social world as it is accepted in the attitude of the natural standpoint. As a result, Schutz rightly dubs his phenomenology "a constitutive phenomenology of the natural standpoint" which, since it prescinds from the reduction, is undertaken "from within the natural standpoint."[2]

As a result of these methodological maneuvers, both consciousness and its world-interpreting meaning structures, whose essential features Schutz uncovers via Husserlian phenomenological reduction in chapter 2, appear as essential features of any life-world since they are invariant across diverse concrete life-worlds. Hence, while the categories and interests ("typifications" and "relevances" in Schutz's terms) by which persons interpret their world vary from culture to culture, it is an essential feature of every such life-world that there are such categories and interests. But if consciousness is essential to the social life-world, it is conversely true that sociality is essential to consciousness since consciousness is immersed in that social world before phenomenological analysis ever illuminates its essential traits and since it is essential to the categories and interests of any life-world that they be socially transmitted and maintained. Because of Schutz's methodological strategies, as I have remarked elsewhere, "The social is not just accidentally affixed to necessary structures of typification whenever they are concretely instantiated, but it is intrinsically necessary to every life-world typification pattern." This fact could be easily overlooked by phenomenological reduction that brackets the natural attitude and the social world in order to concentrate on consciousness and its structures. Schutz further extends his idea of the social character of consciousness when he suggests that even insights into eidetic features of object via a free variation pursued subsequent to phenomenological reduction are still tied to the social typifications through which one experiences the object in the natural attitude. "Ideation can reveal nothing that was not preconstituted by the type," and that type is social from the outset.[3]

Lester Embree correctly sums up the implications of Schutz's methodological fusion of a phenomenological approach to consciousness with the social world when he states that one can separate the individual from intersubjectivity only via a fictitious abstraction for purposes of analysis and that for Schutz any science, natural or social, must be seen as a social phenomenomen as well as individual theorizing. Furthermore, one beginning with a Schutzian phenomenology will not run into the predicament mentioned by the early Beauvoir, namely, of trying to find a way to reinsert a free, autonomous, solitary consciousness into its social milieu. In addition, Sartre's description of the pretheoretical level in terms of the spontaneity of an ontological for-itself instead of the social life-world in which consciousness is embedded from the start and from which it gradually emerges through piecemeal reflection blinded him to the force of social circumstances which he later admitted and which led him to criticize *Being and Nothingness* as excessively rationalistic. With a correct understanding of Schutz's phenomenological methodology, one could also easily see how Jürgen Habermas misreads Schutz in *Zur Logik der Sozialwissenschaften* when he states that for Schutz, whom he conflates with

Husserl, "the monads first spin linguistic intersubjectivity out of themselves." Finally, in *The Theory of Communicative Action*, Habermas takes Schutz and Husserl to task because their concept of the life-world is limited to aspects of mutual understanding and abridged in a culturalistic fashion to the neglect of institutional and personality factors. Habermas never mentions, though, that Schutz, in his own statement of his phenomenological methodology at the end of the first chapter of *The Phenomenology of the Social World*, delimits his own philosophical project in just this way.[4]

In a review of Husserl's *Formal and Transcendental Logic* in 1933, Schutz comments that "To lay bare the achievements of constituting subjectivity, hidden in every theorizing, is one of the preeminent tasks of phenomenology." Just as Sartre and Beauvoir so adeptly reveal hidden subjectivity, whether it lies latent in the extremes of pure theory or crude prejudice, so Schutz's phenomenology pursues a similar course in his theoretical *Phenomenology of the Social World* and, as will be evident later, in his discussion of racial prejudice. Early in *The Phenomenology of the Social World*, Schutz points out how Max Weber's concept of observational understanding (*aktuelles Verstehen*), by which one supposedly can immediately (i.e., without interpretation) read off the meaning of an action such as chopping wood or grasping a doorknob to shut a door, already entails interpretation from the observer's viewpoint. After all, Schutz comments, the wood-chopper might in *his* view be pretending to chop wood or might be working off pent-up energy and the knob-grabber in *her* view might be testing the knob to see how it functions. Weber not only imposes too hasty an interpretation, but he seems to overlook that there is a difference in the meaning an action has for the observer and the agent observed. By conflating his observer viewpoint with that of the one observed and by equating his interpretation with "the observational fact," he conceals from himself his own subjective interpreting activity. It is no wonder, then, that Schutz takes exception to the metaphor in Weber's definition of social action that agents "attach a meaning to an action." To claim that there is an action that awaits conferral of some meaning upon it is once again to ignore the subjective activity that must have already occurred whenever one picks out from the stream of experience an action as an action of a certain type and thus endows it with meaning.[5]

Schutz's analysis of consciousness, through a temporary deployment of phenomenological reduction, attempts to remedy Weber's defects. Through reflection, Schutz uncovers the rarely seen stream of prephenomenal experiences toward which spontaneous acts turn and carve out distinct experiences which become meaning-endowed in that very turning toward them. Beyond such spontaneous acts, actors can in addition undertake planned actions by imagining in future perfect tense a project which will have been completed when the sub-acts leading to its realization are taken, and this "action" phantasied as completed constitutes the meaning of those sub-acts. This effort to recover aspects of experience so familiar that common sense never even notices them, though it recognizes them immediately upon their articulation, also characterizes Schutz's discussion of the process of choice. Once one makes a choice, later reflection tends to simplify, spatialize, and, as a result, falsify the process leading to that choice by reconstructing that choice as if the one about to make it stood at a fork in the road facing two clearly delineated options. In fact, this retrospective glance suppresses the "series of successive and different states which the ego runs through, growing and expanding continuously as it passes between the imaginary tendencies which change during the process of deliberations as the ego changes itself." As such a series unfolds, there never are two neatly defined options, but rather one option undergoes modifications, sub-options develop, then move in other directions, perhaps eddying about another focal option, which generates new suboptions, until one option emerges as preeminent, and "the free action detaches itself from it like too ripe a fruit." As Schutz further evolves his account of consciousness under phenomenological reduction, he illuminates the "typifications," or categories by which actors organize their world, and the systems of interests, or "relevances," which determine foci of attention and the selection of appropriate typifications. He also elucidates *in-order-to motives*, the projects imagined in future perfect tense giving meaning to the sub-acts realizing these projects. Further, he explains *because motives*, the environmental factors affecting an action *a tergo* and discoverable when one searches into the past before the (now past) commencement of that action, into the pluperfect tense, in order to select out the influences that determined that action.[6]

These exemplary phenomenological analyses, not content with a finished act or the naive suppositions of common sense, but intent on uncovering all the hidden "achievements of constituting subjectivity," reach a high point in Schutz's dissection of typification in *Collected Papers 1*. In that book, Schutz points out how one's first performance of an action (A') involves facing a set of circumstances (C') and bringing about a state of affairs (S'). The second time one goes through the action is unlike the first in that the new set of circumstances faced (C") contains a fact lacking in C', namely, that in C" one has already performed the action (A') once. Indeed, the third time one performs the action differs from the second time (with its A", C", and S") in that one has already gone through the action twice. In fact, each time one engages in an action many other circumstances have also altered besides the fact that one has recently performed the action again. And yet, by a typification such as "going to school" or "giving a lecture" or "raising a child," one homogenizes all these unique and irretrievable events because one is interested only in the typicality of A, C, S. One, in effect, "suppresses the primes." Schutz adds that this "suppression of the primes" is characteristic of typifications of all kinds, including linguistic terms. Schutz's insight that every typification fails to do justice to the individual reality it confronts is somewhat typical of Schutz's thought, which, as shall be seen, brings into focus what is left out when one constructs ideal types of another or when one refrains from expressing aspects of one's personality by living up to the typified role expectations of a group to which one belongs.[7]

When Schutz abandons strict phenomenological reduction in chapter 3 of *The Phenomenology of the Social World*, his findings make possible a better understanding of intersubjective relationships. Each person's stream of experience, made up of acts of attention, impressions, surrounding fringes of protention and retention, in their unique order and with their unique intensities, ensure that whatever meaning one gives to another's experience cannot be exactly the same as the meaning given by the other person. Moreover, while one's own stream of experience is given continuously, one who observes another has access only to a continuously unfolding present, with broader segments of the other's past, for instance, out of reach. These discontinuities are reflected in the use of language since every sign, every word, possesses, in addition to its "objective" meaning, that is, the dictionary meaning of a term which abides no matter who uses it, a "subjective" meaning, a fringe of connotations, depending on the stream of (past) experiences one associates with the term. Hence, as Schutz adds, what Goethe means by "demonic" can only be deduced from a painstaking study of his works as a whole, just as what subjective meaning "civilization" carries when uttered by a French person requires careful study of the history of French culture with the aid of linguistic tools.[8]

When the Other appears on the scene, a conscious self adopts an attitude of "other-orientation," although Schutz remains focused on a more epistemological nature of this attitude and does not flesh out the ethical dimensions involved in such an orientation, as Levinas does. When this other-orientation is mutual, complex motivational interactions can occur, such as that between questioner and answerer, a favorite example of Schutz's. The questioner phantasies in the future perfect tense that the person questioned will have answered him and then poses a question. The answerer launches into a project of communicating a response to the questioner. Only after the answerer has completed the in-order-to project of answering, one might raise the question about what was the because motive of that now finished project of replying, and then the respondent, who had been future-oriented and preoccupied with formulating a reply, can in a past-directed reflection recognize that the questioner's question functioned as the because motive of the answerer's project of answering. As Schutz summarizes it, "the question is the because motive of the answer and the answer is the in-order-to motive of the question." Moreover, when two partners share a mutually oriented we-relationship within the same space and time, face to face, each's observations can keep pace with each moment of the Other's stream of consciousness. In addition, each is better attuned to the Other than one's self insofar as one can only grasp one's own experiences with a reflective glance that supervenes upon an act that one no longer lives and that is thus past, but, face to face, one can grasp the Other's living present as it unfurls. Furthermore, in the face to face, one looks at the Other looking back or one looks at the Other looking back at one looking, and one finds oneself thus engaged in "this interlocking of glances, this thousand-faceted mirroring of each other" that Charles Horton Cooley referred to as "the looking-glass effect." Finally, interpretive schemes are immediately revisable in such a face-to-face relationship, and Schutz's favorite instances of interactive activities, such as conversation or making music together in a quartet, involve a mutual coordination of streams of experience and what he calls "growing older together."[9]

Schutz's phenomenology of intersubjectivity underlies his critique of Sartre in his essay "Sartre's Theory of the Alter Ego." In that essay, Schutz at first agrees with Sartre's criticism that Husserl cannot explain intersubjectivity at the transcendental level. In criticism, though, Schutz repeats De Waelhens's opinion that Sartre's view of intersubjectivity is distorted by the antithetical tensions between in-itself and for-itself, and he accuses Sartre of a *petitio principii* in assuming the interchangeability of perspectives without explanation. Schutz's most original criticism of Sartre, though, focuses on whether Sartre's phenomenology adequately captures what occurs in human interactions. Looking at the Other who is living in a setting that one does not define does not lead one to attempt to transform the Other into a utensil. On the contrary, the Other remains a center of activity within the situation that this Other defines. Given this fact, partners seize upon each other as *co-performing subjectivities* when, for example, they speak or make music together. By proposing the alternatives that either the Other looks at one and alienates one's liberty or vice versa, mutual interaction in freedom becomes impossible, and Sartre falls into a "practical solipsism," not all that different from the epistemological solipsism that he himself criticized in Husserl.[10]

Schutz's phenomenology of the social world does not limit itself, however, to describing face-to-face relationships. For when the companion to a we-relationship shakes hands, turns the corner, and vanishes from sight, she becomes a Contemporary, sharing the same time, but no longer the same space with the partner who remains. This partner assumes a they-orientation toward the absent companion and relates to her via a constructed type, based on past experience and also on whatever fragmentary information might be received about this Contemporary via such means as a letter or a report from someone who has visited her. The Contemporary Other is more anonymous than the Other given in the face to face since she is given via inference, and the type of her is much less readily revisable than the typifications constantly being altered as the Other's stream of experience unfolds before one's face. The free, lively Other of the face to face becomes "frozen," as it were, into an ideal type, which, since she is not as unfree as the pure "puppet" constructed by sociologists or economists, still seems able to contravene the distant partner's construction of her (e.g., via a letter). A further modification is introduced when the Other is a Predecessor or Successor who shares neither time nor space with a partner. Since Predecessors or Successors do not participate in the same time, they are even more anonymous and the types of them more inferential and less corrigible, however much one might naively suppose that one's types of them correspond with their meanings and that one's world is the same as theirs.[11]

Schutz's reflections exhibit phenomenological method by retrieving what commonsense knows but never recognizes because it so takes things for granted and by apprehending the eidetic features which are the necessary conditions of the possibility for various types of human relationships. Interestingly, Schutz's phenomenology highlights the dissonances and gaps in intersubjective understanding by emphasizing the noncoincidence of streams of experiences; the subjective connotations fringing objective meanings; the diverse, fragmentary perspectives that each partner has on the other in the face to face and that invite constant revisions; and the partiality of types abstracting from the fullness of Contemporaries, Predecessors, and Successors, who remain shrouded in various degrees of anonymity.

The phenomenological character of Schutz's work becomes most evident when he dialogues with Ernest Nagel about the philosophy of the social sciences in the essay "Concept and Theory Formation in the Social Sciences." Nagel, because of his commitment to a natural scientific method which accepts as verifiable only sensory observable data, is forced to conceive social reality on a behavioristic model that redescribes meanings, purposes, intentions in terms of physically observable behaviors. Schutz argues that Nagel has just assumed that the method of the natural sciences is appropriate for studying the object of the social sciences, the social world, instead of first considering this object to see which methods might be appropriate for it. In reacting against immaterial, invisible notions of mental activity and limiting himself instead to physicalistically, behavioristically truncated notions of human action, Nagel also shows himself prisoner to the prejudices of Cartesian dualism that have governed the natural and social sciences for hundreds of years. Striving to escape unwarranted assumptions and age-old prejudices, as is phenomenology's wont, Schutz offers instead the eidos of the social world, his phenomenology of the social world, his account of everyday life. In the story Schutz tells, interactors grasp each other's meanings and purposes (in-order-to motives) without having to resort to either private, unverifiable introspection or observations of overt physical behavior alone, and thus Schutz's description of life-world interactions enables him to evade the pitfalls of the Cartesian paradigm. Phenomenology also differs from empiricism in that the lifeworld agents it considers are not mere observable objects endowed with meaning by social scientists, as if these social scientists performed like natural scientists, who are the *only* givers of meaning when it comes to the electrons or molecules they investigate. Rather social scientists grasp the meanings of beings who are themselves giving meaning to their world. Agents in everyday life are active interpreters of their

world, intending it by their acts as an intentional object—as phenomenologists would express it. Being intentional, agents can experience
that interlocking of glances by, for example, interpreting how the Other
inteprets their interpreting of them. Social scientists construct ideal
types of how everyday actors interpret their world, and this ideal-typical
method gives fuller play to these actors' subjective meanings than statistical analyses which presuppose but bypass such meaning-bestowals.
Sociological "constructs of the constructs of the actors" in everyday life
are "verifiable" insofar as they are consistent and adequate to what the
actors on the social scene are doing.[12]

In a sense, Schutz's resistance to an empiricist reduction of actors
to objects is consistent with his earliest critique of Max Weber. Like
Weber, with the woodchopper or knob grasper, empiricists have failed
to see that they are not the only bestowers of meaning, that there is an
Other there giving meaning to that Other's world, and that the task of
sociology is to find out what the Other means. Indeed, it could be said
that Schutz's phenomenological basis for the social sciences, his phenomenology of the social world, provides the categories, such as
meaning, action, in-order-to and because motives, typifications, relevances, by which one can give an account of the subjective (in the
sense of "opposed to the observer's") meaning of the actor. One could
summarize Schutz's entire phenomenology as an effort to make it possible that the meaning of the Other can be seen at all, that the hidden
subjectivity of the Other can be revealed.

2. PHENOMENOLOGY AND "EQUALITY AND THE MEANING STRUCTURE OF THE SOCIAL WORLD"

To understand better Schutz's discussion of racial prejudice in his
paper "Equality and the Meaning Structure of the Social World," it is
important to recollect a few biographical details. In 1938 Schutz, an
Austrian by birth, had emigrated to Paris on the verge of Hitler's occupation of Austria. One year later, he came to the United States where
he allied himself with Alvin Johnson's University in Exile, later
renamed the Graduate Faculty of the New School for Social Research.
By the time he delivered his paper on equality at the Fifteenth Sympo-
sium of the Conference on Science, Philosophy and Religion at
Columbia University in 1955, he had experienced social reality in the
United States for sixteen years. It is tempting to speculate that his own

difficult experience as an emigrant and stranger in a new country disposed him to approach the plight of African-Americans in the 1950s with the sympathy that his paper manifests. Whatever may have motivated Schutz's empathy for African-Americans, it is noteworthy that he presented his paper on equality in the same year in which Rosa Parks refused to give up her seat on a bus in Montgomery, Alabama, and sparked the boycott that was a key event in galvanizing the Civil Rights Movement in the United States.

Schutz begins the essay, published in *Studies in Social Theory*, volume 2 of his *Collected Papers*, by reiterating his notion of the social world as taken for granted and its structurization in terms of typifications and relevance schemes that vary according to each social group. Each social group constitutes itself as an "in-group" in reference to groups other than itself, its "out-groups." In the next part of the essay, Schutz connects the notion of equality with structures of relevance. Following Aristotle, Schutz argues that equality and inequality are relational notions which need to be defined in terms of the relevances to which they pertain. Hence, as Aristotle observed, if one has a flute to give, it would be foolish to bestow the flute on someone just because that person is more wealthy, but it would be "just" to consider those who are fluteplayers and to give it to the one who plays the flute best. It is permissible to introduce inequalities (e.g., to give a flute to someone and not another) as long as the reasons for introducing an inequality (that one fluteplayer is better than another) are in accord with a certain domain of relevance (that of fluteplaying). But it makes no sense to introduce inequality in one domain of relevances (fluteplaying) on the basis of reasons that have nothing to do with that domain but pertain to a heterogeneous domain of relevance (that of wealth and money-making). Further, Schutz points out that various cultures and in-groups rank these various domains of relevances to which Aristotle has drawn attention, as when, for instance, a culture values wealth over the art of fluteplaying or the ability to play football over nursing. These ranking of domains of relevances, even though they undergo continuous fluctuation across cultures, are often taken for granted by the in-group as an unquestioned way of life.[13]

Although Schutz has already complexified his study of equality by distinguishing the diverse domains of relevance within which ideas of equality or inequality must be considered and by showing the diverging rankings of these domains of relevance by various in-groups, he dwells even further on the divisions between such groups. In-groups tend to be inherently ethnocentric, usually partaking in what R. M. MacIver called a "central myth," which justifies their relative natural conception of the world as, for instance, "ordained by Zeus" or "mandated by the order of Reason or Nature," although the meaning of such myths can be changed through history, as has, for instance, the meaning of the U. S. Declaration of Independence's tenet that all people are created equal. In-groups often perceive out-groups (which consider themselves to be in-groups) as hostile since they disagree with the "self-evident" truths of the in-group. Since the out-group, in its turn, perceives the in-group perceiving it (as hostile)—and here one sees exemplified most clearly an inter-group "looking-glass effect"—the out-group comes to despise the in-group all the more. The in-group can resort to any number of reactions in the face of out-group resistance, such as seeking reconciliation or hardening itself against the out-group even to the point of ostracizing as "traitors" any of the in-group's own members sympathetic to the out-group.[14]

By diversifying the meanings of equality and expositing the tensions between in-groups and out-groups, Schutz has laid the groundwork for his treatment of racial prejudice, which addresses the issues of subjective and objective interpretation of group membership, equality, and equal opportunity. The *subjective meaning* of a group, that is, the meaning a group has for its members (as opposed to someone outside the group), depends on a shared system of typifications and relevances, whether the members are born into the group or choose it voluntarily. Because one may belong to several groups and since one usually manifests only partial aspects of one's personality in the different groups to which one belongs, one presents a different side of oneself when, for instance, with one's family than when with one's poker group. Further, one ranks the relevances one embraces due to varying group memberships, and, thus, in a crisis, for example, one might give up one's job if its expectations begin to interfere with one's living a healthy family life. The *objective meaning* of group membership refers to how out-group members assign someone membership in a group—an assignment with which the person assigned might agree or disagree. Should outsiders place someone within a group against that person's preference, there would be little difficulty as long as the person so assigned does not fall under the power of those outsiders. Thus, those on the island of Cuba could characterize all citizens of the United States as hard-hearted capitalists, and this fact might not affect the citizens of the United States as long as they are not under

Cuban control. Also, administrative and legislative arrangements classifying someone as a tax-payer or tenant are generally acceptable to those so classified, especially since such a typification impages on only a very superficial aspect of one's personality. It becomes quite painful, however, when those in power identify a person's whole personality with a particular trait or characteristic not of a particular high relevance to that person. Persons who had replaced their allegiance to Judaism with a commitment to Germany found themselves "degraded to an interchangeable specimen of a typified class" when they were declared Jews by Hitler's Nuremberg laws by reason of a grandparent's origin—a fact that they had considered completely irrelevant. The talented African-American applying for a teaching position for which she is quite competent resents it that her skin color is made the basis for rejecting her application since skin color is of no relevance in indicating how one might perform as a teacher.[15]

Schutz's discussion of the subjective and objective meaning of equality lies at the heart of his essay. Schutz turns to the example of Marian Anderson, whom the Daughters of the American Revolution prohibited from using their concert hall in Washington, D.C., because she was an African-American. While opposing the racism of the Daughters since race has nothing to do with a singer's art, Schutz does wonder whether it would be possible to deploy such typifications benignly. Thus, could it not be said, in a highly complimentary sense, that Marian Anderson possesses an unsurpassed ability to sing Negro spirituals at least in part, and in no way detracting from her own individual talent and effort, because she shares the cultural heritage of African-Americans? The example reveals that the mere imposition of a typification from an outsider is not necessarily discriminatory.[16]

Schutz proceeds with another example that illustrates the subtlety of the evil that discrimination inflicts. Justice Henry B. Brown in *Plessy* v. *Ferguson* (1896), which approved the "separate but equal" doctrine, wrote

> If inferiority is inferred from it, it is not by reason of anything found in the act but solely because the colored race chooses to put that construction upon it. . . . Legislation is powerless to eradicate racial instinct. . . . If one race be inferior to the other socially the Constitution of the United States could not put them on the same plane.[17]

Once again Schutz condemns the racism of the comment, but it also represents for him a significant example of an inter-group looking glass. After the court has reached its decision, Brown not only typifies the group, "the colored race," but he also interprets how they will interpret his action. He even explains how that interpretation will be wrong, an act of bad faith, because "the colored race" will "choose" to put a construction upon the decision, arbitrarily, since the court from its subjective viewpoint does not intend to imply inferiority. Brown has thought all this out presumably even before any African-Americans have had a chance to read the decision or to react to it.[18]

Although Schutz does not develop all the implications of this example, it is clear that a phenomenology of the social world that takes account of intersubjective intentionality and the looking-glass effect is better positioned than other theories to account for this particularly insidious aspect of racial prejudice. Not only do in-groups typify out-groups, *but they also typify how those other groups will typify them back* and anticipate how to deflect those typifications from the out-group. What results is a peculiar self-enclosure or self-immunization against critique on the part of the in-group because the out-group is never given the chance to engage the in-group, to represent itself, to contest either the typifications imposed upon them or to reply to the counterarguments already prepared in advance against their objections. Racist in-groups tend to avoid the face-to-face relationship that would afford a more interactive framework within which the out-group might challenge their typifications, although the racist in-group could certainly resist correction or even resort to violence within such a relationship. It is significant, though, that proponents of racial prejudice make themselves even less vulnerable by relating to victims of discrimination as Contemporaries, who are known through more anonymous, less corrigible types. The victims of such prejudice, placed at the distance of Contemporaries, while not being the totally unfree puppets constructed by the sociologist's or economist's types, still seem to have little free input into the constructions formed about them. In his essay "The Stranger, An Essay in Social Psychology," Schutz comments on how *spatial distances* and the shutting out of any possible responses are ingredient in the prejudicial typifications between groups:

> . . . the ready-made picture of the foreign group subsisting within the stranger's home group proves its inadequacy for the approaching stranger for the mere reason that it has not been formed with the aim of provoking a response or a reaction from the members of the foreign group. The knowledge which it offers serves merely as a handy

scheme for interpreting the foreign group and not as a guide for inter-action between the two groups. Its validity is primarily based on the consensus of those members of the home group who do not intend to establish a direct social relationship with members of the foreign group. (Those who intend to do so are in a situation analogous to that of the approaching stranger). Consequently, the scheme of interpre-tation refers to the members of the foreign group merely as objects of this interpretation, but not beyond it, as addressees of possible acts emanating from the outcome of the interpretive procedure and not as subjects of anticipated reactions toward those acts. Hence, this kind of knowledge is, so to speak, insulated; it can be neither verified nor falsified by responses of the members of the foreign group. The latter, therefore, consider this knowledge—by a kind of "looking-glass" effect—as both irresponsive and irresponsible and complain of its prejudices, bias, and misunderstandings.[19]

Ironically the type-construction, which in the social sciences takes more seriously actors' subjective meanings than statistical accounts that record numbers of responses and that could serve as well for the study the behavior of nonconscious atoms, is the very methodology employed by commonsense bigots to make sure that the subjective meaning of their victims is never even seen. Schutz was quite aware that the sociologist's types were prone to a similar occlusion, and hence he insisted on the postulate of adequacy, namely that one test one's types against the experience of those so typed. What Max Weber in his discussion of observational understanding (*Verstehen*) and the empiricist/behaviorist account of social science bring about (but not necessarily deliberately on the theoretical plane), namely, preventing the subjective meaning of the Other from coming to light, the preju-diced person, making use of the looking-glass effect, achieves on a practical level. In so doing they run counter to central value that Schutz's phenomenology of the social world, with its focus on inten-tionality, sought to uphold.

Schutz concludes his discussion of the *Plessy* v. *Ferguson* decision by remarking that African-Americans take segregation as an insult and *with good reason*, in contradiction to Brown's outsider interpretation. The imposition of a typification by an outsider does not necessarily constitute discrimination by itself; what is required in addition is "an appropriate evaluation of this imposition from the subjective view-point of the afflicted individual," as occurs in African-American rejec-tions of *Plessy* v. *Ferguson*. In spite of the rightness of the cause against such discrimination, Schutz recognizes the difficulty of altering the prejudices underlying such institutional discrimination. After all, prejudices are ingrained elements of the interpretations of the social world, one of the mainsprings that make it tick, and they rationalize and institutionalize the "central myth" of an in-group. As a result, they cannot be eliminated by simply informing evildoers that they are cherishing prejudices.[20]

To conclude his essay on equality, Schutz considers the subjective and objective interpretations of minority rights. From their subjective viewpoint, there are minorities that can desire a minimum, such as nondiscrimination at the hands of dominant groups, or there are those insisting on a maximum, namely, special rights and positive services. The first group of minorities pursues formal equality and assimilation with dominant groups, whereas the latter group wants substantive equality and inclines toward separatism. More conservative out-group minorities favor minor shifts within the prevailing relevance system as the "equality to be granted," whereas more radical groups seek an "equality aimed-at" that threatens the system more. In his final discussion, treating equal opportunity, Schutz once again differentiates the objective sense of equal opportunity, understood as "the career open to the talents," from the subjective meaning. The subjective meaning of equal opportunity refers to the meaning that opportunity has for the individual who in objective terms would be eligible to take advantage of such an opportunity. Such an individual would have (1) to be aware of the chance to take advantage of the opportunity, (2) to find this chance compatible with personal relevances and self-definition, (3) to be convinced of his or her ability to live up to the requirements of the position open, and (4) to believe this role accords with his or her other social roles. Obviously, there can be real discrepancies between opportunities considered equal (that is, open to all) from the objective point of view (of those outside of a minority group) and those same opportunities perceived from the subjective viewpoint through which members of a minority group assess whether they are really eligible incumbents of social roles. In Schutz's opinion, equal opportunity in the objective sense is worth fighting for, but more would have to be done to ensure "an equal start for everyone" so that they might feel subjectively that an opportunity is equal.[21]

In all these cases, namely, of group membership, of the meaning of equality, and of equal opportunity, Schutz strives to show how in-group members fashion interpretations that they take to be universal, even though these interpretations in no way accord with the interpretations of out-group members. Here again the business of determining what equality means, particularly when it reaches the nadir of defining equality in terms of equal, but separate, facilities, endangers alterity. Further, the subtle accompanying mechanisms that prejudiced persons deploy and that Schutz illuminates, such as the looking-glass effect, have the tendency to render the subjective meaning of the Other invisible—unless countered by a methodology whose *modus operandi* seeks to render it visible.

3. CRITIQUE

Schutz's methodology, refraining from full-blown phenomenological reduction and undertaking a phenomenology of the natural attitude *from within the natural attitude*, gives the social world its due in a way that Sartre, who finds his pretheoretical basis in prereflective consciousness, does not. And yet Schutz does not abandon Husserl's analysis of consciousness; only the consciousness considered, with its typifications and relevances, appears more clearly socially formed than is the case with Husserl's descriptions of consciousness that often commence with a bracketing of the social world. Although instantiations of typifications, relevances, and consciousness vary from one concrete social life-world to another, eidetic variation discloses that these elements are essential features, invariant across every social world. But, conversely, sociality is invariantly incorporated in every set of typifications and relevances and in every consciousness, however much eidetic discussions of consciousness or even phenomenological reduction may lift consciousness out of its social milieu by prescinding from these social dimensions.

Although Schutz surpasses Sartre by including these social dimensions, he does not sacrifice the attention to consciousness and freedom which is Sartre's undoubted strong point. In spite of being immersed in the stream of consciousness, reflection, for Schutz, can "turn back" on the stream and uncover its unidirectional, irreversible flow. At the same time, reflection can elucidate the spontaneous acts of consciousness endowing meaning on the experiences of the stream by selecting them out and bringing them into relief. Just as Husserl delves beneath the set idea of a house to expose the hidden activities of subjectivity, the many perceptions through a series of spatiotemporal perspectives that, though often forgotten, go into building up the idea of the house, so Schutz does not rest content with the finished act, but brings to visibility the many constituting activities of consciousness, in particular, the adoption of a future perfect project aimed at by the sub-acts leading to the final outcome. Further, Schutz's resistance to empiricist accounts of the social science presupposes that agents are not things, *en-soi*, but active consciousnesses, *pour-soi*, interpreting their world. While because motives may indicate that a past influences the present—as Sartre and Beauvoir would admit—Schutz's account of them implies no mechanistic causality—something with which Sartre and Beauvoir would also concur. For Schutz, persons undertaking a because motive analysis *interpretively* select, on the basis of their interests at hand in the present, *which* pluperfect because motives are to be taken as influences upon the (now past) project they have adopted and executed. Indeed, another example of the ability of reflexivity to escape from mechanistic determinism is to be found in the idea of a reflective phenomenology of the natural attitude, the very achiement of which requires that one have freed oneself in some way from the hold of the natural attitude. To produce a phenomenology of the natural attitude, one must have placed oneself somewhere en route to a transcendental sphere beyond the natural attitude, even if one is not to be located in the full transcendental sphere as the result of a full-blown phenomenological reduction.

Like Merleau-Ponty, Schutz showed himself quite aware that any reflection arises from a prereflective substratum. Schutz speaks of never-captured prephenomenal experiences horizonal to those prephenomenal experiences which consciousness singles out and endows with meaning; of a surf of indiscernible and confused perceptions, physiological reflexes, and forms of involuntary spontaneity that the cone of reflection never illuminates; and of those experiences pertaining to the absolute private core of the person, such as sexual sensations or moods such as grief, that are to some degree ineffable. In addition, typifications inculcated by one's social environment and reinforced by social approval stubbornly resist attempts to recognize or transform them—as was the case with Sartre's crude anti-Semitism or with the internalized myths and norms about the sexes that Beauvoir portrays. Further, in line with Beauvoir's study, such typifications, as Osborne Wiggins and Michael Schwartz note, do not require explicit acts of thought, but rather operate below the level of explicit conceptualization, prestructuring implicitly and automatically the experiential field within which conceptualization can occur. Although such typifications are often inherited and, as Sartre argues, dictate the facts rather than being shaped by them, it is also possible that unhappy experiences with those from a group different from one's own can initiate typifications that could gain momentum, especially if reinforced. One can part with such prejudicial typifications only if one is sufficiently able to let go of them and if one is exposed to positive counterexperiences. It is no wonder, then, that Schutz remarks in "Equality and the Social Meaning Structure" that such prejudices will not "disappear as if touched by a magic wand" when one informs bigoted people that they are cherishing prejudices. Schutz's view here depends upon his having taken the social world seriously, but it does not rule out the chance that rationality can function as a corrective.[22]

For Schutz, consciousness emerges from this lived, prephenomenal, social world that is located somewhere in between an inert in-itself or a clearly and distinctly thinking for-itself—on the hazy undefined terrain that Merleau-Ponty called "the existential." Moreover, since consciousness in Schutz's view is not equated with prereflective consciousness in ontological antagonism toward in-itself, Schutz's account of intersubjectivity does not suffer from the antipathy characteristic of the Sartrean view, since one does not relate allergically to another consciousness appearing on the scene and perceived as threatening to engulf it. Schutz's lack of such ontological commitments permits him to attend phenomenologically to the things themselves, for instance, and to apprehend intersubjectivity as involving a relationship between two co-performing subjectivities.[23]

Schutz's depiction of intersubjectivity can also accommodate the reification central to the thought of Sartre and Beauvoir, but Schutz might re-translate "turning the Other into an object" as "employing inadequate types or typifications from an objective point of view without sufficient responsiveness to the subjective meaning of the Other." Such a redefinition opens up the possibility that not all typifications are reifying. Maurice Natanson suggests just this point in his discussion of "role expectations," which are typifications imposed upon one from an objective point of view beyond oneself, just as there are objective meanings of words as opposed to subjective meanings. Such roles are not per se alienating since, as Natanson observes, one can always transcend the boundaries of the typical, lash into a role with originality, and announce through fresh action that the "I" is still not captive or tame. Similarly, as we have seen, the mere imposition of a typification is not of itself discriminatory, but becomes so only when an appropriate evaluation of this imposition from the subjective viewpoint of the afflicted individual pronounces it so.[24]

But if typifiers seek to reify the Other, they must typify (or universalize) without paying sufficient attention to the subjective viewpoint of the Other. For instance, one might from an objective viewpoint define equal opportunity as "the career open to the talents" and proceed to assign all fault for not taking advantage of such careers to those whose subjective viewpoint this observer never consults. From the subjective viewpoint, however, one might legitimately perceive such an opportunity not as equally open but as beyond one's reach due to the many obstacles beyond one's control, which better-situated others do not encounter at all. If reification entails disregarding the subjective viewpoint of the Other, then Justice Brown's typification of "the colored race" that bars their response before it is ever heard is reifying in the same way that Sartre's democratic anti-Semite's type of "the abstract and universal citizen" suppresses any subjective meaning that might prize Jewish particularity. Equally reifying are the internalized typified roles of Mother or Wife that, as Beauvoir has shown, obliterate the subjective feelings of ambiguity and resentment even before they can be felt.

This human capacity to develop typifications or types inadequate to the subjective viewpoint of the Other or to make use of the looking glass to construct responses rather than give that subjective viewpoint any play reveal processes by which social groups wrap themselves in solipsism and immunize themselves against critique. Since there is always, then, a need to test one's types or typifications of the Other against the Other, the requirement of adequacy applies not only to social scientific *Verstehen*, but also to everyday, life-world *Verstehen*. While this need for recourse to the Other ensures maximal critique, it does not mandate blind compliance with the viewpoint of the Other. Indeed, the fact that the one has a better access to the Other's lived stream of consciousness than the Other does, since the Other can grasp the Other's stream only by stopping and reflecting on that experience as past, establishes at a fundamental level a distribution of knowledge favoring one over the Other—an advantage extending to other dimensions of intersubjective relationships (e.g., one grasps the Other's body language or "expressive movements" in Schutz's vocabulary). Similarly, although Schutz does not develop the idea, it is always possible that the social scientist can have better insights into another culture than that culture itself. The postulate of adequacy need not mean, then, that a social scientist's conclusions are false simply because those whom the social scientist investigates disagree with the conclusions.

Schutz has advanced the discussion of prejudice and discrimination by pointing out that the mere imposition of typifications is not *per se* discriminatory since it also depends on an *appropriate* evaluation of this imposition from the subjective viewpoint of the afflicted individual. The key word "appropriate" suggests that it is conceivable that an individual might find a typification discriminatory in an "inappropriate" way, that is, the typification may not in fact be discriminatory. For instance, a legitimate criticism of someone by someone of another race could be dismissed by the criticized person as "racist" when it is not. On the other hand, it could also be that one might be so afflicted that from a subjective point of view one would not even find an imposed typification discriminatory when it actually is discriminatory. Part of the cruelty of slavery or the subjugation of women has involved inculcating within the minds of those oppressed the belief that their treatment was deserving or fitting. Just because one objects or fails to object to an imposed typification does not necessarily prove that that typification is or is not discriminatory. It is certainly also the case, as Schutz's example from Justice Brown in *Plessy* v. *Ferguson* proves, that the one who imposes typifications might not think them at all prejudicial, while the afflicted person knows better. To determine whether a typification is appropriately evaluated between two parties—a question which presupposes the point to which Schutz has brought the discussion—a *dialogue* needs to ensue between the typifier and the one feeling afflicted by the typification. For such a dialogue to reach discursive resolution regarding the appropriate evaluation of a typification, if such resolution will be possible at all, an unconstrained discourse is called for in which partners would be willing to query their own constructs of each other. Schutz's phenomenology of discrimination thus unleashes a host of problems that set it en route toward critical theory.

This endeavor to determine whether an imposed typification is discriminatory is pitched on an epistemological plane to which Schutz regularly confines himself, with the result that the ethical features of relationships are deemphasized. I have argued elsewhere that Schutz's leariness toward ethics can be traced to a suspicion about how ethical principles and theory serve the interests of in-groups intent on buttressing their "central myths." Also, as remarked above, when Schutz treats of the Other-orientation in *The Phenomenology of the Social*

World, he omits any reference to the ethical dimensions of that relationship. Schutz also seems to leave out a possibility for theoretical ethics
since in his essay "The Problem of Rationality in the Social World" he
explores six different meanings of "rationality," but they all refer to
pragmatic means-ends actions, and nothing is said about "ethical rationality." Such an omission comes as no surprise, though, since Schutz
seems to embrace from the start in his *Phenomenology of the Social
World* Weber's notion of rational action as *zweckrational.* In a sense, the
question of theoretical ethics just was not of interest to Schutz.[25]

On the other hand, Schutz certainly takes account of ethical concerns, as a subset of the general category of relevances. However, there
are openings in his framework to give more prominence to ethics than
seeing it merely as one of many possible relevances since ethics, in fact,
trumps other relevances insofar as the human being is, in Kant's terms,
"the supreme limiting condition in the use of all means." In Schutz's
account of the Other-orientation, the very presence of the Other evokes
an alteration of one's orientation, an attitudinal reconfiguration that
would seem to involve not only the cognitive adjustments that Schutz
discusses but also the ethical dimensions exposited by Emmanuel Levinas. Like Levinas, Schutz locates this tuning-in process at the basis of
all communication, and hence it underlies critical theory itself. In addition, Schutz repeatedly acknowledges throughout his works that the
Other is given as a co-performing subject irreducible to Sartrean *en
soi*—as an end in himself or herself, if Kantian terminology would be
permitted. To be sure, a central doctrine in Schutz's philosophy of
social science is that agents interpreting their worlds cannot be understood if approached as objects who do not confer meanings on their
worlds. Such agents are not passively fitted out with meanings by
behaviorist social scientists who alone are privileged to bestow meanings, as natural scientists do upon molecules or atoms.[26]

Such a Kantian interpretation of Schutz would seem to clash with
Roger Jehenson's reading of Schutz. Jehenson detects in Schutz's
analysis of face-to-face interaction the original form of domination
because this interaction partakes of the pragmatic character of everyday life, where "manipulating objects and handling things and men" is
constitutive. Jehenson, however, contends that Kantian reciprocity
later emerges from the fact that over time each partner will need the
other's assistance and so tolerates being mutually "dominated" by the
other's pragmatic motives. Even if one accepts Jehenson's pragmatic
account of the genesis of Kantian reciprocity, it need not be that one's

reciprocal acts are purely strategic such that one tolerates domination in order to ensure one's own assistance. Rather, it is conceivable that one rises to a generalizing reflexivity beyond one's strategic pragmatic motivations when one recognizes that since *anyone* could find themselves in need it is morally obligatory for *all* to come to the aid of others, in spite of the fact that in any concrete situation one could help others who might not return the favor. [27]

But even though Schutz certainly stresses the pragmatic dimensions of the social world and human interaction, it is by no means clear that his texts would warrant a pragmatic derivation of reciprocity in which the use of things is transferred to persons and the prospects of mutual use prompts reciprocity. On the contrary, Schutz, particularly in his reaction to Sartre, emphasizes how both I and the Other are centers of activity around which things and instruments are organized, and he asserts that "recognizing that the Other lives in a setting not defined by me does not transform him into my utensil." It is as if the Other is experienced from the start as a subject in his or her right, as someone not to be treated as a thing, as a place where all pragmatic thing-usage stops and where even in my pursuit of purposes a different approach is called for: communication rather than instrumentalization. Far from my behavior toward the Other being derivative from my use of things, the Other introduces a disruptive moment in my patterns of thing usage. In addition, the guiding motive of Schutz's phenomenology and his approach to the social sciences, namely, to allow the subjective meaning of the Other to be seen and not suppressed, establishes an agenda on an empirical, social-scientific plane that would be perfectly consistent with a paralleling version of Kantian ethics.[28]

Of course, these descriptions of the experience of the Other do not lead to the deduction of norms from facts, to the naturalistic fallacy. Rather this experience of the Other forms the setting out of which the discourses that determines facts (the sciences) and seeks to argue for norms (theoretical ethics) will arise. This fundamental encounter with the Other, similarly depicted in Schutz and Levinas and in Kant's prelude to the second formulation of the categorical imperative in the *Grounding*, may correspond, as Lyotard remarks, with Kant's "fact of reason," a fact unlike other facts, in which we find ourselves already morally obligated as we begin to think about moral obligation and even to theorize about what our moral obligations might be.[29]

Schutz's methodological distinction between life-world and transcendental phenomenology is of importance for the two-tiered ethical theory that I will soon be developing and that would supplement his phenomenological, descriptive research. It is to the life-world, that substratum from which theory, including phenomenological theory and transcendental phenomenology, issues that Schutz devotes his labors via phenomenology, via a phenomenology that lays the basis for phenomenology itself. Schutz's efforts here resemble Emmanuel Levinas's uncovering, via phenomenology, of the ethical relationship subtending all discourse and theory. This ethical relationship, described by Levinas, forms a counterpole to ethical theory which must always be tested against the face of the Other, and, as a result, Levinas himself does not work out such an ethical theory.

To present such an ethical theory and to justify it requires a discussion of the character of rationality itself—a discussion traditionally situated within the domain of transcendental philosophy. Having determined the distinctiveness of practico-ethical rationality vis-à-vis scientific, empirical rationality, one must then turn to the problem of validating ethical claims. Such claims, unlike empirical claims which are validated through empirical evidence, must appeal to a universal principle for assessing the rightness or wrongness of maxims of action. In order to find such a universal principle that will be sufficiently broad and incontrovertible, one needs to consider the very principle governing the discourse by which one debates if there are moral principles. One finds oneself here at a transcendental level also, considering the principles of discourse that every rational, discursive endeavor must presuppose and observe under pain of performative contradiction. Inscribed into the very structure of discourse itself is an ideal of respect for persons as ends in themselves, entitled to assent to or dissent freely from any claims proposed to them, to introduce or contest assertions, not to be subjected to any authoritarian or violent force, but only the force of the better argument. Such discursive principles stand as an ultimate transcendental backdrop of every discourse, whether Schutz's phenomenology, the social sciences, or the natural sciences, insofar as they propose claims for an Other's reasoned assent or dissent. While such an ethical theory can fulfill functions that Schutz's theory, which is confined to the life-world and is descriptively-empirically oriented, cannot, such an ethical theory, and whatever moral norms are justified in its light, must in turn be supplemented by exposure to the challenging face of the Other over whom moral norms can so easily exercise their imperium. It is to Schutz's great credit that he has given an account how that Other appears, and, though Schutz emphasizes the cognitive dimensions of that appearance, he makes manifest the subtle devices of prejudice through which the subjective meanings of that Other are often banished from sight.

NOTES

1. Alfred Schutz, "The Problem of Transcendental Intersubjectivity in Husserl," *Collected Papers*, vol. 3: *Studies in Phenomenological Philosophy*, ed. I. Schutz (The Hague: Martinus Nijhoff, 1975), p. 82; see also pp. 59–60, 66, 69, 76.

2. Alfred Schutz, *The Phenomenology of the Social World*, trans. George Walsh and Frederick Lehnert (Evanston, Ill.: Northwestern University Press, 1967), pp. 44, 97; Alfred Schutz, "Phenomenology and the Social Sciences," in *Collected Papers*, vol. 1: *The Problem of Social Reality*, ed. Maurice Natanson (The Hague, Boston, London: Martinus Nijhoff, 1962), p. 132; Edmund Husserl, "Epilogue," in *Ideas Pertaining to a Pure Phenomenology and to a Phenomenological Philosophy*, Book 2: *Studies in the Phenomenology of Constitution*, trans. Richard Rojcewicz and Andre Schuwer (Dordrecht, Boston, London: Kluwer Academic Publishers, 1989), pp. 411–12.

3. Alfred Schutz, "Type and Eidos in Husserl's Late Philosophy," in *Collected Papers*, 3:115; Michael D. Barber, S.J., "Constitution and the Sedimentation of the Social in Alfred Schutz's Theory of Typification," *The Modern Schoolman* 64 (1987): 118.

4. Lester Embree, "Schutz's Phenomenology of the Practical World," in *Alfred Schutz: Neue Beiträge zur Rezeption seines Werkes*, ed. Elisabeth List and Ilja Srubra (Amsterdam: Rodolpi, 1988), pp. 123–24; Lester Embree, "Schutz on Science," in *Worldly Phenomenology: The Continuing Influence of Alfred Schutz on North American Human Science*, ed. Lester Embree (Washington, D.C.: Center for Advanced Research in Phenomenology and University Press of America, 1988), pp. 251–73; Simone de Beauvoir, *The Prime of Life*, trans. Peter Green (Cleveland and New York: The World Publishing Company, 1962), p. 435; cf. pp. 13–15 of chapter 2 on Sartre, as well as Jean-Paul Sartre, *Between Existentialism and Marxism*, trans. John Mathews (New York: Pantheon Books, 1974), p. 41; Jürgen Habermas, *Zur Logik der Sozialwissenschaften* [Tubingen: J. C. B. Mohr (Paul Siebeck, 1967)], p. 124; Jürgen Habermas, *The Theory of Communicative Action*, vol. 2: *Life-world and System: A Critique of Functionalist Reason*, trans. Thomas McCarthy (Boston: Beacon Press, 1987), pp. 119–52.

5. Alfred Schutz, "Review: *Formale und transzendentale Logik* by Edmund Husserl, *Literaturzeitung* 54 (1933): 779; *The Phenomenology of the Social World*, pp. 27–29, 42.

6. Schutz, *The Phenomenology of the Social World*, pp. 46–47, 52, 54, 56, 51–62, 67, 74, 78, 84, 91–96; *Collected Papers*, 1:86.

7. Schutz, *Collected Papers*, 1:20–21.

8. Schutz, *The Phenomenology of the Social World*, pp. 99, 102, 107, 123–24.

9. Ibid., pp. 146, 160–62, 163–72.

10. Alfred Schutz, "Sartre's Theory of the Alter Ego," *Collected Papers* 1:197–203.

11. Schutz, *The Phenomenology of the Social World*, pp. 175, 178, 182–84, 187, 190–91, 196, 202, 208, 210.

12. Alfred Schutz, "Concept and Theory Formation in the Social Sciences," *Collected Papers*, 1:48–66.

13. Alfred Schutz, "Equality and the Meaning Structure of the Social World," *Collected Papers*, vol. 2: *Studies in Social Theory*, ed. Arvid Brodersen (The Hague: Martinus Nijhoff, 1976), pp. 229–43.

14. Ibid., pp. 243–48.

15. Ibid., pp. 250–57.

16. Ibid., pp. 257–59.

17. Ibid., p. 260.

18. Ibid., pp. 260–61.

19. Alfred Schutz, "The Stranger: An Essay in Social Psychology," *Collected Papers*, 2:98.

20. Schutz, "Equality and the Meaning Structure of the Social World," pp. 261–62.

21. Ibid., pp. 262–73.

22. Schutz, "Equality and the Meaning Structure of the Social World," pp. 261–62; Schutz, "On Multiple Realities," *Collected Papers*, 1:210–11; *The Phenomenology of the Social World*, pp. 52–53, 70–71; Osborne P. Wiggins and Michael Alan Schwartz, "Psychiatric Diagnosis and the Phenomenology of Typification," in *Worldly Phenomenology*, pp. 215–16.

23. Maurice Merleau-Ponty, *Phenomenology of Perception*, trans. Colin Smith (London: Routledge & Kegan Paul; New York: The Humanities Press, 1962), p. 87.

24. Maurice Natanson, *The Journeying Self: A Study in Philosophy and Social Role* (Reading, Mass.: Addison-Wesley, 1970), p. 66; James Marsh has shown, too, how the mere categorization of another person does not necessarily absorb their otherness, cf. James Marsh, *Critique, Action, and Liberation* (Albany: State University of New York Press, 1995), p. 72.

25. Michael Barber, "The Ethics behind the Absence of Ethics in Alfred Schutz's Thought," *Human Studies* 14 (1991): 131–34; Schutz, *The Phenomenology of the Social World*, pp. 18–19, 144–47; Alfred Schutz, "The Problem of Rationality in the Social World," *Collected Papers*, 2:74–76.

26. Alfred Schutz, "Making Music Together: A Study in Social Relationship," *Collected Papers*, 2:177–78; Immanuel Kant, *Grounding for the Metaphysics of Morals*, trans. James W. Ellington (Indianapolis and Cambridge: Hackett Publishing Company, 1981), p. 43.

27. Roger Jehenson, "Critical Phenomenology of Domination," *Worldly Phenomenology*, pp. 6–7, 18–21; Kant, *Grounding for the Metaphysics of Morals*, pp. 35–38.

28. Schutz, "Sartre's Theory of the Alter Ego," p. 201; it ought to be observed that recently published materials from the Schutz archive suggest the rudiments of a Schutz ethics that makes appeal to the importance of having one's say and being heard in processes of participative citizenry, even if one's arguments are not finally accepted. Such an ethics, if fully developed, might resemble the discourse ethics of Habermas and Apel. See particularly Lester Embree, "The Ethical-Political Side of Schutz: His Contributions at the 1956 Institute on Ethics Concerned with Barrier to Equality of Opportunity," in *Schutzian Social Science*, ed. Lester Embree (Dordrecht, Boston, London: Kluwer Academic Publishers, 1998), pp. 227–307.

29. Kant, *Grounding for the Metaphysics of Morals*, pp. 35–36; Jean-François Lyotard, "Levinas's Logic," in *Face to Face with Levinas*, ed. Richard A. Cohen (Albany: State University of New York Press, 1986), pp. 134–35.

Part 2
SYSTEMATICS
Ethics and
Affirmative Action

The survey of the three phenomenological approaches to forms of discrimination, namely, anti-Semitism, sexism, or racism, shows clearly a continuity both of concern for equality and of fear that an emphasis on equality can nullify alterity. This dialectic between equality and alterity surfaces in Sartre's critique of crude, irrational anti-Semitism and all-too-rational, democratic anti-Semitism; in Beauvoir's ideal of reciprocal relationship between male and female as equal free agents and her distrust of essences and the homogenizing of one's interiority that the internalization of norms effects; and finally in Schutz's impatience with racism and yet his wariness about how in-groups can promulgate an objective (from the observer's perspective and not necessarily "true") view out of touch with the subjective viewpoint of the out-group. Each author displays an appreciation for rationality, for its power to criticize irrational prejudices, and yet each recognizes the importance of submitting one's beliefs, however rational they may appear, to the scrutiny of the Other, to the Jew or woman or African-American.

While it is obvious that each author feels a moral disgust for the different kinds of discrimination he or she treats, there is a reluctance on the part of all three to articulate a theoretical ethics that might justify their moral convictions. This hesitancy about theoretical ethics springs from numerous sources, such as the existentialist mistrust of universal moral laws and the difficulty of applying them, or the descriptive rather than prescriptive method of their phenomenological starting points, or a Nietzsche-like suspicion that moral norms express and mask underlying power motivations. Indeed, the last factor may be the most important insofar as all three of their studies of discrimination provide case studies of how oppression disguises itself as virtue, whether it be an anti-Semitic appeal to democratic values, moral conventions regarding how the virtuous woman ought to behave, or an in-group's promulgation that its folkways are divinely ordained or natural. Only Sartre in his posthumous *Notebooks for an Ethics* ventures a sketch of a theoretical ethics based on discursive relationships that he himself never fully develops.

But it is not enough merely to *have* moral convictions and, at the same time, to be critical of such convictions. Rather, the refusal "to accept unquestioningly any pregiven opinion or tradition" that informed Husserl's as well as Sartre's, Beauvoir's, or Schutz's phenomenological endeavors requires that one give a theoretical account of one's ethical beliefs as well as of one's suspicion of such beliefs. In undertaking a systematic exposition of an ethical theory, which will take seriously the concrete issues of discrimination raised in Part 1, this book repeats in the domain of theoretical ethics what Sartre and Schutz did in *Being and Nothingness* and *The Phenomenology of the Social World* when they presented the epistemological/ontological frameworks for their criticisms of discrimination. One cannot, however, develop a theoretical ethics without addressing meta-ethical questions regarding the kind of rationality one is engaged in, any more than it is possible to do a phenomenological psychology without attending to its transcendental-phenomenological horizons. One cannot responsibly evade reflecting on one's own reflecting.

Hence, these next chapters do not consist of an itinerary through different perspectives as was the case in the first half of this book. Rather, they seek to develop a theoretical ethics that would include an account of its own underpinning rationality and that would be comprehensive enough to deal with the tension between equality and alterity that arose in part 1. On the one hand, Karl-Otto Apel's transcendental pragmatics offers an adequate justification of a Kantian-type ethical theory that would support equality between rational agents. It was upon just this equality, the hallmark of Enlightenment rationality, that Sartre, Beauvoir, and Schutz insisted, even though they never provided an ethical-theoretical justification of their moral convictions with the depth and thoroughness that characterizes transcendental pragmatics.

On the other hand, Emmanuel Levinas's phenomenology of alterity, more than any other theoretical perspective, attends to the question of alterity, which was of equal concern to Sartre, Beauvoir, and Schutz. Levinas's phenomenology brings to light the ethical dimensions of the encounter with the Other who summons one into theoretical discourse in the first place and who serves as a constant source of critique to all theoretical findings and pronouncements.

Apel and Levinas are often taken to represent antagonistic trends in contemporary philosophy, that of German versus French philosophy, modernity versus postmodernity, the concern to justify first principles versus the suspicions that such principles conceal power motivations and suppress differences. But one can conceive these two positions on ethical theory as carrying out different but complementary projects within a common philosophical architectonic. Indeed, it is Husserl's distinction between the transcendental and life-world, or pretranscendental, poles that can serve as scaffolding that unifies and yet differentiates the parts of this architectonic. Apel's transcendental pragmatics, which admits, preserves, and surpasses the insights of hermeneutical, life-worldly phenomenology, focuses instead on the questions of justification and validity on a transcendental plane that resembles (and differs from) Husserlian transcendental phenomenology. Similarly, Levinas, explicit about his debt to phenomenology, pitches his phenomenology of alterity at a pretheoretical level similar to that of Husserl's life-world or of Merleau-Ponty's idea of incarnation.

The next two chapters, attempting to articulate this architectonic, will have to adjust and attune its different levels to each other. Hence, since the architectonic is Husserlian in inspiration and since Levinas's viewpoint is admittedly Husserlian in origin, it will be necessary in chapter 5 to locate Apel with reference to Husserl's phenomenology and to show how his work both criticizes it and harmonizes with it, particularly in developing aspects of Husserl's transcendental level. Secondly, it will be important to spell out Apel's ethical theory and the program of its justification that transcendental pragmatics yields. While this transcendental pole of ethical theory elaborates a notion of equality based on the nature of discourse itself, it also opens toward alterity; but it will require supplementation at a pretheoretical, life-world level from Emmanuel Levinas's phenomenology of alterity, as will be discussed fully in chapter 6. That chapter will commence by situating Levinas's phenomenology of alterity with reference to transcendental pragmatics via Levinas's concept of the Third, and it will consider carefully Levinas's critique of reason, possibly the most controversial aspect of his thought for a transcendental-pragmatic perspective. A final section in chapter 6 will discuss at length the fragile reconciliation, that is, the difference and complementarity, of these two tiers within a single, comprehensive ethical theory. In the concluding two chapters, I will extend this theoretical ethics toward the concrete question of affirmative action. This topic provides a powerful testing case for this ethics because in affirmative action, as in perhaps no other issue, the ideal of equality and concern for alterity meet head on.

5

ETHICS ON A TRANSCENDENTAL TIER

1. THE CRITIQUE OF HUSSERL

Karl-Otto Apel's earlier writings in the *Transformation der Philosophie* show him positively disposed toward the *hermeneutic* phenomenology developed by Heidegger and Gadamer since it opposed the restrictive processes which epistemology has experienced in modern scientific logic, positivism, and naturalism; since it has illuminated processes of meaning-constitution that precede and lie at the basis of scientific thinking; and since it has uncovered the structures of intersubjective interpretation. Although Apel's endorsement of hermeneutical phenomenology is accompanied by critique, his affirmation of hermeneutical phenomenology forms part of a broader critique of the phenomenology that began with Husserl.[1]

Apel frequently marshals the philosophical resources of Heidegger, Wittgenstein, and Peirce against what he sees to be Husserl's excessive emphasis on human consciousness and what he designates as his "methodological solipsism." For instance, in one of his earliest criticisms, Apel states that, in the face of scientific-reductionistic and psychologistic approaches to speech and in imitation of Plato's resistance to the relativizing sophists, Husserl sought to set apart pure "ideal meanings." For Husserl, these meanings remained as fixed stars in a supratemporal, but nonmetaphysical, heaven, over against the meanings realized by chance in the flux of historical, socially transmitted languages. Such a maneuver, however, effectively relegates language to the secondary role of indicating and grasping the meaning-structure of the world that, pre-existing all time and history, is accessible to the isolated consciousness. Against Husserl, Heidegger objected that by conceiving Being in terms of ideas or essential unities one in effect reduces Being to entities, not the visible things on which positivism focused, but those within the realm of unchanging ideas. For Heidegger, in contrast, language functions as the framework for the articulation of Being as it is illuminated in and through the relationships of historical persons, who are Being-in-the-World, socially linked with each other, and so language fittingly serves as the "house" of Being as it assists in the "lighting-up, concealing advent (*Ankunft*) of Being."[2]

Apel compares Wittgenstein's passage from the overly rationalized account of his *Tractatus* to the language-game paradigm of the *Philosophical Investigations* with this continental transition from Husserl to Heidegger. Apel affirms that Wittgenstein refuted the methodological solipsism pervading modernity, such as Husserl's, by his discovery that "one alone and only once" cannot follow a rule and that actions, world-interpretations, and linguistic usage are interwoven in a language as constituent elements of a social life form. Apel faults Husserl for not having made this linguistic turn that Wittgenstein initiated:

> But Husserl, in accordance with the tradition of mentalistic transcendentalism prior to the linguistic turn, went so far as to suppose that a transcendental ego-consciousness that would survive the "bracketing" of the world (including language and communication with other subjects) could constitute, in principle, all timeless meanings by its intentionality. In contradistinction to this methodological solipsism, it has to be pointed out, in my opinion, that the single subject of intentionality even for his or her self-understanding as "I" has to presuppose public, intensional meanings that must be always already carried by language-signs. The subject of intentionality can at best claim to share public meanings by sign-interpretations or to contribute to the publicly sharable meanings of language by his meaning-intentions.[3]

Apel does not deny Husserl's point that it is legitimate and unavoidable for the philosopher to claim any possible meaning to be a virtual correlate of an intentional act, but he insists that one must also admit that the meanings of concepts making possible one's self-understanding as a subject are always mediated by the public meanings of language given in collective experience. Apel, in effect, recommends *supplementing* and *differentiating* Kantian and Husserlian transcendental idealism with the interpretive organon of language-games, which represent different cognitive interests and diverse modes of consciousness's practical engagement with the world.[4]

In later essays such as "Fallibilismus, Konsenstheorie der Wahrheit and Letztbegründung" and those published in the first volume of his *Selected Essays, Toward a Transcendental Semiotics,* one can find Apel's most pointed confrontation with Husserlian phenomenology, and surprisingly Apel there shows himself more accommodating than before toward Husserl. Opposing the rejection of Husserl's evidence-theory of truth by Popperian semanticists, Apel in these essays limns a legitimate niche for linguistically interpreted phenomenon-evidence as *a* truth criterion confirming a correspondence between consciousness and things. By situating such evidence within a more comprehensive theory that encompasses both Peircean semiotics and a consensus view of truth, Apel also contests the sufficiency of such evidence for being a final criterion of truth since it still awaits intersubjective validation. In this regard, Apel favors Peirce over Husserl insofar as Peirce surmounts modern methodological solipsism by placing the responsibility for the redemption of truth claims upon an indefinite community of sign-interpreters, who could reach discursive agreement about the confirmation or falsification of propositions, instead of upon prelinguistic subjects consulting the evidence of their own syntheses of apperception with regard to data.[5]

In order to see clearly Apel's assessment of the value and limitations of Husserl's phenomenology of evidence, it is necessary to consider briefly his rather complex discussion of how one identifies real *denotata* in *Selected Essays.* In that discussion, Apel recognizes the need for public meaning intensions (the conceptual content of names that Frege designated as the *Sinn*) *as well as* intentionality (acts and their intentional correlates according to Husserl) in order to realize pragmatically the semantic dimension of sign-reference.[6]

In contrast to Apel, Saul Kripke and Hilary Putnam react against a mentalistic philosophy of intentionality (such as Brentano's or Husserl's) and the determinative role which Frege allots to public intensions in reference and focus rather upon the extensions of terms. Kripke and Putnam attempt to detach these extensions from the intensions and to connect these extensions of names with the indexical functions that a name assumes in the "original baptism" of an individual. From that point on, one will employ that name as a physical reaction to being causally affected by whatever the "stuff" to be named is, and that "stuff" would evoke such a reaction across possible worlds.

But Apel counters that in order for such an indexical definition to be remembered and transferred by communication one must at least initiate some intensional determination of the extension of the name. Furthermore, in the case of natural kinds that cannot yet be assumed under the head of a general concept, one would have to complement the indexical definition by some description of the phenomenal qualities. Thus, in the case of an original baptism of a undefined natural kind such as "baboo," one can say "baboo" means everything identical in structure with the material baptized at time t and place p by person z, but one must also add "and the structure of 'baboo' may be described by the following list of phenomenal qualities: . . ." In between a purely indexical (and cognitively blind) extensional definition and a complete conceptual (intensional) definition (which would be impossible when one first encounters a newly discovered object of experience whose further determinations would have to be ascertained in the future), it is possible to refer to an object via a description based on a set of intentional properties that supplement indexical definition and prepare it for later conceptual subsumption.[7]

This account of reference would be fully compatible with the semiotics of Peirce, who argues that, above the level of linguistic *indices*, linguistic *icons* present perceptible qualities given with phenomenological evidence in advance of and in preparation for the abstractive logical operation of subsuming phenomena under the heading of a general concept. Thus Peirce and Apel, through nonconceptual sign-types (indices and icons), explain the indispensable evidence basis of human cognition beneath the conceptual level. While acknowledging the causal aspect of referential identifying via indices, Peirce, via his notion of icons, also reserves a place *for the truth core of a Husserlian phenomenology of evidence.*

However, for Peirce and Apel, the evidence of given phenomena, prelinguistic in Husserlian phenomenology, is not yet intersubjectively valid knowledge since conceptual mediation of intuitively given phenomena is still required. In fact, Apel contends that indices and icons "function only inside conceptual signs" since indices like "this," "that," "here," "now," are themselves already determined by conceptual distinctions between "thisness" or "thatness" that are not situation-bound. Similarly, any description of phenomenal qualities would have to invoke conceptual differentiations. However, Apel also cautions that one ought not to fall into the semiotic error of Hegel, who acknowledged only conceptual symbols and neglected situation-bound indexical and intentional signs in his chapter on *sinnliche Gewissheit* (sense certainty) in his *Phenomenology of Spirit*. This discussion of reference by Apel, along with his subsequent criticisms of Searle's arguments for an intentionalistic turn, seeks to uphold the linguistic turn. Thus, Apel concludes, that, although there may be solitary perceptual judgments, after the linguistic turn such "voiceless dialogue" can only be understood as an internalization of the normal public dialogue by speech.[8]

On the one hand, Apel's and Peirce's concession that there is a layer of intuitional iconical evidence that legitimizes the application of predicates to existing objects includes the kind of phenomenological clarification of evidence more appropriate to a correspondence theory of truth than a coherence or consensus model. By this concession, both Apel and Peirce move beyond Habermas, whose consensus theory tends to exclude alternative truth-conceptions, as Apel and H. Offe state.[9]

On the other hand, once Apel admits that there is a dimension where one must resort to an intuitive givenness in order to assess the legitimacy of an empirical proposition, it would seem to be difficult for him to preclude the possibility of another kind of intuitiveness, that of eidetic intuitions, which, according to Husserl, parallel the empirical intuitions of objects. Indeed, Apel's entire discussion regarding reference, identification, the transitions from indexes to icons to the conceptual level, and the constituents of truth determination has not been pitched at an empirical level as if it sought to expound upon any *particular* empirical intuition of any particular empirical object. Rather at every stage of his argument, Apel has proposed to the reader on an eidetic plane an explanation of how *every* identification occurs or how *every* truth claim about the world is established, even though Apel himself does not reflect explicitly in these essays upon the eidetic character of his own inquiry. Moreover, the reader, carefully weighing Apel's claims, has embraced a kind of solipsism—perhaps the most legitimate sense of solipsism of which Husserl speaks insofar as it grows out of the responsibility of philosophers to withdraw into themselves, to refuse to accept unquestioningly pregiven opinions, and to assess for themselves the evidence presented with the same kind of autonomy that has always been a high priority for both Apel and Habermas. Of course, this responsible assessment is required not only for empirical claims but also for the eidetic claims constituting Apel's transcendental pragmatics. Apel himself not only would agree that these claims must be autonomously endorsed by the interlocutor to whom they are proposed, but he himself has devoted considerable methodological self-reflection upon the character of these claims, assessing how they differ from revisable empirical claims—to the point of separating himself from Habermas over their status, as will be shown below.[10]

Although Apel's opening to Husserl might license a kind of Husserlian reflection upon the status of Apel's own claims, Apel still might have the upper hand since the *sufficient* redemption of one's insights always awaits a yet to be attained intersubjectively valid synthesis. Specifically, Apel could correctly point out that the very discourse in which Husserl elaborates the insights leading him to reject or accept eidetic claims would presuppose the very structure of intersubjective communication that Apel's transcendental pragmatics spells out. Paradoxically, even if one were to draw one's interlocutor's attention to some evidence supposedly undermining eidetic features of Apel's transcendental pragmatics, one could do so only by presupposing the very structure of intersubjective communication mapped out by Apel. The features intrinsically constituting intersubjective communication include such things as the four validity claims necessarily implied in communication and open to reflection in discourse, the necessarily presupposed consensual redeemability of validity claims, and the primacy of communicative rationality over instrumental and strategic-purposive rationality.[11]

By embedding all philosophy within a social, discursive context—in line with his whole-hearted endorsement of the linguistic turn and his recognition that socially transmitted conceptual patterns are needed even to convey their nonconceptual substrata—Apel effectively ensures that social influences extend "all the way down," from the heights of theory (including the eidetic claims that present transcendental pragmatics) to the most basic experience. As such, Apel's view would be fully congenial with the work of Alfred Schutz, who allows the social character of the life-world to revolutionize his own phenomenological method and who, as a result, establishes that social world as the encompassing context for all theory, including phenomenology. Given this life-world basis, Schutz in his essay "Type and Eidos in Husserl's Late Philosophy" goes still further by suggesting that even eidetic determinations, discovered after implementing the reduction, depend upon life-world, sociolinguistic constraints.

> It is doubtless possible to grasp eidetically material realms of regions of being, but these regions are not constituted by performances of our consciousness: they are indeed ontological regions of the world, and, as such, given to our experience or, as we may say, imposed upon us. But we have to drive the questioning even farther. Is it pos-

sible, by means of free variations in phantasy, to grasp the eidos of a concrete species or genus, unless these variations are limited by the frame of the type in terms of which we have experienced, in the natural attitude, the object from which the process of ideation starts as a familiar one, as such and such an object within the life-world? Can these free variations in phantasy reveal anything else but the limits established by such typification? . . . Ideation can reveal nothing that was not preconstituted by the type.[12]

If Schutz is right, then phenomenology need not be a form of prelinguistic, mentalistic transcendentalism, in which the transcendental ego-consciousness constitutes all timeless meanings from out of its own intentional resources. In other words, phenomenology need not be equated with Apel's interpretation of Husserl's phenomenology.[13]

There are indeed questions of the accuracy of Apel's interpretation of Husserl's understanding of the social world, especially in light of this book's earlier presentation of Husserl's deep appreciation for the social conditioning unreflectively absorbed by everyone before they adopt a reflective attitude. Furthermore, in phenomenological reduction, properly understood as a reflective attitude taken up toward the world and not a transmigration of one's soul to another ontological domain, the social world remains continually there, present at hand; it does not cease existing but exists for the phenomenologist only now as the intentional correlate of the phenomenologist's consciousness of it. For Husserl, this social world is not denied as a sophist might deny it or doubted as a skeptic might doubt it, but it is bracketed; that is, no judgment concerning spatiotemporal existence is made use of so that the phenomenologist can describe what is given critically, as free as possible from prejudice. In fact, Husserl does not hesitate to affirm that even within the limits of transcendentally reduced pure conscious life, one experiences the world not as a private synthetic formation, but as an intersubjective world, there for everyone, accessible in respect of its objects to everyone.[14]

It is just this experience that prompts Husserl, unwilling to allow any experience to remain anonymous, to undertake in the Fifth Cartesian Meditation a systematic explication of the intentional processes through which the Other becomes present. It is this explication, aimed at bringing to critical clarity the appearance of the Other, that requires him to withdraw to a transcendental sphere of ownness, completely free of whatever refers to the Other. After constituting the Other, Husserl returns to the commonly shared cultural world in which any object given is also given in its possible modes of givenness to Others. Schutz, as mentioned before, finds this transcendental constitution of the Other methodologically problematic and does not believe that one can deal adequately with intersubjectivity in the transcendental sphere. Hence, he opts for understanding the Other as a datum of the life-world to be described by a phenomenological psychology. It is the transcendental constitution of the Other that is the problem for Husserl, and not his solipsism, which, as argued above, ought to be traced back to his commitment to critical reflexivity, that is, his resolve not to accept unquestioningly any pregiven opinion or tradition.[15]

To be sure, Apel's transcendental pragmatics cannot dispense with such a resolve if the autonomy of discourse partners is to be preserved, and, in fact Apel appeals to an autonomous interlocutor in every claim about transcendental pragmatics addressed to his reader. If Apel cannot escape this version of Husserlian solipsism, Husserl, in turn, cannot evade the ideal discursive community, universal validity claims, the priority of communicative over strategic rationality—all of which he presupposes and appeals to even when his zeal for critique drives him to the extremes of theoretical isolation. It is Apel's great service to have articulated the features of the ideal communication community that looms on the horizon of every philosophical discourse and thus constitutes an inescapable, transcendental intersubjectivity, albeit one differing from Hussel's version, which, equally unavoidably, depends on executing the reduction and other phenomenological procedures.

2. APEL'S TRANSCENDENTALISM

Having completed the more difficult task of showing that there is a compatibility between transcendental pragmatics and Husserlian phe-nomenology's descriptive, intuitive-eidetic method, I will now turn to the level of transcendental reflection, an area of easier reconciliation. While Apel himself admits that he has learned from both Kant and Husserl regarding transcendental reflection, it also seems that Apel's uncovering of the intersubjective, transcendental conditions of dis-course brings to the fullest realization the Kantian/Husserlian dynamism not to leave unexamined the ultimate horizons which even the most reflective and self-reflective theoretical endeavors presup-pose. It is on this transcendental level, similar to Husserl's, that Apel has concentrated his efforts and that he has made his greatest contribution to a theory of rationality that includes also the life-worldly level, to which hermeneutic phenomenology has devoted itself. This section will explore this Apelian two-tiered account of rationality, whose two planes resemble those of the ethical theory here being developed, and examine its critique of the ideologies of positivism (via a hermeneutic phenomenology of science's life-world origins) and historicism (via transcendental discussions of truth, validity, and justification). Apel's notion of rationality also provides for societal critique that can make use of social-scientific *Erklären* within a context established by hermeneutical *Verstehen*. However, Apel's pretranscendental level would profit from Levinas's phenomenology of alterity, a phenomenology itself depending on the kind of descriptive phenomenology of evidence, that, as the first part of this chapter has shown, is compatible with a transcendental pragmatic methodology.[16]

Apel's transcendental style of philosophizing emerges clearly in his confrontation with logical atomism and positivism. According to the logical atomism of Russell and the early Wittgenstein, which combined empirical and speech-logical meaning criteria for the first time, the knower grasps the basic empirical elements of the world, assigns them a name, and combines these names into "protocol" propositions and their more complex derivatives which make up the domain of meaningful (= empirical) propositions. The difficulty, though, is to account for the problem of the philosophical statements of logical atomism itself, which constructs its propositions about the meaning of other propositions. These philosophical propositions about the meaning of all possible propositions of speech would have to be meaningless since they are not empirical and do not correspond to observable elements. The young Wittgenstein recognized precisely this paradox when he claimed that whoever understood him would recognize his propositions as meaningless; one would have to throw away the ladder after one had used it to climb to the top. Subsequent logical positivism, objectivistic-physicalist in its methodology, found itself crippled in its ability to reflect upon its own philosophical method because discussions of method appeared to be nonsensical metaphysics, as they had for the logical atomists. Unwilling to discuss the status of its own statements, positivism, from a seemingly neutral (but actually transcendental) pinnacle that concealed its own covert empiricist metaphysics, legislated that only empirical statements were meaningful. Indeed, in Apel's view, this reluctance to self-reflect—in phenomenological terms, this willingness to leave the theorizing on the horizon of one's theoretical focus unthematized and anonymous—has left a transcendental void in contemporary philosophy.

> As I have noted, because of its fear of psychologism, logical empiricism banned the self-reflection of thought from philosophy, calling it an empirical-psychological matter. In addition, it substituted metalanguages and metatheories for the self-reflection of discourse that supposedly necessarily led to antinomies. For these reasons, it rejected the necessity of a nonempirically relevant, transcendental-philosophical self-reflection on the validity claims and conditions of the possibility of knowledge or forms of argumentation, though it subjected this rejection to no relevant reflection. The self-reflection of topical thought is the paradigm for the philosophical rationality of a final grounding; nevertheless, one could claim that, in the great expanse of contemporary philosophy, it has been silently suppressed by the mathematical paradigm of the metatheoretical theory of verification.[17]

Rudolph Carnap attempted to carry on Wittgenstein's critique of metaphysics without taking over his metaphysical presuppositions—to avoid, in other words, an anti-metaphysics based on a disguised metaphysics—via his constructive semantics. However, this semantic theory, which, per agreement of those participating in the discourse, would admit only the pragmatically efficacious propositions of the natural sciences, actually represents not a logico-empirically, but a pragmatically based position that does not in fact terminate metaphysics (of a pragmatic-empirical variety) even though it might seem to decide neither for nor against it. According to Apel, "it is clear here that logical empiricism must give up its particular character and also the claim to being a theoretical critique of metaphysics exactly where it makes itself free of its own metaphysical presuppositions."[18]

Similarly, the later Wittgenstein in the *Philosophical Investigations* abandoned the scientifically inspired copy-theory of speech of the *Tractatus* with its mosaic-theory of signs and objects in the tradition of the Aristotelian philosophy of language and turned instead to a view of language as a use-oriented "basket of tools." Wittgenstein's pragmatism, which surpassed most forms of American pragmatism in its radicality, located various linguistic uses within a variety of everyday language-games and thereby contributed to illuminating the "Being-in-the-World" of everyday language, as Heidegger was simultaneously doing on the continent. Wittgenstein's pragmatism also inclined toward relativism insofar as these language-games stood as the ultimate measures of thought, each beside the other, without any overarching organization and with no criterion for their assessment other than that they proved themselves functional within life-forms. Finally, Wittgenstein restricted the role of philosophy to the more humble, therapeutic role of clearing up those disturbances in the functioning of language which had produced philosophical problems, but, as in the *Tractatus*, he continued to deny to his own statements the status of a theory.[19]

Apel, however, refuses to attribute the validity of the convincing arguments of Wittgenstein's own critique of language to the fact that they produce therapeutic effects. Rather, these arguments at root involve a whole new insight into the *essence* of speech, the meaning rules of which vary from one language-game to another, and they present such games as being related to each other by a "family-resemblance" instead of by the Aristotelian "unity of analogy." Wittgenstein would have to affirm that it lies in the essence of human speech use that there is no unity of analogy in the manifold of language-games, that language uses are tied to life-forms, and so on. In Apel's terms, *Wittgenstein is actually articulating a transcendental philosophy of the preconditions for the possibility and validity of meaning and understanding.* However, Wittgenstein himself was unable to affirm meaningfully that this was what he was doing because he conceived of his later philosophy as offering no general doctrine, but as only having the practical function of bringing philosophy to peace through the speech-critical clarification of thought, on a case-by-case basis. For Apel, Wittgenstein's self-interpretation of his later philosophy is on a par with his conception of the *Tractatus* as a ladder to be discarded. In the later philosophy, Wittgenstein failed to recognize that philosophical language does not function practically as if it were one among the many institutionalized language-games, in which speakers send and receive reports and in which speech usages and pertinent behavioral practices appertain to a surveyable and generally describable functional unity. Rather the philosophical language-game acts as a *meta-institution*, through which all institutionalized language-games and life-forms first receive their articulation, their justification, and/or their revolutionary new grounding. Although Wittgenstein, like many pragmatists and life-philosophers before him, no longer felt the earnestness of the problem of a reflexive self-justification of philosophy, Apel insists that the language-game of Wittgenstein's own philosophy and the language-game of philosophy in general cannot be placed on the same level as the other language-games whose description they make possible and comprehensible.

> This language game [philosophy] cannot, however, be satisfactorily thought of as a historically contingent language game among innumerable other ones; rather, it must be considered as that reflective language game in which one has always laid claim to the circumstance that, with regard to all possible language games, one can make statements with an a priori universal claim to validity (for instance with Wittgenstein: that all language games stand in relation of "family-resemblances" to one another as parts of "forms of life.") And as far as philosophical discourses are supposed to make sense at all, the participants must also always in principle impute that, only in this language game, all claims to validity that in other language games may be exposed as debatable, can be redeemed or refuted in a sense that is not only a conventional one. In short, philosophers must honor the fact that the language game of argumentative discourse is foundational, since it is unsurpassable, or otherwise risk a performative self-contradiction.[20]

Apel's accusation that Wittgenstein falls into a *Logosvergessenheit* (forgetfulness of reason)—a play on Heideggerian *Seinsvergessenheit* (forgetfulness of Being)—must be seen as the outcome of Apel's determination not to exempt philosophy from reflecting on what is horizonal, including the status of the very claims that it itself authors. Likewise, transcendental pragmatics, by not allowing the philosophical language-game to lapse to the level of the other language-games whose structures it elucidates, resembles phenomenology, which illuminates the hidden subjectivity prone to surrender itself to the various forms of naturalism and objectivism that are of its own making.

In fact, Apel utilizes his transcendental approach to criticize the way in which positivism eliminated subjectivity by treating it as an object to be causally explained away. Apel, concurring with Gadamer, notes that objective, natural-scientific cognition itself presupposes an understanding of meaning (*Verstehen*) of the natural scientists among themselves. In fact, if two experimental psychologists were to replace their mutual communication with an explanation of the causal motives effecting their partner, each would treat the other as a scientific object, but not as a member of the communication community of scientists. However, for their experiments to be meaningful, each would have to have recourse to *some* other communication community of scientists.

Thus, the ultimate horizon of the argumentative transcendental communication community stalks every positivist argument to eliminate subjectivity since such an *argument* must always appeal to the co-subject of the argumentation process.[21]

Apel wields his transcendental weaponry not only against positivism and ordinary language philosophy, but also against post-Husserlian continental philosophy, represented most preeminently by Heidegger and Gadamer. At first, though, as seen above, Apel praises the great achievement of Heidegger's hermeneutical phenomenology insofar as it overcame the Cartesian-Kantian subject-object paradigm ruling in the logic of the natural sciences in favor of a deepened appreciation of the "existential fore-structure" of intersubjective understanding (*Verstehen*). This existential fore-structure, or "Being-in-the-World," implied the surpassing of epistemological idealism and, through *Mitsein*, of the methodological solipsism that Apel attributes to Husserl. Language assumes a prominent role for Heidegger, as it did for Wittgenstein, insofar as it informs *Verstehen*, which itself is essential to the constitution of the data of experience, including positivism's empirical "protocol-sentences," for which the natural sciences provide a causal explanation. As a result, the subject-subject relationship through which interlocutors reach agreement about something precedes the subject-object relationship paradigmatic for the causally oriented natural sciences.[22]

By articulating the structures of Being-in-the-World, from which all knowledge and language take their start, Heidegger, in Apel's opinion, uncovered "the quasi-transcendental presuppositions of a new type of theory of knowledge." Drawing on Theodor Litt, Apel highlights the transcendental level of Heidegger's fundamental ontology since it takes place on a reflective plane which is in principle different from existence and the history-immanent understanding of Being, which *Being and Time* makes understandable. One cannot say of this thinking which sets forth the *essential* existentiality, the finitude, and the historicity of the human understanding of Being that *it itself* is *only* existentially, finitely, or historically conditioned since it itself is the presupposition of affirming and understanding that all viewpoints are existentially, finitely, and historically conditioned.[23]

Furthermore, according to Apel, Heidegger's focus on the Being of beings provides a critical counterpoint illuminative of the ultimate philosophical presuppositions of his logical, empirical, and pragmatic critics, who dismiss his talk of Being as empty or meaningless. While logicians find Heidegger's talk of Being out of sync with the usual pattern of a subject of predication referring to an object, while empiricists chide him for not making a verifiable existential claim, or while pragmatists dismiss his claims for having no practical payoff, Apel reconstructs a Heideggerian response to the effect that Heidegger's claims are meaningless only in light of the meaning-criteria of these critics. Following his earlier pattern of showing the camouflaged metaphysics underlying positivism's elimination of metaphysics, Apel takes these critics of Heidegger to task since, however much they might seek the demise of metaphysics, they employ meaning-criteria laden with metaphysical presuppositions that clearly emerge in the light of Heidegger's seemingly empty notion of Being. Indeed, these critics' meaning-criteria pertain to a realm of thinking that limits itself to the technical-instrumental disposability of this-worldly objects, which places humanity at the service of this disposability and which, in the end, conceives humanity as itself nothing more than a disposable object. By distinguishing the manipulable from that which is not reducible to manipulation, the *Seienden* from the *Sein*, Heidegger in a kind of transcendental manner effectively exposes the ultimate, hidden metaphysical presuppositions about Being that underpin the very critics who attack his own speech as meaningless.[24]

In spite of Heidegger's own acumen at exposing the hidden but neglected presuppositions of the Western philosophical tradition and his important contribution to the problem of the constitution of meaning, Apel warns that one ought not blind oneself to his deficiencies in the area of truth/validity, that is, the question of the general and intersubjective bindingness of philosophy. Apel argues that hermeneutical phenomenology à la Heidegger and Gadamer originally distanced itself from forms of transcendental idealism and, as a consequence, has declined to mediate its view of historical-substantial thinking through the kind of noological reflection developed by Descartes or Hegel (and Husserl). As a result, hermeneutical phenomenology cannot inquire into the conditions of the possibility of the general validity of truth claims, including the propositions lying at its own basis. Thus, it sacrifices the Greek and modern ideal of a generally valid science for a concrete exploration of the "now, for us" lived, historical situation of conversation in which one relates to others and Being. Apel, however, suggests that Heidegger's own distinction between concrete existentielle properties and noncontingent existential structures indicates a self-layering of reflection. Had Heidegger pursued these levels of reflection to the end, he might have come to recognize that philosophy acquires legitimization for its statements not only from the listening of the hearer to the call of Being, but also from the ever-to-be-renewed self-layering of reflection that finally extends to thinking about thought itself and thought's intersubjective validation.[25]

Apel anticipates that Heidegger probably would have rebuffed such charges because the posing of questions of meaning-validity instead of world/meaning constitution would have meant a return to the "metaphysics" he had left behind. In Apel's view, however, while Heidegger's attack on metaphysics rightly targeted the instrumental rationality that proceeds from a subject-object paradigm, such an attack does not touch the rationality of discursive communication in which the validity of claims is weighed.

> I naturally do not mean that Heidegger's philosophy in general or the *hermeneutic turn* in general, are to be rejected, rather, I mean this: The overcoming of the *relativistic historicism* of the nineteenth century, which is suggested by Heidegger and Gadamer, is in truth no overcoming, but rather a continuation and augmentation of it. This is so because their viewpoint has freed itself from all scruple about principles through an arbitrary stroke, namely through the prohibition of reflection upon one's own universal validity-claims. Here occurs the "*Holzweg*" of the forgetfulness of logos [*Logos-Vergessenheit*]. But here I understand by "logos" not the logos of the "framing" [*Gestells*] of, for example, "instrumental reason," which Heidegger and Derrida have placed in question with some right. Rather, I refer to the *logos of discursive communication, posited in language*, which every self-critique of reason, even that of argumentative skepticism, presupposes continually as the condition of the possibility of one's own validity claim and of which it must take account.[26]

Indeed, when Heidegger issues his own philosophical claims in *Being and Time* and elsewhere, he stands on the terrain of *logos*, that is, of discursive communication, insofar as his own works appeal to the uncoerced assent of his philosophical interlocutors.[27]

Apel's critique of Heidegger and Wittgenstein depends upon a dialectically conceived architectonic that recognizes the indispensability of both *world-engagement* and *reflection* for the attainment of knowledge. While Wittgenstein's rooting of thought in life-forms and language-games and Heidegger's basing of thought upon Being-in-the-World have been key philosophical breakthroughs in the twentieth century, Apel asserts that they have not overcome the truth that Descartes discovered at the opening of modernity and Hegel later reaffirmed. That truth is that thinking itself reflexively assures itself of the standpoint of general validity, and, in effect, this truth of generally valid self-consciousness is, as Litt's account of reflexivity's layers suggests, presupposed by every generally valid presentation of hermeneutic thinking.[28]

In terms of the Husserlian framework, Heidegger and Wittgenstein focus upon the pole of lived engagement, the life-world, which precedes philosophical reflection and stands opposed to the Husserlian phenomenological-transcendental plane anticipated by Descartes. Within this architectonic or philosophical division of labor that Apel delineates, there would always be a legitimate place for Heideggerian disclosure or the opening up (*Sinn-Eröffnung*) or lighting up (*Lichtung*) of Being. But it also seems inescapable that one must attempt to present one's findings to others, to convey them in language, perhaps in a language reformed in the light of those findings. Finally, one will, for example, write a book like *Being and Time*. In so doing, one steps onto the region first explored by Descartes and one presupposes Apel's transcendental structures of argumentation—but this region and these structures would be empty without the often unreflected soil of the lifeworld which gives birth to all validity-claims and which also forms the presupposition of transcendental reflection, as it did for Husserl.

This section has revealed that Apel's philosophical style involves bringing to light the horizonal presuppositions that philosophical positions usually resist recognizing precisely because these presuppositions run exactly contrary to the tenor of the positions themselves. Thus Apel exposes the shrouded empiricist metaphysics underlying logical atomism and positivism's dismissal of metaphysics, the nonrelativity of the Wittgensteinian philosophical language-game making possible the relativity of every other language game, the co-subjectivity taken for granted by objectivist views intent on eradicating all subjectivity, the *verstehende* base of *erklärenden* explanation, the nonconditional character of the fundamental ontology that accentuates the unavoidability of historico-social conditioning, the veiled metaphysics of those who deride Heidegger's talk of Being, and the transcendental presuppositions of Heidegger's rejection of the transcendental approach. With an almost Derridean glee, Apel continually points out how fundamental philosophical positions are haunted by a horizon or shadow at odds with their own philosophical projects—an absence haunting their presence. In thematizing these fundamental, but unexamined presuppositions, Apel exhibits the spirit of phenomenology, unwilling "to accept unquestioningly any pregiven opinion" or to allow prejudices to remain latent and uncontested.

It is in his confrontation with the fallibilism of Hans Albert's critical rationalism and of Jürgen Habermas's view of his own philosophy as a reconstructive science à la Chomskyan linguistics that Apel achieves a transcendental tour de force (if one would excuse the combative metaphor). Hans Albert, in the wake of Karl Popper's *The Logic of Scientific Discovery*, opposes any philosophical foundationalism in favor of a program of unlimited rational criticism. Albert carries out this attack on foundations via a syntatic-semantic, purely deductively based argument, which, as Apel indicates, ignores the pragmatic presuppositions of argumentation. In addition, Albert's pancritical rationalism, namely, that one "can fundamentally doubt everything," draws its power from the ceaseless discrediting of scientific theories for which Popper's theory of falsifiability calls. Apel, though, criticizes this ideal of unlimited rational criticism by showing that there are certain transcendental presuppositions of argumentation (e.g., that only the force of the better argument should prevail, that all other force should be excluded, that communicative rationality ought to prevail over mere strategic argumentation) that any doubter must make use of as he or she sets about to give arguments aimed at disproving an extant theory. Even if one attempts by argumentation to cast doubt upon these transcendental presuppositions of argument, one will inevitably rely upon them. In a typical Apelian paradox, the indubitable structure of argumentation is the condition of the possibility of dubitability, and fallibilism rests upon infallible suppositions in the sense that even to challenge such suppositions one must utilize them.[29]

Jürgen Habermas's "*universal* pragmatics" maintains the *universalism* of the four validity claims (to truth, rightness, truthfulness, and comprehensibility) and the *universal* "idealization" that the validity of such claims could be justified through the possible consensus of all conceivable partners to an argument. However, when Habermas considers the statements asserting his own universal pragmatics, for instance, those at the heart of his *The Theory of Communicative Action*, he considers them similar to claims made within reconstructive sciences such as those of Chomsky or Piaget; that is, they are at once pitched at a more general level than concrete empirical statements and yet open to empirical refutation.[30]

Apel disputes Habermas's attribution of an empirical-reconstructive status to these core beliefs of *The Theory of Communicative Action* regarding the four validity claims, the necessarily presupposed consensual redeemability of validity claims, and the primacy of communicative rationality vis-à-vis instrumental or strategic-purposive rationality. In Apel's view, these core beliefs are more than empirical since they constitute the transcendental conditions of the possibility of every discourse in which hypotheses would be tested and thus of every effort to produce an empirical refutation. The central theses establishing Habermas's *universal* pragmatics assume a transcendental status in Apel's *transcendental* pragmatics since they are constitutive of argumentative discourse, and they appear as indisputable since they would have to inform even the argumentation that would dispute them. Although empirical claims are always testable against empirical evidence, claims laying out the conditions of the possibility of discourse are distinctive in these two senses: (1) they transcend any concrete discourse since they are at play even in the concrete discourse that would dispute them and (2) they are identifiable, not by the fact that some empirical evidence would confirm or disconfirm them, but rather by the fact that they cannot be disputed without performative self-contradiction.[31]

Apel's self-reflexive methodology here reaches a high point: not only in making explicit the implicit structures of discourse accompanying any concrete discourse, but in examining the status of the statements presenting these structures. Unlike empirical statements which one can easily imagine being disproved, when one tries to imagine a disproof of the principles of discourse, one can only envision such a disproof as taking place within a discourse which must observe those very principles as it sets out to disprove them. Husserl, too, had urged a similar reflexivity upon one's own claims when in *Cartesian Meditations* he suggested the possibility that some claims might possess a unique type of evidence insofar as they present to critical reflection a state of affairs with the "signal peculiarity" of "the absolute unimaginableness (inconceivability) of their *non-being*, and thus excluding in advance every doubt as 'objectless,' empty." Once again Apel illuminates the philosophical shadow of counterpositions—in this case of a critical rationalism and universal pragmatics, both seemingly under the spell of the boundless fallibilism and revisability that are the hallmarks of the empirical sciences.[32]

Wolfgang Köhler has charted the course of what has become an extensive debate over the epistemic status of the core beliefs of *The*

Theory of Communicative Action. Habermas, A. Berlich, and A. Wellmer highlight the fallibility or incompleteness of the philosophical *expression* of these core beliefs, but for Apel the limitations of expression do not undermine the transcendental-pragmatic conditions for fallibilism since such conditions would be presupposed even by those who criticize the deficient expressions. To avoid arrogance on the part of philosophy, Habermas resists locating it on a higher plane than the sciences and contends that one can locate the transcendental dimension of validity claims in their accompanying sense of unconditionedness. That sense of unconditionedness rests on that fact that one inevitably envisions all rational agents concurring with such claims, but this sense of unconditionedness is thoroughly compatible with the fallibility of every such claim. Apel, of course, would emphasize that the core-beliefs are distinctive in that they would spell out the conditions of the possibility of the fallibility of any and every claim, and thus seem eidetic in nature rather than empirical. However, even eidetic claims must be advanced within a philosophical exchange, within what Max Scheler called the *Streit* (conflict) of intuitions, and in such an exchange these claims must be open to revision. However, once again Apel could claim that this very *Streit* cannot dispense with the very conditions of discourse that *The Theory of Communicative Action* spells out. This oscillation between Apel and Habermas can be perpetuated *ad infinitum* since it depends on the point of view one takes on the core-beliefs, that is, whether one focuses on the impossibility of imagining a critique of such beliefs without the conditions they describe being in place (Apel and Husserl) or whether one concentrates on the sociolinguistic setting of interrogation in which such beliefs must be proposed to an interlocutor.[33]

3. TRANSCENDENTAL-PRAGMATIC ETHICS

While it is impossible in this limited space to present fully Apel's discourse ethics or to address all the criticisms raised against it, still we cannot evade the question of the justification of an ethics prohibitory of discrimination—a question that has arisen in the accounts of discrimination given by Sartre, Beauvoir, and Schutz and that must be addressed before turning to a discussion of the ethics of affirmative action. One can, of course, operate with implicit ethical norms, but the assumption of responsibility for unexamined horizons to which

Husserl summons philosophers will not permit one to bypass the task of justifying one's ethical principles. This section will attempt to present discourse ethics and the arguments justifying it, to preempt the usual misunderstandings of it, and to suggest its benefits, particularly those useful for combating discrimination.

As soon as one inquires about whether there are ethical norms and how and whether they might be rationally grounded, one embarks upon a discourse and also upon a discourse of practical reason. While Apel obviously presupposes a distinction between practical and speculative/factual discourse, Habermas, in his essay "Discourse Ethics: Notes on a Program of Philosophical Justification," has gone further than Apel in specifying the difference between these discourses, which take as their launching point for reflection two different kinds of claims, descriptive and prescriptive. While the descriptive claim "This culture practices sexism" can be justified by appealing to empirical evidence (e.g., statistical surveys), the prescriptive claim "Sexist comments ought not be made" cannot be justified by empirical evidence (since such evidence might suggest to the contrary a widespread practice of people making sexist comments). Rather, one must appeal to some kind of principle in the light of which sexist comments can be proved to be immoral.[34]

But where to find such a principle? In the taken-for-granted everyday life-world, there are numerous linguistic practices, such as narrating stories, playing games, telling jokes, reading poetry, or ordinary conversation. But it is also possible within that life-world to embark upon a different kind of enterprise, to engage in the distinct type of language-games known as the sciences, in which one's purpose is *not* to take for granted what is given in everyday life but rather to give an account of that everyday reality. Further, it is the prerogative of philosophy to undertake a particularly critical stance toward even these various critical scientific standpoints and to describe the structures of language-games in general or to examine the features or norms of argumentation, utilized but not yet made explicit by scientific language-games themselves. In the structure of argumentation that philosophy makes explicit and that ought to govern philosophy itself (as well as the sciences), the ideal is that parties honestly seek to convince each other and that they show themselves sincerely willing to revise beliefs if a better counterargument surfaces. It is on this highly self-reflective plane, on which one strives as much as possible not to partake naively in the unexamined presumptions but instead strives to put such presumptions to the discursive test, that the question rises as to whether one's ethical norms have any rational justification. It is on this highly self-reflective plane, where a culture strives to be as self-critical as it ever becomes and to distinguish what is universal from what is particular or relative, that Apel searches for an incontrovertible principle, intrinsic to the self-reflexive language-game of philosophy itself and its ideal of unconstrained argumentation. Unlike the principles intrinsic to less self-critical language-games, a principle intrinsic to this self-critical activity of philosophy will be less likely to fall prey to later progressive stages of critical reflection since it will be intrinsic to the very activity that might undermine it.

According to Apel, anyone who seriously argues has already recognized implicitly a groundnorm of the in-principle equal entitlements of every communication partner in the sense of an "ideal speech situation." According to this ideal speech situation, as Habermas explains it, each subject with competence to speak ought to be entitled to the following: to take part in a discourse; to introduce questions and assertions; to express attitudes, desires, and needs; and not to be prevented by internal or external coercion from exercising all these entitlements. In brief, the normative structure of discourse itself requires that each participant be treated as a Kantian end in him- or herself, not subjected to force or violence, and addressed only with arguments that appeal to one's reasoned, autonomous assent. On this basis, it can be shown that sexist comments treat women in a way that is at odds with the respect due them as discourse partners, a respect that would be accorded them even in the very discourse that would seek to determine whether sexist comments were justifiably immoral or not. It is evident that discourse and the ethical norms intrinsic to it mandate and justify the kind of equality sought after by all the phenomenological opponents in the first part of this book.[35]

A standard objection that immediately comes to mind is that one can imagine any number of concrete counterexamples or thought-experiments in which discourse is not carried on in compliance with these norms. However, those in a discourse who present such counterexamples against the ideal speech situation would be shocked were they to be forcefully forbidden to bring up such counterexamples. They would be shocked precisely because interlocutors within a philosophical conversation such as the one being carried on *here* and *now* expect that the principles of the ideal speech situation will govern their discourse, even *this* discourse in which the ideal speech situation is up for debate, even *this* discourse in which one is advancing empirical counterexamples in which the norms of ideal speech were not observed. In effect, those who advance such empirical counterexamples are not being sufficiently (self-) reflective upon the norms intrinsic to the discourse in which they themselves are here and now participating and, as a result, of the performative contradiction into which they fall as they dispute the norms of the ideal speech situation. Wolfgang Kuhlmann has remarked on how it is possible for one to withdraw oneself imaginatively from the situation of argumentation (in which one is actually involved) and consider argumentation presuppositions as theoretical objects at a distance rather than as the presuppositions of which one is already taking account. Kuhlmann's verdict that "Ultimate grounding cannot be produced in the attitude of the reflexionless, self-forgetful theoretican" could also apply to the many opponents Apel engaged in the last section, opponents who were not sufficiently cognizant of the character of their own claims.[36]

However, more is involved than simply not being sufficiently self-reflective on the present discourse in which one is engaged. The one who disputes the norms governing argumentation by referring to counterinstances adopts an "outward" orientation, attempting to refute a position by pointing out empirical facts in a manner reminiscent of the sciences. However, what is required is that one undertake an entirely different orientation, an "inward" focus, in which one seeks to become *self-reflective* upon expectations one adopts as soon as one enters upon an authentic philosophical argument. Of course, one often anticipates such an authentic discourse only to find that one's interlocutor is proceeding dogmatically and is unwilling to entertain objections or to listen to a new point of view; at such a point, one retreats from any expectation of authenticity and settles for a game of competitive philosophical sparring. Moreover, in retrospect one can often recognize when one has deserted the high plane of authentic philosophical discussion for a game of one-upmanship, in which one has listened very little to the Other. Because of situations such as these, in which there is also a kind of ethical disappointment since one has not taken the Other seriously or has not been taken seriously oneself, Apel and Habermas repeatedly affirm that the norms of the ideal speech situation often function counterfactually. That is to say, these norms are noticed even and perhaps especially when they are *not* put into practice in a discourse; they make themselves present markedly and paradoxically by their absence.[37]

Finally, Habermas and Apel uphold the ethical structure of discourse against counterexamples of distorted communication by pointing out that various forms of manipulation or strategic uses of the structure of discourse to achieve covert perlocutionary effects are themselves parasitic upon the original mode of language-use in which communicative rationality is the norm. In fact, one has to conceal such strategies if they are to be at all successful.[38]

The norms of the ideal speech situation can also seem less than universally binding if one considers the resistance of skeptics. However, skeptics who refuse to enter discourse forfeit any ability to claim rationality for their skeptical position. In addition, skeptics who *do* enter philosophical discourse and argue against there being moral norms succumb to a performative contradiction insofar as they presuppose the norms of the ideal speech situation in order to make their argument. Skeptics who undertake to argue that there is no rational basis for ethical norms need only be confronted by the fact that this position entangles them in the practical inconsistency of having no rational basis for what they must constantly presuppose in acting. Of course, pointing this out to skeptics would establish a rational foundation for moral norms only if they were willing to observe some principle of practical consistency. It is conceivable that die-hard skeptics might counter that to observe that principle or, for that matter, even to be rational at all depends on the free choice of the skeptic, which no reasoning can compel. Faced with such recalcitrance, Apel admits that his arguments may not have the power to change the *will* of someone who refuses to be rational or to enter a philosophical argument; however, ethical theory never claimed the power to change wills, but only the ability to correct mistaken arguments and to identify behavior as irrational and immoral. The problem of an ultimate grounding, Apel observes, is a different question than the existential question of converting the stubborn.[39]

Apel acknowledges that one cannot logically deduce from universal discursive principles the norms appropriate for concrete, historical situations. Instead, at the level of application, there is room for what Aristotle called *phronesis*, for the "context sensitivity" that Gilligan and Murphy require, and for "application-discourses" in which the interests of all concerned by a concrete decision are taken into account. Furthermore, in moving from the universal norms of discourse to concrete situations, Apel faces the problematic fact that one group might be governed by the principles of discourse whereas another group, with which it deals, might not be so governed. In such dilemmas, which are often those of international politics, the discursively oriented group may have to resort to strategic action, but, of course, its long-range goal ought to be to replace eventually strategic interaction with discursive, consensual conflict regulation.[40]

Because of these tensions between principles and applications, Apel has developed the idea of a dialectic between the *ideal* communication community, which one can envision as realizing the discursive norms of equality and mutual respect, and the *real* communication community, necessarily and rightly concerned about its own self-preservation and yet pervaded with obstacles to the realization of the principles of the ideal communication. He further proposes two long-range regulative principles mandating efforts both to realize the ideal communication in the real situation and to ensure the survival of the human species qua real communication community. He even stratifies his own ethical theory on two planes, an A level of ultimate grounding and the derivation of first principles, corresponding to Weber's characterization of Kant's ethics as an ethics of conviction (*Gesinnungsethik*), and a B level of application, corresponding to Weber's ethics of responsibility (*Verantwortungsethik*). This dialectic between principles and applications, between ideal and real communication communities, and between the A and B levels establishes within Apel's ethics a movement toward the excluded Other, as I shall explain by the end of this chapter, and it is this movement that Levinas's phenomenology of alterity will amplify.[41]

Some would argue, however, that basing an ethics upon the norms implicit in theoretical discourse and leaving the application of these norms to concrete cases to a discourse between those to be affected by the final group decision precisely tends to exclude Others for many reasons. In the first place, discourse ethics runs the danger of submitting resistant individuals to group totalitarianism or allowing those who are verbally articulate to subjugate those less verbally gifted. Indeed, the fear of such possibilities might be exacerbated when one considers the competitive character of much *de facto* philosophical discourse or when one ponders Nietzsche's view that those who pride themselves on their rationality are most adept at hiding even from themselves their own true motivation. Postmodernists have taken the lead in this critique of critical theory (and transcendental pragmatics), and it is no wonder that Apel should cite Jean-François Lyotard, who warns that the search for consensus can impose a false conformity upon the heterogeneity of language-games and quash both dissent, the source of creativity, and sensitivity to differences.[42]

Apel's response, typical for his transcendental style of philosophizing, is that Lyotard, by these very arguments, is himself seeking to establish a consensus with his reader. While there is some validity in this transcendental revelation of the consensus-seeking shadow of an argument against consensus, still Lyotard would no doubt find this another instance of a transcendental viewpoint subsuming whatever is different or dissenting under itself—and there is some validity to Lyotard's claim also, as the following chapter on Levinas will argue. It seems that a better interpretation of transcendental pragmatics (and one more in accord with the Levinasian themes to be presented below) might be that the very notion of consensus is aimed at making sure that one *not* impose one's view upon another since one cannot claim universal validity for one's own opinion as long as the Other freely and autonomously withholds assent and so blocks the emergence of consensus. Apel himself provides grounds for such an interpretation when he contrasts discursive argumentation (and unfortunately the word "argumentation" in English perhaps connotes competitiveness) with the vying to be found in sports.[43]

> For in argumentative discourse, people do not struggle for victory, rather—as Popper would say—they allow the arguments in place of themselves to struggle and they watch to see which [arguments] will prove themselves the stronger. That is to say, those involved in argumentation are not primarily interested in their personal victory, rather, with the help of the presentation of a struggle among arguments, that is, among argumentation-strategies, they hope to come nearer to finding the *truth to which all could give their assent*.[44]

Of course, a Nietzsche-immersed postmodernist might be suspicious of this metaphor of arguments playing themselves out apart from their authors, whose appearance as disinterested spectators can so often cloak interests they would prefer to remain latent. In response, Apel could reassert that, whenever ulterior motives guide the discourse, they effectively distort the communication in which only the force of the better argument ought to prevail. Furthermore, a subsequent, authentic discourse would be required to exhume such buried motivations.

There are numerous advantages that Apel's discourse ethics affords. For instance, it provides nonrelativistic, universal norms calling for respect for persons *as equals* and nonviolence. Such norms would be acceptable to communities from diverse life-worlds especially since any discourse between communities regarding whether there might be any norms binding on members from both groups would already presuppose these norms of discourse itself. Moreover, discourse ethics would be perfectly compatible with the natural and social sciences, each of which, insofar as they are governed by the unconstrained force of the better argument, already presupposes the transcendental norms of discourse ethics. As a further advantage, Apel claims that his discourse ethics explains Kant's "fact of reason" even as it avoids the naturalistic fallacy.

> Therefore one does not need to contest the claim that the reflexively ascertained transcendental normative conditions of argumentation belong to the "facticity" (in the sense of "fore-structure") of human "Being-in-the-World." One means thereby something like what Kant called the "fact of reason." One can thus decipher this unique fact— again thinking with Heidegger against Heidegger—in the sense of an "a priori perfect," as the *necessary fact of the having recognized the normative conditions of argumentation*. Thus, one shows that one in no way falls into the *naturalistic fallacy* when one deduces normative consequences from *this* fact. One draws these consequences in no way from a *contingent anthropological fact*, rather from the circumstance, which is incontestably true, the one as a meaningful arguer *necessarily* has recognized the *normative* conditions of the possibility of argumentation. This, so it seems to me, is Kant's so-called "fact of reason," which I have here interpreted in the sense of the normative unity of theoretical and practical reason.[45]

Apel's discourse ethics also offers resources suitable for tackling questions of prejudice and other forms of exclusion because, like phenomenology, it rescues the subjectivity that objectivist (subject-object) theoretical approaches suppress. It recovers this subjectivity by pointing out the intersubjective context that all the sciences presuppose insofar as they engage in unconstrained argumentation at all. Thus the hidden subjectivity that Apel recovers is a hidden *intersubjectivity*, in which each participant is *equal* to every other in the ability to author claims, to raise questions, and thus to be taken seriously as a discourse partner—and it is just this fundamental equality that all forms of discrimination negate.

Furthermore, the ethics derived from Apel's transcendental pragmatics retrieves a lost sense of solidarity through its overcoming of the traditional ethics based on methodological solipsism. Apel's ethics thus would no longer condone the view that just as each individual thinks for him- or herself alone, so each must assume responsibility alone for the actions in which he or she is involved. For instance, Apel criticizes Nobel Prize–winner Friedrich Hayek, who, in the face of worldwide overpopulation, recommended that in order to restore equilibrium to the human biosphere, it would be best to leave those dwelling in the so-called Third World in their hunger rather than to help them. Since discourse ethics entails a deontology in which discourse participants are to be accorded respect as ends in themselves and not to be subordinated as means to the projects of others, Apel resists such a crude, utilitarian social Darwinism. In addition, Hayek's solution, monologically determined without regard to how Third World inhabitants might think, would be unacceptable to an ethics based upon discourse with its mutual search in solidarity for solutions to questions of truth and ethics, in which the viewpoint, needs, and questions of each participant must be taken seriously.[46]

As a further benefit, Apel's discourse ethics implies the abolition of all asymmetries. In a discussion on Rawls, Apel explains that when one acts strategically in an argument, intent on the triumph of one's own interests, one simply cannot determine whether a truth or moral claim is rationally able to be grounded or validated. Thus, the search for truth or rational grounding demands that one not be so fixated upon one's own interests so as to be unable to give adequate consideration to competing opinions. Since the very structure of the discursive process thus forbids one to neglect counterpositions and actually enjoins one to take them into account, especially those stances contrary to one's own, it is not surprising that Apel urges that discourses continually strive to include points of view not yet party to the discourse, such as those of future generations.[47]

> First, in earnest argumentation—already with the positing of the question—we have already recognized in principle the *responsibility in solidarity for the solution of problems* and *in such problem-solving the equal entitlements* of all members of a *real* communication community, of all presently existing humanity. We have, secondly, with the necessary, contrafactual anticipation of an *unlimited ideal communication community* already in principle recognized that all *valid* problem-solving—including ethically relevant problems—must *be able to win the assent* of all participants in the unlimited ideal communication community, if they were able to discuss these problems.

Therein it is implied that this responsibility for problem-solving belongs to those living members of a real communication community who are capable of discourse and that this responsibility extends also to the possible problems of those who are not yet capable of discourse and also to the foreseeably existing members of the unlimited communication community. This occurs in two aspects. First, for the sake of the *coherence of all valid problem-solutions* one can in principle exclude no potential member of the unlimited argumentation community in the search for consensus. Second, due to the recognition of the *in principle equal entitlement of all potential discourse* partners one must responsibly take account of the foreseeable problem situations and the needs of the foreseeably existing members.[48]

The ideal communication community continually impels the real communication community beyond its boundaries in an effort to include the perspectives of those who, as Kantian ends-in-themselves and potential parties to a discourse, deserve to have their say. In the above-cited passage, Apel seems to derive this responsibility for the excluded other, not directly from the excluded other, but rather, epistemologically, that is, from the intrinsic dynamism of rationality itself and its need to consider all viewpoints as it seeks to arrive at the valid solution of its problems. Such an argument at the least shows that Apel by no means countenances the exclusion of the less articulate that some characterizations might attribute to him. It is also true that—as a matter not of epistemological completeness but of ethical principles—Apel's first long-range principle, mandating the implementation of the ideal communication in the real one, and the principles of his level A ethics serve as a guiding telos in the real communication community. This telos calls for the "setting aside of those impediments, which stand in the way of the application of the pure discourse principle" and represents a real impetus to ensure equality *and* to include excluded alterity.

However, as shall be seen in the next chapter, there is a difficulty in reaching the Other when one begins with one's own principles as a starting point. As Levinas shows, when faced with the Other, one is summoned to adopt a receptive attitude different from that in which one articulates principles. In this exposure to the Other beneath the level of the Third *where principles are articulated*, the fact that the initiative of the Other takes precedence over one's response maximizes self-critique, renders the course of discourse more tentative, and transforms the meaning of human solidarity. Levinas's account of the

Other supplements, reinforces, and especially radicalizes the tendencies toward alterity already to be found in Apel's thought.[49]

The journey through the existential phenomenologists, Sartre and Beauvoir, reveals that various forms of discrimination are wrong because they perpetrate a kind of reification, the reduction of free for-itself to an itself, and this reification can also be construed as thwarting an ideal of reciprocity between equal free agents. Sartre's and Beauvoir's existentialist perspective, however, permits little ethical justification for the ideal of reciprocity that pervades their extensive criticisms of discrimination, although Sartre seems to anticipate such a justification in his unpublished notebooks. Apel, in my opinion, has articulated the features of this ideal, exhibited it as a presupposition of every authentic discourse, including the existentialist discourse of Sartre and Beauvoir, and supported it with the argumentation that had been lacking.

Similarly, Apel's transcendental pragmatics accords with Schutz's phenomenology which takes its intersubjective bases more seriously than other phenomenologies, even as Apel makes possible the ethical theory that Schutz never attempted. In Schutz's insight into the subtleties of looking-glass type constructions that occlude the input of the excluded victim of prejudice as well as Schutz's awareness of how the need for social scientific adequacy impels the scientist to consult the actor, one detects the trace of the ideal of unconstrained discourse, obliterated by discrimination and yet demanded by science.

At the same time, the route through the phenomenologists indicates a suspicion of rationality itself, an awareness of the danger that it might suppress difference, unless it speaks *with* the Other it speaks *of*. Apel's transcendental pragmatics by its own intrinsic dynamism would resist such suppression, but in this very trajectory it can be supplemented by Levinas's phenomenology which, I will try to show, heightens the very critical rationality on which the Frankfurt thinkers pride themselves by elucidating the ethical context from which theory itself arises. Perhaps the phenomenological reading I have given of Apel's transcendental pragmatics will allow for some reconciliation with Levinas the phenomenologist, who needs to be taken not for a postmodern enemy of transcendental pragmatics but a kindred soul.

NOTES

1. Karl-Otto Apel, *Transformation der Philosophie*, vol. 1, *Sprachanalytik, Semiotik, Hermeneutik* (Frankfurt am Main: Suhrkamp Verlag, 1973), pp. 24, 32–48, 80, 117, 171, 177, 258, 262–63, 298, 302.

2. Ibid., 1:87–105.

3. Karl-Otto Apel, *Selected Essays*, vol. 1, *Towards a Transcendental Semiotics*, ed. Eduardo Mendieta (Atlantic Highlands, N.J.: Humanities Press, 1994), p. 141.

4. Ibid., pp. 65, 77–78; Karl-Otto Apel, "Towards a Reconstruction of Critical Theory," *Philosophical Disputes in the Social Sciences*, ed. S. C. Brown (Sussex: Harvester Press and Atlantic Highlands, N.J.: Humanities Press, 1979), p. 129; Karl-Otto Apel, *Toward a Transformation of Philosophy*, trans. Glyn Adey and David Frisby (London and Boston: Routledge & Kegan Paul, 1973), pp. 137, 147, 158; Karl-Otto Apel, *Understanding and Explanation: A Transcendental-Pragmatic Perspective*, trans. Georgia Warnke (Cambridge, Mass., and London: MIT Press, 1984), pp. 56–57.

5. Karl-Otto Apel, "Fallibilismus, Konsenstheorie der Wahrheit and Letztbegründung," in *Philosophie und Begründung*, ed. Wolfgang R. Köhler, Wolfgang Kuhlmann, and Peter Rohs (Frankfurt am Main: Suhrkamp Verlag, 1987), pp. 126–29; *Selected Essays*, pp. 182–83.

6. Apel, *Selected Essays*, pp. 136–41.

7. Ibid., pp. 141–50.

8. Ibid., pp. 150–72

9. For an admission of the need for this autonomous evidence of consciousness by Apel, see "Pragmatic Philosophy of Language Based on Transcendental Semiotics," *Selected Essays*, pp. 234–35; see also pp. 185, 192.

10. Edmund Husserl, *Ideas Pertaining to a Pure Phenomenology and to a Phenomenological Philosophy*, Book I: *General Introduction to a Pure Phenomenology*, trans. F. Kersten (The Hauge, Boston, London: Martinus Nijhoff, 1982), pp. 7, 8–9; Edmund Husserl, *Cartesian Meditations: An Introduction to Phenomenology*, trans. Dorion Cairns (The Hague, Boston, London: Martinus Nijohff, 1960), pp. 1–6, Edmund Husserl, "The Vienna Lecture" in *The Crisis of European Sciences and Transcendental Phenomenology: An Introduction to Phenomenological Philosophy*, trans. David Carr (Evanston, Ill.: Northwestern University Press, 1970), p. 286.

11. Apel, *Selected Essays*, pp. 141, 182; Karl-Otto Apel, "Normatively Grounding 'Critical Theory' through Recourse to the Life-world? A Transcendental-Pragmatic Attempt to Think with Habermas against Habermas," in *Philosophical Interventions in the Unfinished Project of Enlightenment*, ed. Axel Honneth, Thomas McCarthy, Claus Offe and Albrecht Wellmer, trans. William Rehg (Cambridge, Mass., and London: MIT Press, 1992), p. 142.

12. Alfred Schutz, "Type and Eidos in Husserl's Late Philosophy" in *Col-*

lected Papers, vol. 3: *Studies in Phenomenological Philosophy*, ed. I. Schutz (The Hague: Martinus Nijhoff, 1975), p. 115.

13. Ibid., p. 114; *supra*, chapter 4, pp. 1–2, 10–11; Apel, *Selected Essays*, pp. 141, 182.

14. Husserl, *Cartesian Meditations*, pp. 35–37; *Ideas*, 1:60–62; *supra*, chapter 1, pp. 4–6.

15. Husserl, *Cartesian Meditations*, pp. 91–92; Alfred Schutz, "On Multiple Realities" in *Collected Papers*, vol. 1: *The Problem of Social Reality*, ed. Maurice Natanson (The Hague: Martinus Nijhoff, 1962), pp. 257–58; Alfred Schutz, "The Problem of Transcendental Intersubjectivity in Husserl," in *Studies in Phenomenological Philosophy*, pp. 51–91.

16. Cf. Apel's essay, "Scientistics, Hermeneutics and the Critique of Ideology: Outline of a Theory of Science from a Cognitive-Anthropological Standpoint," in *Toward a Transformation of Philosophy*, pp. 46–76, and also pp. 80, 136, 256, 266; *Selected Essays*, pp. 65, 182, 243; Karl-Otto Apel, "The Problem of Philosophical Foundations in Light of a Transcendental Pragmatics of Language," in *After Philosophy: End or Transformation?* ed. Kenneth Baynes, James Bohman, and Thomas McCarthy (Cambridge, Mass., and London: MIT Press, 1987), pp. 268–69.

17. Apel, *Transformation der Philosophie*, 1:302–308; Karl-Otto Apel, *Transformation der Philosophie*, vol. 2: *Das Apriori der Kommunikationsgemeinschaft* (Frankfurt am Main: Suhrkamp Verlag, 1973), p. 41. The translation is mine.

18. Apel, *Transformation der Philosophie*, 1:308–20.

19. Ibid., pp. 151, 174, 261, 268–69; *Towards a Transformation of Philosophy*, p. 20.

20. Apel, *Selected Essays*, p. 245; *Transformation der Philosophie*, 1:269–73, 331–34; *Towards a Transformation of Philosophy*, p. 33.

21. Apel, *Understanding and Explanation*, pp. 193, 197; *Selected Essays*, pp. 11, 13, 19, 23, 59, 65–66; *The Transformation of Philosophy*, pp. 78, 97, 155, 197.

22. Apel, *Transformation der Philosophie*, 1:24–27, 264; 2:53–58, 151, 165, 261. Heidegger's Being-in-the-World achieves the same end as Apel's insistence that the pragmatics furnishes the context for formal logic and for semantical-syntactical approaches.

23. Apel, *Transformation der Philosophie*, 1:25, 247.

24. Ibid., 1:297–98.

25. Ibid., 1:32–34, 42–44, 272–75; 2:18.

26. Karl-Otto Apel, *Diskurs und Verantwortung: Das Problem des Übergangs zur postkonventionellen Moral* (Frankfurt am Main: Suhrkamp Verlag, 1988), pp. 386–87. The translation is mine.

27. Apel, *Transformation der Philosophie*, 1:41.

28. Apel, *The Transformation of Philosophy*, p. 49; *Transformation der Philosophie*, 1:49, 247, 274–75; 2:18–27.

29. Karl-Otto Apel, "The Problem of Philosophical Foundations in Light of a Transcendental Pragmatics of Language," pp. 250, 255, 256–62, 263, 266–67, 276.

30. Jürgen Habermas, "Philosophy as Stand-In and Interpreter," *Moral Consciousness and Communicative Action*, trans. Christian Lenhardt and Shierry Weber Nicholsen (Cambridge, Mass., and London: MIT Press, 1990), pp. 15–16.

31. Karl-Otto Apel, "Normatively Grounding 'Critical Theory' " pp. 127–28, 141–43, 147, 153.

32. Husserl, *Cartesian Meditations*, pp. 15–16.

33. Wolfgang R. Köhler, "Zur Debatte um reflexive Argumente in der neueren deutschen Philosophie," in *Philosophie und Begründung*, ed. Wolfgang R. Köhler, Wolfgang Kuhlmann, and Peter Rohs (Frankfurt am Main: Suhrkamp Verlag, 1987), pp. 315, 318–19, 326; Herbert Schnädelbach, "Transformation der kritischen Theorie," in *Kommunikatives Handeln: Beiträge zu Jürgen Habermas' "Theorie des kommunikativen Handelns*," ed. Axel Honneth and Hans Joas (Frankfurt am Main: Suhrkamp Verlag, 1986), p. 34; Jürgen Habermas, "Entgegnung," in *Kommunikatives Handeln: Beiträge zu Jürgen Habermas' "Theorie des kommunikativen Handelns*," pp. 349–52; Wolfgang Kuhlmann, "Ethik der Kommunikation," in (*Funk-Kolleg*) *Praktische Philosophie/Ethik*, ed. Karl-Otto Apel, Dietrich Böhler, Alfred Berlich, and Gerhard Plumpe (Weinheim-Basel: Fischer Verlag, 1984), p. 297; Max Scheler, "Phenomenology and the Theory of Cognition," in *Selected Philosophical Essays*, trans. David R. Lachterman (Evanston, Ill.: Northwestern University Press, 1973), pp. 152–55; Apel, "Normatively Grounding 'Critical Theory,' " pp. 148, 151, 153, 160.

34. Jürgen Habermas, "Discourse Ethics: Notes on a Program of Philosophical Justification," in *Moral Consciousness and Communicative Action*, pp. 45–57; Apel recognizes this distinction insofar as he accepts the whole Kantian framework; distinguishes, for example, empirical facts from the fact of reason; and attempts to avoid naturalistic fallacy, and so forth. Cf. Apel, *Diskurs und Verantwortung*, pp. 49, 99.

35. Apel, *Diskurs und Verantwortung*, p. 116; Habermas, "Discourse Ethics," p. 89.

36. Apel, *Diskurs und Verantwortung*, pp. 111–12; Kuhlmann, "Ethik der Kommunikation," p. 298.

37. Apel, *Diskurs und Verantwortung*, p. 50; Kuhlmann, "Ethik der Kommunikation," p. 298.

38. Apel, *Diskurs und Verantwortung*, p. 101; Jürgen Habermas, *The Theory of Communicative Action*, vol. 1: *Reason and the Rationalization of Society*, trans. Thomas McCarthy (Boston: Beacon Press, 1984), pp. 288–95.

39. Apel, *Diskurs und Verantwortung*, pp. 174, 348; *The Transformation of Philosophy*, p. 268.

40. Apel, *Diskurs und Verantwortung*, pp. 142–49, 212–19, 298–99; cf. Klaus Günther, *The Sense of Appropriateness: Application Discourses in Morality and Law*, trans. John Farrell (Albany: State University of New York Press, 1993).

41. Apel, *Diskurs und Verantwortung*, pp. 142–49, 212–19, 298–99; *The Transformation of Philosophy*, 276–85.

42. Apel, *Diskurs und Verantwortung*, p. 158.

43. Ibid.

44. Ibid., pp. 235–36. My translation.

45. Ibid., pp. 48–49, cf. also pp. 35, 138; Apel, *The Transformation of Philosophy*, pp. 124, 249, 255–57. My translation.

46. Apel, *Diskurs und Verantwortung*, pp. 62–63, 184, 198; *Transformation der Philosophie*, 1:61.

47. Apel, *Diskurs und Verantwortung*, p. 283.

48. Ibid., pp. 202–203. The translation is mine.

49. Ibid., p. 147.

6

PHENOMENOLOGY OF ALTERITY AT THE PRETRANSCENDENTAL LEVEL

1. THE FACE AND THE THIRD

Levinas, like his predecessor Husserl, believed that the transcendental level, where for Apel one becomes self-reflexive about the very processes of argumentation by which one argues for any philosophical position at all, presupposes a level of lived experience from which theory and theory about theory arise. In his preface to *Totality and Infinity*, Levinas specifically identifies his own effort to retrieve this forgotten, founding level, even of philosophy itself, with the endeavor of the later Husserl to return to the life-world as the soil of theory itself.

> Notions held under the direct gaze of the thought that defines them are nevertheless, unbeknown to this naive thought, revealed to be implanted in horizons unsuspected by this thought; these horizons endow them with a meaning—such is the essential teaching of Husserl. What does it matter if in the Husserlian phenomenology taken literally these unsuspected horizons are in their turn interpreted as thoughts aiming at objects! What counts is the idea of the overflowing of objectifying thought by a forgotten experience from which it lives.[1]

Although Levinas's project seems to unfold at a life-world level prior to theory, he clearly dissociates himself from what he takes to be Husserl's excessively cognitive portrayal of this pretheoretical domain in terms of "thoughts aiming at objects." Indeed, from Levinas's early *Theory of Intuition in Husserl's Phenomenology*—a mostly expository book introducing Husserlian phenomenology to France and opening up the possibility of a theory of being in all its diverse spheres—Levinas had his misgivings about Husserl's intellectualistic tendencies. Because of Levinas's opposition to Husserl's conception of the life-world, the terms "pretheoretical" or "pretranscendental" have been used here to refer to the locus where Levinas presents his phenomenology of alterity, that is, his description of the eidetic features of the ethical relationship with the Other at the origin of theory.[2]

Before discussing this phenomenology of alterity, it is important to acknowledge that in everyday life persons generally operate with what Schutz describes as the reciprocity of perspectives, anticipating that the Other's reactions to objects will correspond to our own and that differences in relevances are irrelevant for the common purposes at hand. By extension, it seems plausible that we also anticipate that just as we treat the Other, so the Other will treat us. These expectations of reciprocity assume a kind of normativity in common sense—a normativity that becomes visible when interruptions of such expectations take us aback. For instance, we are surprised when the Other walks through a plate-glass window that the Other and we both seemed to have recognized or when the well-educated colleague refers to an object by an inappropriate word. Or we are disturbed when we treat someone politely who in the next moment acts rudely in return. In some ways, Apel's transcendental pragmatic account of the normative expectations of reciprocity operative on the theoretical plane of argumentation finds a correlate in these unreflective reciprocal expectations pervading everyday life and present every time one uses a word or utters a statement, expecting that what one says will be understandable to the Other, as it usually is.[3]

However, Levinas, in his phenomenological attempt to return to "the things themselves" without resting in any unexamined presuppositions, illuminates in this experience of intersubjective life a new dimension that becomes visible when one stands facing the Other. According to Levinas's phenomenological descriptions, when one faces the Other, one finds oneself called into question with regard to the naive right of one's powers and summoned to respond to the Other. The Other is given from a *moral* height, inviting one to service and responsibility (as opposed to a height that might derive from the Other exercising an *immoral* domination over the I). Perhaps since the moral character of this height becomes recognizable particularly when it is given in conjunction with the Other's destitution, Levinas repeatedly associates moral height with the destitute. I recall one example of such a conjunction of moral height with destitution when in an open-air restaurant in Guadalajara, two small boys asked my friend and me if they could eat whatever we left on our plates—in their presence after that question, we could only feel responsible to them, something had to be done, some response given. Of course the Other invites us to an ethical response in less dramatic situations, as when we feel obliged to embark upon a discourse with another or just to allow the other to pass through a door before us. This sense of being pulled out of ourselves by the Other's presence/need/destitution/moral height seems strikingly at odds with the experience of everyday ethicality that might build upon Schutz's descriptions, namely, the reciprocity, mutuality, predictability, and equality typical of the reciprocity of perspectives.[4]

Levinas insists that this distinctive phenomenological experience of the Other's moral height must take its departure point from the I facing the Other; "we know this relation only in the measure that we effect it . . . alterity is possible only starting from *me*." Jean-François Lyotard develops Levinas's attempt to isolate this moment when the I experiences the Other's summons by claiming that one actually adopts two separate attitudes within a communicative pragmatics: one of experiencing the Other's prescriptive, which is meant to be executed, and the other of treating the Other's statement of a prescriptive as a "denotative," to be subjected to reflective examination and assessment. It is one thing to be the addressee of another's order and another to take up the attitude of commenting on the other's order, and, as a commentator, one becomes an addresser (no longer an addressee) and one, in effect, neutralizes the Other's order to examine it. While the receiver of the order stands in asymmetric relation to the order-giver, the commentator functions symmetrically with others.[5]

Just as one can distinguish between the attitudes of receptivity toward the Other's prescriptive and of reflexivity upon the validity of that prescriptive, so one can separate the experience of the Other's moral summons from appraising the prudence of complying with whatever concrete demands the Other presents, e.g., assessing whether the Other is likely to reciprocate for generous initiatives on the Other's behalf or take advantage of them. Expectations that the Other ought to behave reciprocally lie on the horizon of any experience of the Other's moral height, and it is always possible that one may have to make focal a caution about the Other and to restrain the impulses to serve the Other that the Other elicits. However, one adopts protective measures with reference to an Other who on some level awakens one's responsiveness, even if that response involves only the consideration of whether to respond with openness or circumspection.

For example, when the police arrive on the scene where an aggressor is waving a knife against all comers, the aggressor's behavior puts one on guard, blocking the generous responses appropriate in other settings. Nevertheless, the aggressor even in the midst of his threatening behavior still issues a kind of plea for ethical treatment that fundamentally shapes and constrains all subsequent police responses. For instance, the police might begin testing whether a less threatening approach on their part might defuse his anger. If those efforts prove unsuccessful, the police may be prepared to use force, but only that minimally necessary to disarm the aggressor, and then only as a last resort and with regret. Even though the Other's threatening actions in this case promise no reciprocity and no respect for his interlocutors, the look of terror and desperation in his eyes nevertheless appeals to the police to refrain from inflicting any unconstrained violence upon him. One might argue that it is law or public pressure that really constrain the police, but a counterresponse would be that laws and public pressure against police brutality themselves have been developed in response perhaps to past instances where overwhelming police power has been brought to bear on relatively powerless individuals, who even in their deaths still haunt the public conscience. Thus, the moment of experiencing the Other's prescriptive that Levinas distills out of experience is distinct from any demand that the Other act reciprocally and separate from any attempt to "record the correspondence or the non-correspondence" of the Other's return with one's going unto the Other. Levinas sums up his effort to distinguish these dimensions of experience when he remarks, "War presupposes peace, the antecedent and non-allergic presence of the Other; it does not represent the first event of the encounter."[6]

This lived ethical relationship of facing the Other—and the technical terms "same and other" refer to this facing—poses certain problems if one attempts to "stop and think about it" since one must place oneself at a distance from the relationship and introduce modifications that diminish its ethical force, in much the way that adopting a denotative attitude neutralizes the moment of receiving the prescriptive. In thinking about relationships, one conceives them as reversible, able to be read indifferently from left to right and from right to left, as Levinas asserts in "The Breach of Totality" in *Totality and Infinity*. In so thinking of the Other as a B interchangeable with another conceived as A, the Other (B) is placed on the same plane with A, and the ethical height of B, which might be given to A facing B, is obscured. In fact by looking upon the parties to a relationship as interchangeable, one actually takes up a position C outside of the relationship between A and B and does not see the relationship as A might if A were facing B.[7]

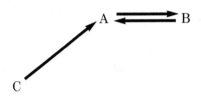

FIGURE 1

One need not adopt viewpoint C only in regard to a relationship between two *other* people, A and B. In self-reflection, it is also possible to take up a distance toward oneself in relationship with another, to look upon oneself as if one were an A in a relationship with B, and thus conceive the relationship in which one is involved as reversible. But one would then be placing that relationship, as one did in looking upon a relationship between two other people, within a system visible from the outside, from point C, reabsorbing, thereby, the transcendence of the Other within the unity of the system. By contrast, Levinas is attempting to describe how the Other appears when one takes up the position of an I facing an Other *before one ever reflectively removes oneself from that facing by adopting a reflective posture on the relationship.*

FIGURE 2

Since the correlation of the same and other are meant to capture the experience of an I facing an Other, it is important to resist the temptation to construe the relationship between the same and the other as reversible, as is so often mistakenly done. What this entire analysis shows is that the very process of reflection has the effect of concealing one's experience of facing an Other since it distances one from the very experience which Levinas is inviting his reader to consult and since it leads one to conceive the facing relationship as reversible between interchangeable, equal variables. But this critique of reflection's limits itself results from another kind of reflection, phenomenological reflection, disclosing the height of the Other which is the condition of the possibility of recognizing the distortion that the first kind of reflection introduces. One is here reminded of Merleau-Ponty's idea of "radical reflection," reflecting on the point where reflection makes its break with the unreflected and introducing distinctions, such as between subject and object, that are actually blurred in the lived experience.[8]

In *Totality and Infinity*, Levinas develops the implications of his description of the face of the Other, which in its destitution offers ethical resistance, that is, the resistance that has no resistance or physical power. For example, since war and violence happen against the background of this prior ethical relationship in which the Other obliges one with the primordial expression "you shall not commit murder," Levinas conceives his own thought as providing an alternative to Hobbes, whose politics rests upon an initial encounter of war. Furthermore, Levinas contests Enlightenment notions of rationality that, like the one employed by Sartre's democratic anti-Semite, require interlocutors to renounce their uniqueness for the sake of the universal. On the contrary, when one conceives universality and rationality as arising out of the speech relationship between interlocutors, the subject does not abdicate uniqueness or dis-individuate, but is called upon by an Other to respond, to deliver an apology, in a way that upholds and even augments that uniqueness. In a sense, Aristotle proceeded in just the opposite direction from Levinas, spinning out universal theories about whose sex or whose nationality or whose physique (e.g., that of a slave or free person) would qualify them to be an interlocutor instead of submitting such theories to testing in the speech relationship. In addition, this ethical mandate of the Other supervenes upon an I already distinguished from any pantheistic totality or Hegelian Absolute Spirit and individuated through what Levinas calls "enjoyment." Moreover, in singling out or "electing" its recipients, this ethical mandate turns them to the resources of their interiority and confirms them in their uniqueness and strength, as they undertake responsibilities for which they cannot be replaced.[9]

Levinas's phenomenological descriptions of these eidetic features involved in the encounter with the Other in fact furnish an a priori foundation and the philosophical matrix from which Levinas undertakes throughout the course of *Totality and Infinity* to reinterpret traditional philosophical categories and problems such as freedom, truth, language, violence, commerce, history, suffering, death, eros, procreation, and time. It is no wonder, then, that Levinas can claim in his introduction that ethics, that is, the moral relationship with the Other, is an "optics" and in his conclusion that "Morality is not a branch of philosophy but first philosophy."[10]

The phenomenological recovery of the face not only compels a rethinking of traditional philosophical positions, but it also acts back on the very phenomenological method Levinas utilizes to elucidate the face in the first place. For Levinas, the relationship with the Other is not to be treated in terms of thematizing intentionality, the "consciousness of . . .," that is the trademark of phenomenology. According to Levinas, "intentionality remains an aspiration to be filled and fulfillment, the centripetal movement of a consciousness that coincides with itself." Although intentionality does not designate voluntary intention only, it still retains the initiating and inchoative pattern of the voluntary, according to which "the given enters into a thought which recognizes in it or invests it with its own project, and thus exercises mastery over it." Hence, when faced with the Other, the Other defects from any intentionality aimed at disclosure, in which the Other might appear in plastic form as an image or portrait; instead phenomenality defects into a face, a failing of all presence, less than a phenomenon, "already a poverty that hides its wretchedness and calls upon me and orders me." Although Levinas emphasizes how the Other uproots intentionality, tearing "consciousness up from its center," at other moments, he acknowledges, without clarifying, that the Other is given through an "intentionality of a wholly different type," "unique in its kind," other than the usual "noesis-noema structure." Levinas's phenomenology has, in effect, uncovered an "object" (the Other), which is not really an object to be approached through an "intentionality," which is not really intentionality. The Other approached ethically constitutes a new "region of being," which is really unlike every other region of being. Thus the Other effectively calls for paroxysms in phenomenological method such that one can wonder whether one is even practicing phenomenology in the usual sense.[11]

To be sure, via phenomenological method Levinas has distinguished the asymmetric experience of the Other's height from the symmetrical experiences of reciprocity, mutuality, and equality that Schutz and Apel make evident on pretheoretical and theoretical planes. These asymmetrical and symmetrical dimensions of experience are thoroughly intermingled in everyday life: at one moment one finds oneself holding an Other accountable for not behaving reciprocally or treating oneself equally and at another moment one finds oneself taken up into responsibility for an Other without any regard for recompense. Indeed the example of knife-wielder's encounter with the police shows how both strands of experience can be at play in a single incident. However, since Levinas has distinguished theoretically these two dimensions of experience, he himself attempts to provide a theoretical reconciliation of them.

Rather than simply attempting to *think* from the face to reversible equal relationships, a passage that ends up obscuring the moral height of the Other, as he has shown in "The Breach of Totality," Levinas attempts to show how the symmetrical idea of equality already contains within it as a strand of meaning the asymmetrical height of the Other. Just as Husserl constituted the idea of a house by revealing the underlying meanings that go into building up the final meaning of house, that is, the various spatiotemporal perspectives on the house through which one passes in order to build up such a final meaning, so Levinas seeks to unpack the notion of equality, to generate it, out of a series of personal experiences of the Other. Thus for Levinas when one serves another and then finds that the Other, in turn, is at the service of a third person, one discovers that one is the Other's equal (since both are servants of a Third) and that oneself, the Other, and the Third are equal (in service of each other). Levinas is not offering here a genetic account of the psychological origins of the notion of equality; that is, it is not as if a child arrives at the idea of equality after having observed that the Other whom the child serves is at the service of another Other, and so on. Rather, Levinas could be seen as moving back from an already constituted level of the Third to a stratum of meaning, of unequal obligation, that is an ingredient in the notion of equality in the same way that Husserl moved backward from the constituted house, for instance, to the constituting activities through which the idea of "house" is gradually built up. Both Husserl and Levinas are concerned more with phenomenological meaning constitution than with a psychological account of how a concept is learned for the first time. By this procedure, in which the engine of movement is personal obligation to another (e.g., the Other's to the Third), Levinas ensures that the idea of equality and reciprocity is not severed from one's ethical responsibility to the Other. [12]

When Glaucon, in his purely strategic account of justice at the opening of *The Republic*, points out that omnipotent beings would never accept any equalizing justice since they could inflict injustice without suffering it and that only less-than-omnipotent beings would agree out of interest in their self-protection to the constraints of equality, he concurs with Levinas that equality itself is derivative. Whereas for Glaucon equality is derivative from the self-interest of those who are threatened by their lack of omnipotence, for Levinas it is derivative from the sense of ethical responsibility for the Other that the Other evokes. One might concur with Thrasymachus and Glaucon that motives such as self-interest and the desire to dominate others often prevail in this world, but if one does not accept their reductionistic account of human motivation, then the very treatment of others as equals may reveal the presence of nonstrategic, moral motivations. In a world of such mixed motivations, a world where others constitute a distinct threat to oneself, to have recognized them as equals at all could well be an act of moral service, a risking of oneself for the Other, in which the symmetry of equality already bears the mark of the asymmetry of the face to face.

While the analytic level of the Third is generated from the face to face—and these two levels, intermingled in lived experience, are analytic levels in Levinas's exposition—the level of the Third has its own dynamics and even acts back upon the level of the face to face. One is impelled to move to the level of the Third by the Other since the "unlimited initial responsibility . . . justifies this concern for justice" and "the extraordinary commitment of the other to the third party calls for control, a search for justice." Once on this plane, Levinas notes, there is an "incessant correction of the asymmetry of proximity in which the face [of the Other] is looked at." In other words, there may be moments when the standard of equality requires us not to place ourself at the Other's service and to insist that the Other treat us equally, perhaps for the Other's own good. Not only must we adjudicate the Other's demands with our own, but broader questions of adjudication appear when the Third person appears on the scene, asking for the same ethical treatment that the Other calls for in a dyadic relationship and summoning the community to a "search for justice, society and the State, comparison and possession, thought and science, commerce and philosophy." Thus, the quest for universal principles of precisely the type that Apel articulates must be situated beyond the anarchic moment of the face to face and at the moment of ordering introduced by the Third. At this level, the level of philosophy and the founding of institutions such as the egalitarian and just State, "which is to be set up and, especially to be maintained," I experience with others a "copresence on an equal footing as before a court of justice," "a terrain common to me and the others." Here "subjectivity is a citizen with all the duties and rights measured and measurable which the equilibrated ego involves."[13]

A dialectic between the levels, however, ensues as Levinas worries whether on the tier of the Third, in one's concerns for justice and philosophy, one can lose sight of the experiential basis underlying these concerns. After all, "justice, society, the State and its institutions, exchanges and work" run a constant risk of "having their center of gravitation in themselves and weighing on their own account." To offset just this possibility, Levinas insists that equality—a preeminent value at the level of the Third and certainly in Apel's transcendental pragmatics—is itself generated from an originary experience: the welcoming of the face. In sum, the idea of equality "cannot be detached from the welcoming of the face, of which it is a moment."[14]

Having uncovered via a kind of phenomenological disinterment the hidden strand of "ethical" inequality within the common sense/philosophical notion of equality, Levinas in *Otherwise than Being* recapitulates the transition from the face to the Third and from the Third back to its more ancient *arche*.

> It is not that the entry of a third party would be an empirical fact, and that my responsibility for the other finds itself constrained to a calculus by the "force of things." In the proximity of the other, all the others than the other obsess me, and already this obsession cries out for justice, demands measure and knowing, is consciousness. A face obsesses and shows itself, between transcendence and visibility/invisibility. Signification signifies in justice, but also, more ancient than itself and than the equality implied by it, justice passes by justice in my responsibility for the other, in my inequality with respect to him for whom I am a hostage.[15]

Some final methodological points are in order. On the one hand, there is the Husserlian distinction between life-world and transcendental planes, and Levinas specifies the locus of his phenomenology of alterity at the life-world level. On the other hand, there is the Levinasian analytic distinction ("analytic" because these levels are intermingled in everyday experience) of the asymmetry of the face and the symmetry of the Third. It is important not to conflate these two sets of distinctions. One cannot reduce the life-world to the asymmetry of the face because there are also practices of reciprocity, documented by Schutz, pervading the life-world in which the face comes to appearance. Nor can one claim that the Third is confined to a theoretical level since there are experiences of equality (e.g., via the reciprocity of perspectives) in everyday life and Levinas includes as part of the Third institutions such as law and the economy, which operate within the life-world.

Further, one can draw various connections between and within different levels, for example, by claiming that the reciprocity and equality characterizing the exercise of theory (e.g., in Apel's account of discourse ethics) can be traced to the reciprocity of perspectives making possible a common world in everyday life. Levinas, too, argues that those who theorize have learned to be self-critical, mistrust themselves, and hold their drives in check. Such characteristics of theorizing indicate that sedimented within the activity of theorizing is the ethical experience of the Other from whom one learns to place oneself in question. Likewise, it is tempting to speculate about the relationship between the ethical height of the Other and Schutz's reciprocity of perspectives experienced both immediately and unreflectively within the life-world. It may be well that one's desire to share a common world with the Other who asks for such sharing motivates one's regular assumption of the reciprocity of perspectives. Levinas himself detected just such a desire at the base of the universality of language, which is "correlative with the generosity of the subject going to the Other . . . to establish, by gift, community and universality . . . to offer things which are mine to the Other." Following Levinas and by supplying an ethical foundation to the thesis of the reciprocity of perspectives, one ends up giving an ethical twist to what is for Schutz a predominately epistemological principle.[16]

2. THE CRITIQUE OF REASON

It is no secret that Jacques Derrida raised critical questions about *Totality and Infinity* three years after its publication in his essay "Violence and Metaphysics, An Essay on the Thought of Emmanuel Levinas," and that Levinas takes up several of Derrida's challenges ten years later in *Otherwise Than Being*, without mentioning Derrida specifically. Derrida argues that Levinas is forced to utilize language to speak of infinite alterity which is supposedly unutterable, that his critique of phenomenology via the Other must nevertheless appeal to phenomenological evidence of the Other, and that his attempt to think the Other beyond ontology inevitably presupposes ontology and discloses Being. For Derrida, it is as if Levinas attempts to escape the violence of language, phenomenology, and ontology by seeking to present the Other apart from these intermediaries. Nevertheless, Levinas ends up concealing his own philosophical pretension to nonphilosophy, and by propounding a nonphilosophy aloof from *logos* he runs the risk of being doctrinaire. The only recourse, in Derrida's view, is to embrace the admittedly flawed enterprises of language, philosophy, and ontology, whose violence is less than the worst violence of all—the silence that refuses the give and take of discourse and that ultimately terminates in dogmatism. Derrida sums up his criticisms of Levinas by accusing him of being an "empiricist."

> But the true name of this inclination of thought to the Other, of this resigned acceptance of incoherent incoherence inspired by a truth more profound than the "logic" of philosophical discourse, the true name of this renunciation of the concept, of the aprioris and transcendental horizons of language, is *empiricism*. For the latter, at bottom, has ever committed but one fault: the fault of presenting itself as a philosophy. And the profundity of the empiricist intention must be recognized beneath the naiveté of certain of its historical expressions. It is the *dream* of a purely *heterological* thought at its source. A *pure* thought of *pure* difference. Empiricism is its philosophical name, its metaphysical pretension or modesty. We say the *dream* because it must vanish *at daybreak*, as soon as language awakens.[17]

Ironically Derrida, mistaken by many to be seeking the destruction of philosophical discourse, here criticizes Levinas's outmaneuvering of philosophy because it is insufficiently philosophical, insufficiently self-reflective upon its own viewpoint and its own route of access to what it investigates, insufficiently transcendental, if you will. Derrida's pointing to the philosophical presuppositions which Levinas is reluctant to acknowledge, since they seem to run counter to his whole philosophical project, puts Derrida paradoxically in league with Karl-Otto Apel. Indeed Apel, too, criticizes the postmodern "total critique of reason," among whose proponents one might rank Levinas because they participate in a kind of *Logosvergessenheit*, lacking in self-reflection upon their own speech-communicative presuppositions. Derrida detects in Levinas the very fault which Apel attributes to Derrida and Rorty who, in Apel's view, are scarcely able to write or speak without developing performative self-contradictions that spring up between their performative introduction of universal validity claims and those claims' contents, which tend to deny all universal validity claims.[18]

But it would be unfair to overlook how Levinas is self-critical of his own discourse. At one point in *Totality and Infinity*, Levinas stops and wonders whether his own book encompasses the same and the other within the totality of a single panoramic vision that places them alongside each other, on the same plane.

> The same and the other cannot enter into a cognition that would encompass them; the relations that the separated being maintains with what transcends it are not produced on the ground of totality, do not crystallize into a system. Yet do we not name them together?[19]

This self-reflective turn places figure 2, which represents oneself as an "I" facing the Other, in a new light, since in Levinas's text, one is not actually inserted in the position of that "I" in the figure but is rather reflectively observing oneself as if one were an I looking face-to-face at another. In reflection, one will thus inevitably take up some position C_1 (see figure 3) over against one's "I" facing the Other, and one will necessarily place oneself at one remove from *being* that "I" who faces the Other.

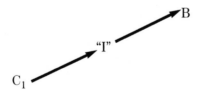

FIGURE 3

To be sure, Levinas has improved upon the reversible relationships (figure 1) conventionally prevalent in common sense and philosophy by uncovering the Other as the other appears, from a height, to the I facing the Other (figure 2), even though that facing relationship must necessarily be construed within a reflective framework still at some distance from the lived relationship (figure 3). That the facing relationship (figure 2) is being reflectively grasped in the same way that one reflectively grasps reversible relationships (figure 1) is shown by the introduction of the C-position in figure 3. But since this reflective grasp has improved upon the C-position of figure 1 that only conceives relationships as reversible, the C-position in figure 3 has been subscripted with the numeral 1. The reflective position of C_1 in figure 3 is thus distinct from and superior to that of C in figure 1.

This latest moment of Levinas's own self-reflection (diagrammed in figure 3), however, still threatens to bring the same and the other into the kind of correlation that Levinas has been at pains to avoid, and, as a result, he seeks once again to disrupt such a correlation in the passage immediately following that from *Totality and Infinity* cited above. In this new passage, Levinas points out that, although the discourse stated within his own book—"the said"—lays out the same and the other alongside of each other, the height of the Other is nevertheless preserved, or reasserts itself, insofar as his entire discourse is nevertheless addressed to the Other in a "saying" relationship that subtends the contents of the discourse itself.

> The formal synthesis of the word that names them together is already part of a discourse, that is, of a conjuncture of transcendence, breaking the totality. . . . And if I set forth, as in a final and absolute vision, the separation and transcendence which are the themes of this book, these relations, which I claim form the fabric of being itself, first come together in my discourse presently addressed to my interlocutors: inevitably across my idea of the Infinite the other faces me—hostile, friend, my master, my student.[20]

The height of the Other that is leveled out in the very reflective discourse that conveys it reappears in the fact that even that discourse is addressed to an Other.

Two consequences follow from Levinas's analysis. First of all, it would seem that the relationship between the I and the Other must ultimately be *lived* since the height of the Other to whom one relates seems inescapably deflated in *thought*. Levinas comments, "We know this relationship only in the measure that we effect it," and he insists that the face does not consist in figuring as a theme under one's gaze but rather in expressing itself, an event which "is not achieved by some sort of modification of the knowledge that thematizes, but precisely by 'thematization' turning into conversation." However, in *Otherwise*

Than Being, Levinas warns that there is a danger in a facile subsumption of the ethical relationship as a part of the bipolarity between the lived and the thematized, "to which Husserl's phenomenology has habituated us." This bipolarity in the end can tend to favor thematization, the reduction to theory of what is irreducible to theory, and a conflation of the intelligibility of an impersonal logos with intelligibility as proximity (that is, as the lived face to face).[21]

Secondly, Levinas's self-reflection on his own discourse reveals the limits of *any* and *every* discourse. For Levinas is well aware, even in *Totality and Infinity,* that philosophical discourse by its nature synthesizes diverse terms, brings them into a conjuncture, and locates them as parts of the same system, revealed synoptically and panoramically. As a result, Levinas asserts that it is impossible for a total reflection to do justice to the approach of the Other (since the Other's height will be deflated and the total reflection will be addressed to an Other, who, "emancipated from the theme that seemed a moment to hold him, forthwith contests the meaning I ascribe [to him]" and so fractures the total reflection). This impossibility of a total reflection, however, involves no negative impugning of the finite subject, but rather indicates the surplus of the social relationship itself.

> The impossibility of total reflection must not be posited negatively—as the finitude of a knowing subject who, being mortal and already engaged in the world, does not reach truth—but rather as the *surplus* of the social relation, where the subjectivity remains in face of . . . , in the straightforwardness of this welcome, and is not measured by truth. The social relation itself is not just another relation, one among so many others that can be produced in being, but is its ultimate event. The very utterance by which I state it and whose claim to truth, postulating a total reflection, refutes the unsurpassable character of the face-to-face relation, nonetheless confirms it by the very fact of stating this truth—of telling it to the Other. Multiplicity therefore implies an objectivity posited in the impossibility of total reflection, in the impossibility of conjoining the I and the non-I in a whole. This impossibility is not negative—which would be to still posit it by reference to the idea of truth contemplated. It results from the surplus of the epiphany of the other, who dominates from his height.[22]

In *Otherwise Than Being,* Levinas commences with this interplay between the stated discourse, "the said," and the relation to the Other underpinning that said, "the saying"—an interplay which culminates

Totality and Infinity's effort to protect alterity by spelling out the limits of reason. But certainly Derrida and Apel could respond that rational reflection itself gives an account of this saying and thus brings it under the canopy of the said. And yet here once again in his later work, Levinas asks just such a question of himself, namely, whether his very discussion, a thematizing, a synchronizing of terms, a recourse to systematic language, does not bring "back into the bosom of being all signification allegedly conceived beyond being."[23]

He answers first of all by indicating that the very contestation of the saying by the said implies that one has already recognized the difference between the said and the saying. In addition, Levinas highlights the time lapse between the statement that describes the asymmetries of the saying relationship and a later reflection that reflects on the conditions of that statement. This later reflection explains how this earlier statement regarding the asymmetries of the saying relationship in fact embraces them within its panoramic view and thus lays these asymmetries out "alongside of each other," synchronizing the diachronous and leveling out what is not to be leveled. As a result, the ("panoramizing") conditions of the earlier statement, discovered in a later reflection, are at odds with the saying relationship (and the asymmetries) that earlier statement intended to describe. But for Levinas, such a lapse also occurs in the case of skeptic who states his skepticism, which philosophy later refutes because the conditions of the skeptic's claim (namely, that it claims validity) are at odds with the claim itself. But the skeptic acts as if his or her skepticism and the later analysis of the conditions of its statement did not resound in the same time, as if philosophy synchronized what was not meant to be synchronized, because skepticism returns again and again and philosophy seems unable to repress it. In a similar way, the absorption of the saying within the said would always be subtended by a saying relationship in which that absorption is said, and that new saying relationship could subsequently be absorbed into a new said by a *later* philosophical reflection, but this reflection itself would be subtended by another saying relationship, and so on *ad infinitum*. The criticism that philosophy cannot escape enclosing the saying with the said ignores just these temporal discrepancies and above all the inability of the saying to be synchronized with the said.[24]

Reflections such as these evoke a final philosophical reflection on philosophy itself, which, being a manifestation of the said, inevitably betrays the saying. And yet philosophy can "reduce the betrayal of the saying in the said," as Levinas himself has done in his own philosophy, his own "said," which upholds the diachrony between saying and said and which differentiates the asymmetry of the same/other relationship from the symmetry of a reversible one (cf. figures 1–3). In line with Derrida's analysis, Levinas remains something of an empiricist insofar as he points to the saying which continually eludes the clutches of the said, which even in its moment of triumph over the saying must always be directed to another. Apel falters here insofar as he does not quite seem to understand the diachronous relationship between the said and saying, so intent is he on corralling the saying within the said. While Apel, following Husserl's lead in refusing to leave presuppositions unexamined or horizonal, begins with discourse and moves "upward" to illuminate its transcendental presuppositions, Levinas, no less Husserlian, heads "downward" toward the saying relationship "that obliges the entering into discourse" in the first place and that looms on the horizon of whatever is said in such a discourse, even when that said makes that saying itself its focus.[25]

The theme of the inability to integrate the saying with the said plays itself out in another key when it comes to temporality. Consciousness through memory gathers together the temporal dispersion of its past into a present, into a simultaneousness, and the historian recuperates all divergencies into a present in which nothing is lost and everything is presented and represented. Memory and history function like the said, bringing everything into a synchronous assemblage. However, whereas my memory starts from my present and returns to a prior present which it draws into the present it starts from, the ethical call of the Other, through which I find myself chosen before I choose, indebted before contracting for anything, at no point begins in the chosen my present, freedom, or choice. In contrast, my present, my freedom, my choice are always experienced in a setting where the Other's call has already made itself felt, and my action is thus always a response *after the fact* to that call, which always comes as a past always more past than my present. The linear, regressive movement of memory or historiography back along the temporal series toward a remote past could never reach the absolutely diachronous past which proceeds from the hither side of consciousness in the ethical mandate of the Other, by which consciousness finds itself already obliged. It is no wonder that Levinas describes the experience of the Other's command as resembling aging in which one loses time without recovering it. In other words, the Other's ethical plea pertains to the "untamable diachrony of non-historical, non-said time, which cannot be synchronized in a present by memory and historiography, where the present is but the trace of an immemorial past."[26]

Insofar as Levinas insists on a diachronous saying or an immemorial past refractory to synchrony in the said or the present of history and memory, he remains a kind of empiricist in line with Derrida's portrayal. However, in *Otherwise Than Being* Levinas cedes to Derrida that the saying must be given through a said that inevitably betrays it, that is, with the less than perfect means of philosophy. Similarly, Levinas grants that the immemorial past is given in the present, albeit through a trace that fails to inscribe that past within the present. In addition, in *Otherwise Than Being*, the Other is not presented as outside, in front of, or present *immediately* to the same, but rather as given in a *mediated* fashion—*within* the same. To convey this change, Levinas makes use of a new set of metaphors not found in *Totality and Infinity*, such as maternity (the Other's demands within the same), feeling too tight in one's skin (because of being called beyond it), or inspiration (recognized in the respiration it arouses). In order to express further how the ethical injunction is inside one before one even becomes conscious of it or how one becomes conscious of it always after it has completed its enjoining, Levinas reverts to Merleau-Ponty's notion of incarnation. One's bondedness to the Other is no more a decision of consciousness than is one's bondedness to one's body; rather, one's consciousness always emerges from out of a gray obscurity in which there is no clear separation between itself and its body and its relation to the other and in which such distinctions are always a subsequent product of reflection. By the way, this incarnational level at which the Other impacts the subject justifies situating Levinas's analyses at a pretheoretical level, on the soil out of which theory itself arises, on a plane analogous to the late Husserl's view of the life-world, at a pole counterpoised to Apel's transcendental examination of what theory already enacted must have presupposed.[27]

In order to emphasize the trace of the Other *in* the same, instead of presenting the Other as an unmediated datum, Levinas also resorts to the theological metaphor of creation, which in Genesis obeyed God's command before the creation was even there to hear the command. It is as if as the creation and the reader of the biblical account are so taken up with God's command that they are not aware, until later, that the conditions were not even in place for that command to be obeyed. Likewise, the Other's ethical demand so galvanizes one's response that only later does one reflectively recognize that demand in one's response. Although this rich creation imagery permits one to find the Other in the same, at the same time it does not reduce the Other to the same, since, like the creation, one also realizes later that the demand of the Other in no way depends upon one's own resources, as if one's free commitment or decision to contract with the Other lay at the origin of one's duties to the Other. Levinas repeatedly conveys this theme of the Other given in the same through diverse imagery, as when he speaks of how the Other's command is stated in the mouth of the one commanded or of how the Infinite (the human Other and/or the divine?) is not a theme but "passes" in the act of saying.[28]

Just as Apel's methodology involves pointing out the hidden presuppositions which diverse positions are reluctant to acknowledge, including what anyone who seriously argues already presupposes, so Levinas's attunement to the Other in the same will enable him to find the Other's ethical plea in the response, including the response of embarking upon a discourse with another. Since that plea comes from on high and commands asymmetrically, the equality between discourse partners already includes, often unrecognized by them, an ethical response to alterity and the inequality of its appeal.

This brief exposition of Levinas's critique of reason makes evident a project, begun in *Totality and Infinity* and continued in *Otherwise Than Being*, to think what is otherwise than being. Further, Levinas thinks what is otherwise than being without thinking of it as nonbeing, which would still belong to a system in common with being, as if it were being's dialectical other, as Hegel held. In thinking the otherwise than being through the saying/said distinction and his analysis of temporality, one also comes to see more clearly what stands opposed to the otherwise than being, namely, being itself. For Levinas, essence, *esse*, designates the process or event of being, as opposed to the static *ens*, and the work of essence, which "fills the said," is exposition, truth, and philosophy. In these activities, essence appears as a unity, univocal in all its appearances, which are absorbed in the intersection of their relationships and which do not retain any supplementary identity other than that which is due to the reference of each term to all the other terms. Essence absorbs every subject, encloses everything within itself, in such a way that "any radical non-assemblable diachrony would be excluded from meaning." Essence stretches on indefinitely without any possible halt or interruption—since any interruption would have to *be* in order to interrupt—without respite or any possible suspension. One can discover the spirit of essence in every effort to avoid disruption, to balance accounts, and maintain equality and equilibrium.[29]

This notion of essence, exhibited so clearly in philosophy, and perhaps in some of Apel's transcendental pragmatic strategies that show the reason at play in efforts to criticize reason, finds itself disequilibrated, however, in the ethical relationship with the Other.

> Essence, in its seriousness as *persistence in essence*, fills every interval of nothingness that would interrupt it. It is strict bookkeeping where nothing is lost nor created. Freedom is compromised in this balance of accounts in an order where responsibilities correspond exactly to liberties taken, where they compensate for them, where time relaxes and then is tightened again after having allowed a decision in the interval opened up. Freedom in the genuine sense can be only a contestation of this book-keeping by a gratuity. This gratuity could be the absolute *distraction* of a play without consequences, without traces or memories, of a pure pardon. Or, it could be responsibility for another and expiation.[30]

On the basis of this idea of a gratuity beyond book-keeping of essence, Levinas develops a novel notion of human solidarity that will be crucial to the discussion of affirmative action in the final two chapters. If one's sense of ethical responsibility begins with oneself, such that one is only accountable for what one does, one could wash one's hands of the faults and misfortunes that do not begin in one's own freedom or in one's present. But if the ethical relationship begins with the Other, one finds oneself responsible for the Other even if one is innocent and has done nothing—exactly the opposite to the thinking of Job and his friends who thought that "in a meaningful world one cannot be held to answer when one has not done anything." Thus, the ethical relationship dissolves the strict quid pro quo measuring characteristic of essentialist ways of proceeding. Furthermore, if because of the Other's weakness, failure, or evil, one is burdened with a certain suffering imposed "by-the-other," a reserve for one's egoism could open up since one could still pride oneself on one's innocence or resent this externally imposed suffering. However, for Levinas, the Other's ethical plea invites one to extirpate that egoism even more, to eliminate that reserve for one's egoism, by converting one's suffering "by-the-other" into suffering "for-the-other," that is, to look upon one's suffering as expiating for the other and substituting for the other and to refuse to distinguish any more one's being innocent from one's being accused—all one is is accused. As Levinas puts it, "The for-the-other keeps all the patience of undergoing imposed by the other."[31]

Since many of the institutions and cultural enterprises founded on the appearance of the Third, including philosophy and Apel's transcendental pragmatics, exhibit some of the behaviors typical of essence, that is, totalizing and filling in every interval, one might be tempted to devalue them or dispense with them. Such a depreciation would be foreign to Levinas's own purposes, for he is readily aware of the importance of dealing with the problems of adjudication that arise, not at the level of proximity, but only with the appearance of the Third. In commenting on the transition from proximity to the Third, Levinas asserts that "the extraordinary commitment of the other to the third party calls for control, a search for justice, society and the State, comparison and possession, thought and science, commerce and philosophy, and outside of anarchy, the search for a principle." If one has truly turned oneself outward toward the Other, one above all would take account of the Other's turning outward toward the Third, that is, of the Other's *extraordinary commitment* to the Third. It is as if Levinas envisions one as being guided by this example of the Other to care for the Third in such a way that one would be unable to escape the necessity of struggling on behalf of all, seeking equality, doing philosophy, and realizing institutional justice. Not to ascend to the level of the Third would be to violate the generosity and goodness generated in proximity.[32]

3. ETHICS ON TWO TIERS

Having established these two possible approaches to ethics, that of transcendental pragmatics and the phenomenology of alterity, I will seek to contrast them, point out their similarities, and seek to reconcile them while preserving their autonomy.

In a battle to secure their terrains, each against the other, Apel could rightly assert that Levinas's phenomenology, his books, are themselves forays into discourse, thereby presupposing the ineluctable structures of communication described in transcendental pragmatics. Similarly, Levinas could argue that Apel, in authoring his transcendental pragmatics, or anyone, in undertaking a discourse, in taking up a query and offering an account, has already paid heed to the Other's appeal which shows itself in the very solicitude of the reply. Furthermore, while Apel could claim that there would be no cognizance of the "saying" except through the said that presents it, Levinas might counter that even the said that presents the saying is always accompanied by a saying that ever eludes the said seeking to domesticate it.

Stark differences in methodology and starting points characterize these positions. Transcendental pragmatics, by spelling out the conditions that anyone who seriously argues presupposes, is in a position to justify or invalidate behaviors or philosophical positions performatively contradicting those conditions; but a project of justification or invalidation would seem all but impossible for a phenomenology of the Other, which prides itself on being anarchic, prior to, and critical of universalizable principles. While Apel must resort to a third-person account (i.e., from a position of C outside the lived relationship), as must any philosophical position that takes wing at the level of the Third, Levinas seeks to take his point of departure from the I, facing the Other. However much Levinas might be unable to avoid giving a third-person observer's account of how the world is given to that I, he struggles to burst the integument of the third-person perspective to reach the I whose lived relationship to the Other resists subsumption under a third-person theoretical stance. Although Apel's laudable emphasis on intersubjective adjudication of claims to truth makes room for phenomenological insight and although he must, as an heir to the Enlightenment, allow a space for autonomous, solitary, personal assessment of claims to validity as a moment in the search for truth, Levinas has uncovered a reserve in which there will always be a place for a first-person philosophy. For face to face with the Other in a solitude charged with responsibility and thus far from any selfish solipsism, one finds oneself elected and "unable to shirk," radically individualized by infinite responsibilities, incapable of mitigating obligations or exempting or excusing oneself by appealing to any principle or consensus. Nevertheless, the principles, consensuses, or consultations that Apel recommends can advance the kind of responsible self-criticism that enables one to be *really* at the service of the Other.

These divergences in levels, methods, first- and third-person perspectives, starting points, and strengths and weaknesses between transcendental pragmatics and the phenomenology of alterity ought not blind one to their similarities. Both views emphasize the importance of solidarity, of responsibility, one for the other, even though they vary regarding the bases of the solidarity. For Apel, solidarity arises in the self-reflection by which any discourse partner discovers the consistency of treatment due all discourse partners; for Levinas, solidarity commences in the exigency beginning with the Other that does not allow one to wash one's hands of faults and misfortunes that do not begin in one's own freedom. Both strive to include the excluded—Apel, because of the dynamism of reason seeking adequate solutions and the self-consistency required of any rational interlocutor who would not want to be excluded him- or herself, and Levinas, because any totality is always summoned from its exteriority.

Both standpoints foster a kind of philosophical fallibilism since discourse mandates continual testing and justification of one's position and since the Other never allows discourse to be "the unfolding of a prefabricated internal logic," but rather renders it always adventurous and uncertain. Paradoxically, in each case their fallibilism depends on unshakable premises: on the incontrovertible structure of discourse which even its opponents must employ or on descriptions of the alterity that abides persistently and irrecusably, like the eyes in the tomb that look at Cain, even when the Other is denied, explained away, or murdered.

One can find in both perspectives a style of reflection in the tradition of Platonic reminiscence, though Levinas at times rejects aspects of that tradition. Thus Apel reminds interlocutors of what they already know, that is, already have acknowledged, whenever they embark upon argumentation, and the later Levinas continually recalls respondents to the command discernible in their response. Both viewpoints synthesize intersubjectivity with an autonomous I, with Apel ceding a place to the I, which, for Levinas, is the departure point for alterity. These many convergences on significant matters suggest a compatibility between Apel and Levinas, even though the fissure between the level of the face to face and the Third, latent until Levinas elucidated it, highlights variances in methodology and perspective that cannot be eliminated. Because of their mutual concurrence on the central importance of ethics and human solidarity, it is doubtful that any other philosophy on the plane of the Third would be as compatible with Levinas's phenomenology of alterity as transcendental pragmatics or that any philosophical perspective born in the milieu of French postmodernism would be more appealing to transcendental pragmatics than the phenomenology of alterity.

A more systematic reconciliation is possible if one considers the phenomenology of alterity and transcendental pragmatics as part of a common phenomenological architectonic. Such an architectonic extends from the pretheoretical level of the face to face where, as Levinas expresses it, "I am bound to others before being tied to my body," to the post-theoretical, transcendental meta-level of the philosophical language-game unveiling the presuppositions implicit in other institutionalized language-games. Both outlooks manifest the Husserlian resolution not to leave horizons unexamined, and, following Husserl's pattern, elucidate presuppositions being made use of but not admitted, reflections on the character of one's own claims, and reasoning about the character of reasoning itself, especially one's own reasoning. Like Husserl, each exposes a hidden subjectivity, whether the ethical intersubjectivity latent within argumentation in Apel's case or the so easily obscured subjectivity of the Other in Levinas's.

The subtlety of self-reflection becomes most evident when Apel examines Habermas's central claims about discourse in *The Theory of Communicative Action* and finds that they are not merely reconstructive-empirical claims, but distinctive transcendental claims which even those who would dispute them must employ. Similarly, Levinas's self-reflective acumen is evident when he presents his phenomenology of alterity and then recognizes how his very presentation of alterity betrays the height that his phenomenology reveals. Insofar as Lyotard's interpretation of Levinas is accurate, there is also a careful self-reflexivity involved in differentiating the experiential attitude of one receiving a prescriptive from the Other and the theoretical attitude of one who delivers an opinion of whether the prescription is universalizable or not. While the addressee of the command feels its urgency, the commentator shifts from being an addressee to an addresser who "neutralizes the executive force of the order," as Lyotard has put it. Indeed, it is precisely these subtle shifts in attitude that Lyotard rightly educes from Levinas's own thought that lie at the root of the distinctions between the lived face to face and the reflexivity of the Third. Without sufficient attention to the distinctiveness of one's attitudinal stance—the hallmark of phenomenological method—one would not be even able to recognize these diverse strata.

Moreover, beyond the compatibility of these varying philosophical projects, there are ways in which each needs the other. The frequently heard objection to Levinas's thought, namely, that it promotes an uncritical heteronomy, indicates an area where Levinas needs Apel since it can be the case that the Other asks a response that would not be ethical and to assess the Other's request one may have to resort to ethical first principles. Such an objection to Levinas's thought overlooks Levinas's own comments on the need to be critical of the Other.

For Levinas himself acknowledges that "The ego can, in the name of this unlimited responsibility, be called upon to concern itself also with itself," and he agrees that the third party provides an "incessant correction" of the asymmetry of proximity. In these contexts and in others, Levinas clearly perceives the danger that would exist if there were only the anarchic level of the face to face, without the level of the Third, the level of principles. For Levinas, it is perfectly permissible to look upon oneself through the eyes of the Third, that is, to see oneself as a member of the universal kingdom of ends and as a person to whom others owe the respect that one holds for them. In some sense, the very idea of duties to oneself, owed by oneself and by others, involves a transference to oneself of the obligations experienced when facing others, as if one looks upon oneself as if one were an Other.[33]

Furthermore, since the unlimited responsibility for others prompts one to be concerned for oneself, it is a further step, but one fully consistent, to construe insistence upon one's dignity in a relationship with the Other as a part of one's responsibility to that Other. To allow the Other to abuse oneself or to take advantage of oneself is not to be of service to the Other; on the contrary, to hold the Other accountable for the Other's behavior is indeed part of assuming responsibility not only for the Other, but also for the Other's responsibility—as Levinas is accustomed to say. In the process of removing oneself from the inordinate, asymmetric demands of the face to face to inquire about what sorts of behaviors are not to be tolerated if the Other is to be held accountable—and here one takes up an attitude at one remove from that of receiving a prescriptive in order to assess whether the Other's prescriptive is valid—one will benefit from the discourses of justification and application that transcendental pragmatics has developed.[34]

Similarly, caricatures of transcendental pragmatics can portray it as a version of cold-hearted rationalism, out to convict the rest of the world of its irrationalism through "argumentation," with all the unpleasant connotations that that word carries in nonphilosophical contexts. Such comments, however, ignore the vulnerability that entering discourse requires of all its participants, who, as Apel notes, are not engaging in the equivalent of medieval "tournaments." In addition, as mentioned above, reason itself requires that the point of view of all to be affected be considered if the solutions it seeks are to be sufficiently comprehensive. Transcendental pragmatics is not devoid of its own Levinasian emphases.[35]

And yet, these arguments which begin with the character of reason and discourse itself and lead them toward the Other may perhaps run the risk that Levinas sees in the state, politics, and techniques insofar as they "are at every moment on the point of having center of gravitation in themselves, and weighing on their own account." In fact, if one commences with the intrinsic dynamism of rationality itself and its search for solutions, it is possible that one might remain ensconced within Lyotard's denotative attitude, in which one comments on and assesses previously experienced prescriptives, neutralizing their executive force, constantly assuming the position of addresser rather than addressee. Although one must adopt such a denotative frame of mind eventually in any rational discourse, an initial relaxing of one's guard, for which Levinas incessantly calls, in order to permit the entrance of the Other's questions, objections, or interpretations, more easily overlooked in the denotative posture, is more likely to enrich whatever judgments one finally arrives at. In addition, it would seem that this exposure to the Other would achieve its critical potential the less that one's motive for receptivity to the Other depends upon looking upon the Other as a source of missing data for the rational solution one seeks and the more that one places in abeyance one's own agenda and opens oneself to the Other for the Other's sake, because the Other asks for such an opening. Paradoxically, if highly self-critical transcendental pragmatics is to be fully self-critical, it would profit from such an ethical yielding to the Other—and yet such a yielding will not be as full as it could be if one yielding is too centripetally focused, concentrating on the enhancement of one's own self-critical capacity. Moreover, the critical potential of discourse may be more effectively realized to the extent one approaches the discourse that transcendental pragmatics recommends with a Levinasian slant, in order to be taught by the Other rather than to point out the Other's shortcomings, although the possibility of indicating such shortcomings can never be ruled out—for the Other's sake.[36]

This uneasy synthesis between transcendental pragmatics and the phenomenology of alterity within a common architectonic would not only enhance both its components, but would also provide a framework for better resolving problems and philosophical tensions, such as the one between the conflicting values of equality and alterity that have surfaced in the previous discussions of discrimination in its various forms. Jean-Paul Sartre, in his writings on anti-Semitism, racism, and homophobia, understood fully the need for impartial rationality to uphold equality and also for confrontation with the Look of the Other to escape any denial of alterity in the name of equality. For all his existentialist suspicion of practical rationality and any ethics of principles, Sartre, by recognizing violence as a refusal of the discursive in his *Cahiers pour une morale*, anticipated transcendental pragmatics, just as his account of the Look captured some of the ethical dimensions that come to the fore in Levinas's description of the face. Likewise Simone de Beauvoir, in her analysis of misogyny, relied upon the eidetic descriptions of *Being and Nothingness* and an idealization of reciprocal relations between equal freedoms, although she too was wary of the oppressive uses of essences and moral norms whose internalization inflict violence upon women. In a strikingly Levinasian move at the end of *The Second Sex*, she recommends generosity as the way out of the dilemmas of inequality and self-donation to cultural pursuits without self-conscious preoccupation for equality as the route to equality between the sexes. Alfred Schutz, too, anticipated transcendental pragmatics by his emphasis on intersubjectivity between co-performing subjectivities in the life-world who require intersubjective testing to attain adequacy in social and social-scientific understanding and to overcome the fragmentation and impediments to discourse that Schutz adeptly delineates. Schutz's very understanding of these obstacles to understanding keeps him mindful of the Other, given more cognitively than ethically, in Other-orientation.

But if the transcendental/alterity architectonic developed here is complex enough to accommodate the various concerns of the predecessors of Apel and Levinas, the proof of its value can also be shown in its ability to deal with one of the thorny ethical and epistemological questions of the day, where the currents of equality and alterity pointedly collide: affirmative action.

NOTES

1. Emmanuel Levinas, *Totality and Infinity: An Essay in Exteriority*, trans. Alphonso Lingis (The Hague, Boston, London: Martinus Nijhoff, 1979), p. 28.

2. Habermas supports just such a point when he argues that the presuppositions of the communicative practice of everyday life are at least partly identical with the presuppositions of argument as such in Jürgen Habermas, "Discourse Ethics: Notes on a Program of Philosophical Justification," in *Moral Consciousness and Communicative Action*, trans. Christian Lenhardt and Shierry Weber Nicholsen (Cambridge, Mass., and London: MIT Press, 1990), pp. 100–101.

3. Emmanuel Levinas, *The Theory of Intuition in Husserl's Phenome-nology*, trans. Andre Orianne (Evanston, Ill.: Northwestern University Press, 1973), pp. 4, 12, 26, 43, 44, 92, 94, 119, 131, 132, 155–56. Richard Cohen comments on how Levinas's critique of Husserl in that book is based on his reading of Heidegger; of course, the lived experience of being-in-the-world for Levinas would come to include ethical dimensions to which Heidegger did not pay sufficient attention. Cf. Richard Cohen, "Levinas, Rosenzweig and the Phenomenologies of Husserl and Heidegger," *Philosophy Today* 36 (1992): 165–78.

4. Levinas, *Totality and Infinity*, pp. 35–36, 73–77, 84, 100–101, 199, 200–201; see Emmanuel Levinas, *Otherwise Than Being, or Beyond Essence*, trans. Alphonso Lingis (The Hague, Boston, London: Martinus Nijhoff, 1981), pp. 83–85, 117; see Jean-François Lyotard, "Levinas's Logic," in *Face to Face with Levinas*, ed. Richard Cohen (Albany: State University of New York Press, 1986), pp. 125, 130, 139, 145, 151–52. In referring to the Other's destitution, there is no implication that the Other is only a passive victim. bell hooks rightly objects to presentations of the Other as a victim by pointing out that she belongs to the "'we' who inhabit marginal space that is not a site of domination but a place of resistance." Levinas's Other who is destitute is also critical, outspoken, placing in question the same and the totality. I have argued against those who would interpret Levinas's view of alterity as passivity. See *Ethical Hermeneutics: Rationality in Enrique Dussel's Philosophy of Liberation* (New York: Fordham University Press, 1998), pp. 116–24. See bell hooks, *Yearning: Race, Gender, and Cultural Politics* (Boston: South End Press, 1990), p. 152; for a criticism against Levinas's view of the Other as interpreted by Enrique Dussel, cf. Ofelia Schutte, "Origins and Tendencies of the Philosophy of Liberation in Latin American Thought: A Critique of Dussel's Ethics," *Philosophical Forum* 22 (1991): 280, 283, 288.

5. Levinas, *Totality and Infinity*, p. 40; Lyotard, "Levinas's Logic," pp. 123–29, 130, 139, 145, 147, 151–52.

6. Levinas, *Totality and Infinity*, pp. 36, 199.

7. Ibid., pp. 35–40.

8. Maurice Merleau-Ponty, *Phenomenology of Perception*, trans. Colin Smith (London: Routledge and Atlantic Highlands, N.J.: Humanities Press, 1962), pp. 62, 219.

9. Levinas, *Totality and Infinity*, pp. 53–60, 198–201, 218–19, 220–26, 245–47.

10. Ibid., pp. 29, 304. It should be noted that although Levinas is depicting the eidetic features of the *ethical* relationship with the Other, he is not implying that there are not other types of relationships with the Other. Indeed, the erotic and filial relationships described in section 4 of *Totality and Infinity* captures some of the modifications the ethical relationship undergoes in other contexts, but there is essentially an ethical dimension even to those relationships.

11. *Otherwise Than Being*, pp. 48, 50, 90, 96, 101; *Totality and Infinity*, pp. 23, 49, 207, 294; cf. Michael Barber, "The Vulnerability of Reason: The Philosophical Foundations of Emmanuel Levinas and K. O. Apel," in *The*

Prism of the Self: Philosophical Essays in Honor of Maurice Natanson, ed. Steven Galt Crowell (Dordrecht, Boston, London: Kluwer Academic Publishers, 1995), p. 97.

12. Levinas, *Totality and Infinity*, pp. 212–14.

13. Levinas, *Otherwise Than Being*, pp. 128, 157–61.

14. Levinas, *Totality and Infinity*, p. 214; *Otherwise Than Being*, pp. 128, 159.

15. Levinas, *Otherwise Than Being*, p. 158.

16. Levinas, *Totality and Infinity*, pp. 82–83.

17. Jacques Derrida, "Violence and Metaphysics, An Essay on the Thought of Emmanuel Levinas," in *Writing and Difference*, trans. Alan Bass (Chicago: University of Chicago Press, 1978), p. 151 (italics in original); see also pp. 109–53.

18. Ibid., pp. 109–53; Karl-Otto Apel, "Die Herausforderung der totalen Vernunftkritik und das Programm einer philosophischen Theorie der Rationalitätstypen," in *Concordia* (Frankfurt) 11 (1987): 19; Karl-Otto Apel, *Diskurs und Verantwortung: Das Problem des Übergangs zur postkonventionellen Moral* (Frankfurt am Main: Suhrkamp Verlag, 1988), p. 114. Robert Bernasconi cautions against reading "Violence and Metaphysics" as a critique instead of a "deconstruction" of *Totality and Infinity* in "The Trace of Levinas in Derrida" in *Derrida and Differance*, ed. David Wood and Robert Bernasconi (Evanston: Northwestern University Press, 1988), p. 18.

19. Levinas, *Totality and Infinity*, p. 80.

20. Ibid., p. 81; see also pp. 47, 195, 221, 295–96 where this dialectic between the saying and the said also is present.

21. Ibid., pp. 39–40, 51; Levinas, *Otherwise Than Being*, p. 167.

22. Levinas, *Totality and Infinity*, p. 221; see also pp. 39, 80, 290, 294.

23. Levinas, *Otherwise Than Being*, pp. 5, 155.

24. Ibid., pp. 156, 167–71.

25. Ibid., pp. 156, 162; Levinas, *Totality and Infinity*, p. 201.

26. Levinas, *Otherwise Than Being*, pp. 9–11, 51, 56, 57, 75, 87–89, 104–105, 133, 154.

27. Ibid., pp. 67, 76–77, 104, 106, 108, 111–12.

28. Ibid., pp. 12, 113, 116, 147–49, 150, 151–55.

29. Ibid., pp. 9, 30, 94–96, 134–35, 155, 158–59, 163, 187.

30. Ibid., p. 125. (Italics in original.)

31. Ibid., pp. 116, 122, 124–25.

32. Ibid., pp. 157, 161.

33. Ibid., pp. 128, 158.

34. Ibid., pp. 84, 117.

35. Apel, *Diskurs und Verantwortung*, p. 236.

36. Levinas, *Otherwise Than Being*, pp. 9 159; Lyotard, "Levinas's Logic," pp. 125, 130, 145.

7

THE TWO-TIERED ETHICS AND THE AFFIRMATIVE ACTION DEBATE

Definition, Equality, and Compensation

These next two chapters will attempt to show the relevance of the two-tiered ethics, developed in the last two chapters and emerging out of earlier discussions of prejudice, to the affirmative action debate. Affirmative action is a legal concept that has been developed through legislative, executive, and judicial activities since *Brown* v. *Board of Education of Topeka, Kansas* in 1954. Although this concept has played a significant role in decisions regarding education, admission to professional schools, hiring, promotions, layoffs, and many other areas, the following two chapters will discuss only the underlying principles of affirmative action (e.g., deontology, equality, compensation, etc.) rather than take up the myriad, intricate applications of these principles. In addition, these chapters will also try to bring to the surface many of the basic philosophical presuppositions underlying the debate on affirmative action (about equality, solidarity, the nature of the political realm, etc.). Given that many today consider affirmative action as a form of reverse discrimination and think it to be as unfair as the discrimination it seeks to correct, I will show how the ethical theory developed in the last two chapters would support a delimited approach to affirmative action as an *ethical* legal policy. Further questions about the legal and constitutional appropriateness of affirmative action, however, would require extensive considerations in the philosophy of law that lie beyond the scope of this book.

This chapter will begin by arguing that the debate has coalesced around certain deontological concerns that have served to delimit the meaning of affirmative action. It will then present an alternative notion of equality to the one usually used in arguments against affirmative action. This notion implies that one must take seriously the injury of systematic discrimination, which, in turn, calls for compensation—the most promising rubric for justifying affirmative action, in my opinion. The issue of affirmative action will serve as a catalyst for further reflections on the two-tiered ethics itself. The next chapter will take up the issue of whether affirmative action provides adequate compensation, chiefly by arguing against those who claim that it is inadequate and that it often introduces new injustices. Here it will be necessary to address the problems of over- and underinclusion, the type of causal reasoning used to warrant or oppose compensation, and the plight of those displaced by compensation.

Throughout these chapters, a mutual interplay will unfold between the transcendental and the pretheoretical levels of ethical theory, between transcendental pragmatics and the phenomenology of alterity. Due to the scarcity of space and the complexity of what is being attempted, I will be able to sketch only briefly how theoretical justifications for affirmative action on the basis of transcendental pragmatics might be developed. Also, I will concentrate on affirmative action with reference to African-Americans, whose history of being discriminated against warrants affirmative action on their behalf in exemplary fashion. Finally, although affirmative action functions in many of the practical areas mentioned above (e.g., layoffs, promotions), I will focus on affirmative action hiring practices, which have frequently been the theme of the philosophical debates.

1. DEONTOLOGY AND THE DEFINITION OF AFFIRMATIVE ACTION

While the gravity of past injustices seems to cry out for rectification through some such measure as affirmative action, Alan Goldman raises an ethical concern about those to be excluded by affirmative action from positions for which they were competent. Goldman argues that rational contractors would adopt a rule giving initial prima facie rights to positions to those who best qualify. Such contractors would recognize that to allow jobs or positions in professional schools to be awarded capriciously would flout one's right to compete with others, to be judged on the basis of one's performance, and to have the equal opportunity to acquire the goods attached as rewards to such jobs and positions. Although Thomas Nagel has questioned whether economic and social benefits ought to accrue to one simply because one possesses abilities and Judith Jarvis Thomson has disputed that competence alone entitles one to a job, Goldman rightly perceives that those competent for a job who are rejected for positions on other grounds than their ability are likely to have the sense that they have been excluded without warrant and thus to experience a kind of personal violation. Indeed, it is precisely this kind of personal violation that minorities themselves have experienced insofar they have been refused employment for which they were able on the basis of an irrelevant reason, namely, their race. In a sense, having acquired a competence that one brings to an employment opportunity and being rejected on grounds that have nothing to do with competence is much like not having one's claim to validity taken seriously in a discourse. Hence, Goldman claims that the harms that merit any compensatory hiring must be direct, clear, and measurable since another's deontological right, based in what all rational contractors would assent to and trumping any utilitarian purposes to which it might be sacrificed, is at stake. Although Goldman allows that in some cases someone at one time unjustly deprived of a job might later merit to be hired even if he or she has not maintained competency at the level of the present job occupants, he upholds the general principle that granting preference arbitrarily to the undeserving is not merely inefficient, it is unjust. So firmly committed is Goldman to hiring on the basis of competence that he states that one would never be able to charge that discrimination or reverse discrimination was involved as long as standard criteria are used in actual hiring decisions. Presumably, to prefer over other nonminority candidates a minority candidate who had demonstrated *equal* competence—the standard understanding of affirmative action—would not involve unjust reverse discrimination and so be permissible for Goldman.[1]

Others object to any arbitrary disregard of the competence requisite for positions, but without expressing as much concern for those who are competent but displaced, as Goldman does. These critics of affirmative action, such as Nathan Glazer, Barry Gross, and Ernest Van den Haag, bemoan the extent to which affirmative action candidates may have lacked the qualifications for the positions they receive in labor, business, or education. Robert Simon suggests that affirmative action hirings of those insufficiently competent could harm the very groups such hirings were supposed to help, as, for instance, in cases where an unqualified professor, hired under affirmative action, might provide a demoralizing example for the very students that professor was hired to inspire.

African-American authors such as Thomas Sowell and Stephen Carter criticize affirmative action when it entails the lowering of standards since it diminishes minority striving for excellence and fosters the false impression that minorities obtain important positions only because they belong to minority groups. Hence, Carter concludes that it is better to search for "the blacks among the best and not the best among the blacks." Goldman, too, contends that when standards are abridged because of a mistaken belief that all credentials are misleading or all tests biased, one effectively undercuts any reason for making required reforms in education and culture and further jeopardizes present minority efforts to acquire requisite skills. In all these cases, a program aimed at those previously excluded, if it neglects the importance of qualifications, can have the effect of marginalizing them all the more.[2]

In fairness to the initiators of affirmative action, however, it should be mentioned that they intended neither to exclude the competent nor to reduce standards of excellence. Affirmative action, according to Robert Drinan, was not designed to hire incompetent persons, but to rectify the fact that many among the qualified had been excluded on the same kinds of arbitrary grounds (e.g., racism) that the critics of affirmative action today abhor. In addition, the originating Health, Education and Welfare (HEW) guidelines for affirmative action required instead of "strong" reverse discrimination a "weak" version that stipulated that qualifications must be met first, in accord with Goldman's proposals. But, of course, the proponents of affirmative action, with their own eyes fixed on traditionally excluded groups, realized that more was needed *in addition to* competence if such formerly excluded groups were to be included, and abundant evidence exists that affirmative action did play a key role in securing placements for minorities that might not have been available to them before.[3]

Cornel West has provided a definition of affirmative action that takes account both of the possible exclusion of minorities that might result if nothing beyond competence were considered for hiring and of the dangers for both nonminorities and minorities that affirmative action programs present if they downplay the importance of ability. West points out that that job-hiring choices are made on reasons of merit *and* on "personal grounds," which can be influenced by racist perceptions. West then adds that the choice ought not to be between merit or race, but between merit influenced by race-bias against minorities or merit with a special consideration for traditionally excluded minorities and women. Hence, like Goldman, West upholds a notion of affirmative action that considers merit first, but that at a secondary level works against the exclusion of minorities and women that might result if competence were the only determinant. While West's definition still countenances preferences for competent women and minorities over white male competitors and entails therefore a kind of exclusion to be considered later, this exclusion is less irksome than one which neglects the importance of ability from the outset.[4]

West goes on to criticize conservative rhetoric about race-free hiring criteria since in the end he believes it would allow many discriminatory practices to remain intact. There is no doubt that he would include Sowell and Carter among the conservatives, even though in some respects the title "conservative" does not accurately apply since Sowell recommends potentially expensive educational programs to develop skills and habits and since Carter favors taxes particularly targeted for inner-city schools and war on poverty programs. In fact, Sowell's and Carter's opposition to affirmative action rests upon a theoretical perspective that places a premium on the self-critique of African-Americans who, they believe, need to establish themselves on their own, without special advantages. Carter exhibits this self-critical attitude, for example, when he addresses what many African-Americans consider to be an excessive scrutiny directed by the FBI and other policing agencies upon black elected officials. Instead of criticizing the excessive scrutiny, Carter responds, "if we really believe our enemies are using our leaders' behavior to hold us down, our practical solution must surely be to insist that our leaders be more pure than Caesar's wife."[5]

While such self-criticism on the part of African-Americans constitutes a laudable emphasis among black "conservatives," this criticism ought not blind one to the subtlety of anti-black prejudice and its long history or to the indifference to the plight of African-Americans outside the African-American community. West, who insists on competence and criticizes "black nihilism" like the conservatives, also shows himself aware of these factors extrinsic to the African-American community, as does a "liberal" like Derrick Bell, who, deeply pessimistic over the success of white racism in manipulating even the best of legal structures, has come to wonder whether legal remedies such as affirmative action are of any worth.[6]

The question of what exactly constitutes equal competence requires a much more thorough discussion than is possible here, but the spectrum of positions presented here do seem to converge in their recognition of the need for equal competence as at least a precondition for affirmative action. Those in favor of affirmative action seem fully aware that any deemphasis on competence will have deleterious results for the very groups affirmative action was meant to aid. For example, because of instances of misapplied affirmative action in the past, the present beneficiaries of affirmative action policies may have felt questioned by their peers in regard to their own competence, which, paradoxically, may have as a result been taken at times with as little seriousness as that of their predecessors who were refused hiring on the basis of skin color. West's definition of affirmative action, by allowing a central role for merit and yet providing for preferences after merit criteria have been met, thus addresses the concerns of both the critics and proponents of affirmative action.

This emphasis on merit seems to depend upon a kind of right to be taken seriously for what one has to offer, one's competencies—which is not to say that one has a right to be hired in a job. The right to be taken seriously for one's competencies parallels the right to be taken seriously in discourse, that is, to introduce questions and assertions, which deserve reasoned response and which ought not be overruled by any arbitrary internal or external coercion—which is not to say that one must be agreed with. No utilitarian telos, such as maintaining a discriminatory social order or, in contrast, eliminating prejudice from society, justifies inattention to this right to be taken seriously. Thus, by insisting that affirmative action beneficiaries be equally competent with those they displace, the competence and worthiness to be hired of those displaced is acknowledged. Their displacement is not a matter of a racial politics dispensing with competence or ignoring their worthiness to be hired. Rather, two people are equally competent for a position, and the need for compensation for a history of discrimination tips the scale in favor of one candidate, just as other factors than competence must when candidates are equally able.

The dual-layered ethics presented in the previous chapter is readily applicable to these issues. On the one hand, a justification of these rights to be taken seriously in discourse and in the pursuit of employment could appeal to the very presuppositions of discourse, even the discourse that might call such rights into question. On the other hand, it also seems to be the case that a Levinas-like concern or vigilance for the Other, the person excluded, neglected, or left out, has implicitly been operative in creating, limiting, and prolonging affirmative action. The referent of the expression the "Other in need of inclusion" seems to have undergone continual transmutation, at one moment designating those unhired in a discriminatory society; at another, those denied employment by affirmative action programs that did not take competence sufficiently into account; or at another, those whom a process of inclusion leaves excluded even in their being included because they are unfairly thought to be undeserving of the posts they attained. In the present, this Other in need of inclusion could designate those who might be left behind now if affirmative action were to be abolished *in toto* because of its past abuses.

2. EQUALITY

Perhaps one of the most troubling features of affirmative action for many is that by privileging minorities at the expense of majorities it seems to violate the essence of justice, namely, that one ought to act consistently and impartially toward all. In using criteria such as race or sex to tip the balance in hiring judgments regarding equal competitors, one seems to be engaging in the very kind of discrimination—now against white males—that produced the plight of racial minorities and women in the first place. As Barry Gross puts it, " . . . the very favoring of someone over another because of his race or sex is wrong. But if it was wrong before, why should we think it right now?" Similarly, Alan Goldman feels uneasy over the prospect of violating rights of those competent in the present so that competent minority-group members will not be denied rights in the future.[7]

Those who oppose affirmative action because it violates equality conceived as the consistent treatment of all, without privileging some on the basis of sex or race, provide a historical narrative regarding how the civil rights movement came to transgress the limits of equal opportunity, construed as "impartiality regarding race," in favor of the race-based privileges of affirmative action. According to Gross, the civil rights movement at first favored only a formal principle of equality of opportunity that never guaranteed substantive equality. Although this principle would guarantee that everyone has an equal chance to compete, they need not end up with roughly equal results or roughly equal shares of the world's goods. This principle never prescribed removing every sort of block to the equality of successful results. In the view of Sowell and Carl Cohen, Title VII of the Civil Rights Act of 1964 intended only this formal equal opportunity since its wording explicitly forbids any discrimination against whites. Subtly, via a series of administrative guidelines, executive orders, and court decisions, affirmative action, intent on substantive equality of results, came to replace the formal equality of opportunity that had banned hiring on the basis of any racial or sexual categories. The nondemocratic character of these policies is further evinced by the fact that, as Sowell observes, preferential policies have repeatedly been rejected in public opinion polls in the United States, although it is important to know how the questions in such polls were worded and to recognize that other polls indicate strong approval of affirmative action.[8]

Interestingly enough, the defenders of affirmative action suggest a competing narrative. Michel Rosenfeld remarks that in the wake of *Brown* v. *Board of Education* it became evident that, after centuries of official racial segregation, a mere return to color blindness through lifting of legal barriers or instituting voluntary measures did not lead to school integration. Hence, states had to resort to race-conscious remedies, including race-related assignments to particular schools. Similarly four of the justices in *Regents of the University of California* v. *Bakke* (1978) concluded that unequal needs and unequal conditions could permit equal protection to go beyond mere equality of treatment. In the light of this history, Rosenfeld concludes that the principle of equality of opportunity never existed as an end in itself but rather as a means to restore individuals' prospects to what they would have been had no social deprivation taken place. In other words, the inner dynamic of equal opportunity leads beyond mere formal equality, the refusal to employ any racial classifications, to positive measures making use of racial classifications to ensure a restoration of the victims of discrimination to actual equality of opportunity. To paraphrase Rosenfeld's point in Alfred Schutz's terms, affirmative action came into being after it was recognized that the struggle to attain *objective* equality of opportunity would not achieve its goal due to the severity of past injustices, unless government also acted to promote *subjective* equality of opportunity.[9]

Owen Fiss's account of the history of the remedies for discrimination parallels Rosenfeld's. According to Fiss, at first the state excluded African-Americans from public institutions until this exclusion occupied judicial attention in the late 1940s and the following decade. At this stage of the struggle to achieve civil rights, it would have been adequate for judges to interpret the Equal Protection Clause of the U.S. Constitution's Fourteenth Amendment via a mediating principle that Owens dubs the "anti-discrimination principle." This principle would allow the state to discriminate among persons only on the basis of a justifiable criterion (e.g., only those who pass a civil service examination are entitled to civil service positions). At the same time, it would prohibit the state from acting arbitrarily, as would occur if the criterion upon which it based its action were unrelated to its purpose (e.g., whiteness ought not be a criterion for civil service positions since whiteness is irrelevant to performance in such positions).[10]

While of particular appeal to mechanistic forms of jurisprudence willing to ask only whether means fit ends, the anti-discrimination principle has subsequently—and paradoxically—been used by some groups to justify bigoted policies. For instance, racially restrictive housing against blacks might be tolerated if there were also equal restrictions against whites in other areas, and, since both groups seem equally discriminated against, there would seem to be no discrimination at all. Similarly, one could argue that the state would not engage in any racial discrimination if it failed to withhold liquor licenses from clubs discriminating against African-Americans, since it was the clubs that practiced the racial discrimination and the state showed itself neutral in granting licenses to *all* clubs, whether they had discriminatory admissions policies or not. In either case, a veneer of equality and nondiscrimination is upheld, even though injury and exclusion is inflicted upon African-Americans. Fiss points out that these instances resemble cases in which "facially innocent criteria" are employed to conceal discriminatory ploys, as when a city claims that the costs of building a swimming pool are prohibitive as a disguise for its efforts to avoid desegregation. Fiss concludes that it is ultimately impossible to justify affirmative action on the basis of a reading of the Equal Protection Clause through the mediation of the anti-discrimination principle since affirmative action must use race or sex as a criterion even though it may not be directly related to the purpose to be achieved. Affirmative action discriminates—albeit for the sake of women and minorities and not like the discrimination that earlier excluded them—and so cannot pass the test of the anti-discrimination principle.[11]

Those who would rule out affirmative action because it violates such an anti-discrimination principle, like those who utilize facially innocent criteria for exclusionary purposes or those who laud only the "appearance" of nondiscrimination in state policies, often appear indifferent about the impact that such "nondiscriminatory" policies would have on the welfare of excluded racial or sexual groups. In contrast to just this unconcern, Fiss, convinced that anti-discrimination readings of the Equal Protection Clause will rule out affirmative action, returns to the original intent of the Equal Protection Clause, which was to safeguard African-Americans from hostile state action. He thus interprets the clause through a "group-disadvantaging principle" that would prohibit actions, such as covert racism disguised by facially innocent criteria, that would result in harm to a disadvantaged minority group. Positively, this group disadvantaging principle would endorse policies that attempt to improve the conditions of a disadvantaged group, such as affirmative action, even though it must discriminate in their favor on the basis of race or sex.[12]

The histories narrated by Rosenfeld and Fiss reveal a common pattern, namely, the failure of nondiscrimination to remedy the exclusion of groups disadvantaged by past discrimination and a subsequent turn to more aggressive affirmative action policies—a pattern reiterated in Harvard University's efforts to become integrated, according to former president Derek Bok.[13]

Fiss's turn to a group-disadvantaging principle, however, leaves the misimpression that affirmative action policies are not quite egalitarian. To defend the equality of affirmative action policies, Ronald Dworkin has articulated a new definition of equality that such policies actually embody. Dworkin distinguishes between *equal treatment* and the right to *treatment as an equal*. For instance, if there is only one dosage of a remedy left for two children suffering from a disease, one dying with it and the other only uncomfortable with it, they deserve not equal treatment but treatment as equals. That is, the interests of each have to be treated as fully and sympathetically as the other's. A fully sympathetic treatment, however, would involve giving the dosage to the dying child, while offering emotional support to the other child who is left in a more prolonged state of discomfort. In fact, it would be wrong to decide on equal treatment, such as flipping a coin between the two children, since the dying child has so much more to lose. In affirmative action and its preferential deployment of racial classifications—and Dworkin reminds us that their mere deployment is not forbidden by the Equal Protection Clause—special treatment for those injured by prior discrimination, with sympathy for whites displaced as a consequence, would represent treatment as equals even though it does not involve equal treatment. Dworkin finishes his discussion with the paradoxical statement, "We must take care not to use the Equal Protection Clause to cheat ourselves of equality." Similarly, the late Justice Harry A. Blackmun speaks paradoxically when he claims "in order to get beyond racism, we must first take race into account" and "in order to treat some persons equally, we must treat them differently." These paradoxes suggest that employing race-neutral principles such as nondiscrimination or superficial conceptions of equality ("treating everyone the same") can have the historically evidenced result of maintaining the unequal status of large segments of people damaged through previous discrimination.[14]

These diverse positions on affirmative action, presupposing diverse definitions of equality and accompanied by buttressing historical narratives, compete with each other at what Levinas has called the level of the Third, which calls for "comparison (e.g., of rights)," "measure (e.g., of the legitimacy of differing claims)," and the "copresence on an equal footing as before a court of justice." The opponents of affirmative action envision human relationships with the strict reversibility and reciprocity that for Levinas marks the level of the Third. Hence, for these adversaries of affirmative action, if one does not want racial or sexual categories to be used against oneself, one ought not use them against others. Moreover, the discrimination of affirmative action appears as inconsistent and wrong as the discrimination of the Jim Crow laws. The standard notions of impartiality and consistency employed here readily appeal to commonsense thinking and find their echo in the repeated commonsense rejection of affirmative action as promoting inequality and, therefore, appearing to be a less than moral policy.[15]

For Levinas, however, beneath this commonsense portrayal of relationships and its accompanying conception of equality, lies the experience of the "I" facing the Other, without being able to take up a third-person perspective from outside the face to face and without conceiving of the I and Other as reversible. As the "I" faces the Other, the Other commands from a height—a height Levinas regularly associates with the Other's suffering—a suffering that places in question the "I," its universalizations, ethical beliefs, and notions of equality insofar as these have not taken sufficient account of the Other's affliction. Ideas of equality ought not be detached from the welcoming of the face, for if they do, like the adjudicatory institutions of the state they might fall prey to "having their center of gravitation in themselves and weighing on their own account." When notions of equality are detached from the welcoming of the face, they readily appear to proceed from a war of all against all instead of from the irreducible responsibility of the one for all. However, when notions of equality are linked with the face, "the equality of all is borne by my inequality, the surplus of my duties over my rights."[16]

Thus, in attempting to discuss equality with reference to affirmative action, it is of crucial importance that one take account of the affliction of those who have been treated as Other through centuries of racial discrimination. This devastation that African-Americans have suffered calls for a type of rectification (and not necessarily the exaggerated goals of equal results or equal shares of the world's good that Gross imputes to affirmative action) and points to a need for careful reflection on the meaning of equality itself. Rosenfeld exhibits this thinking "back behind" the principle of equality when he explains how after *Brown* a guiding principle of color blindness proved insufficient to reinstate those formerly excluded and how remedies beyond mere formal equality of opportunity seemed called for. Similarly, Fiss's account of how one can deploy "facially innocent criteria" or an antidiscrimination reading of the Equal Protection Clause in order to justify an evasion of responsibility for disadvantaged groups penetrates beneath the abstract level of the Third to the need of the excluded Other discoverable in the face to face.

But what is happening when one confines oneself to the level of the Third, insisting on the centrality of principles such as that all ought to be provided only with formal equality of opportunity, that all should be treated the same, or that one ought never use classifications of sex or race in hiring, and so forth? Such principles can serve as armaments in the charged atmosphere of adversarial politics, and one can employ them with an aggressive argumentative style, ruthlessly hunting down an opponent's inconsistencies and contradictions. As Nietzsche saw, it is further possible to conceal the power dimensions at work in such argumentation by convincing others and even oneself that one is *only* being rational. Likewise, one's self-righteous outrage over what one takes to be violations of equality and fairness can confirm a sense of one's own virtue and purity of motivation. However, to the extent that one does not take sufficient account of the historical plight of those formerly excluded by discrimination and that exclusion's continued repercussions—at least as a component in the discussion—one runs the risk of simply defending principles for principles' sake. By taking such a stand on principles, one confines oneself to the level of Third without heeding the face to face out of which the Third arises and from which it undergoes questioning. Limiting oneself to the plane of the Third would be tantamount to flipping a coin when confronted with the two children in Dworkin's example. The Levinasian face to face supplies beneath the level of the Third a critical counterpoint that seems to have been implicitly guiding the defenders of affirmative action in their critical examination of commonly espoused principles and universalizations. Indeed, phenomenologists such as Sartre, Beauvoir, and Schutz displayed similar suspicions about generalizations on the nature of equality, even though they lacked the ethicotheoretical framework that Levinas affords.

Of course, it would only be a piece of totalizing violence on my part to assert that all those who oppose affirmative action on the level of principles are engaged merely in Nietzschean power struggles, concealing power motivations beneath a veneer of rationality and ethical self-righteousness. It is certainly conceivable that there are those opposing affirmative action who are thoroughly and sympathetically acquainted with the suffering of victims of centuries of discrimination, but who do not think that affirmative action is an appropriate and/or moral response to that suffering. In such a case, although both sides in the affirmative action debate might differ on the value of affirmative action as a means to rectifying and relieving suffering, they would at least be bound together in their common ethical concern for those who have suffered—they would in fact share the Levinasian foundation for which this book has been arguing. In the current antagonistic climate, recognition of such unity on such a fundamental level could play a great role in dissolving the antipathies and preparing the way for constructive solutions. Finally, however, the Levinasian perspective cannot convict opponents of their Nietzschean motivations; all it can do is present the appeal of the Other, who invites one to examine oneself.

Ethical principles at the level of the Third are not simply to be held suspect because of the face to face. For example, Dworkin's distinction between treating others equally or treating them as equals demonstrates that the face to face does not only function *antagonistically* toward the level of the Third. Rather, Dworkin takes the face to face as a hermeneutical starting point for *positively* rearticulating principles at the level of the Third. Thus, exposure to the unique need of the dying child, to the concrete circumstances of that child's predicament, subverts a principle of *equal treatment* even as it inspires the formulation of the new principle of *treatment as equals*. Similarly, in the case of affirmative action and in the face of the unique suffering of African-Americans, Dworkin dispenses with the principle of equality, interpreted as "everyone ought to be given *equal* (or the same) *treatment*," and formulates positively a new principle of equality demanding that each person ought to be treated *as an equal* in the sense that that his or her unique needs and circumstances (including injustices suffered) ought to be taken with the same seriousness as anyone else's. On the basis of this new conception of equality, reestablished at a deeper level, Dworkin recommends, as does Blackmun, that some people be treated differently than others. The argumentation of Rosenfeld and Fiss, too, by taking account of the face to face that inspires and informs their argumentation, model how principles can be developed via an interaction between the level of principles and that of the face to face—an interaction recommended at the end of the previous chapter.[17]

In addition, one could fashion a justification on the tier of transcendental pragmatics, at the level of the Third, for the results at which the defenders of affirmative action, such as Dworkin, arrive. For the affirmative action debate, itself a discourse, presupposes the structure of discourse that Apel has presented. While this structure of discourse implies an equality among discourse partners in their right to advance and question claims, this equality involves much more than each participant formally having an equal right to speak. For discourse itself, according to Apel, involves exchanging a monological approach for a dialogical one, allowing the Other to make in incursion in one's life, and thus taking seriously the Other's needs, claims, and arguments. As such, the equality constitutive of discourse according to Apel cannot be reduced to the merely formal reciprocity or reversibility that sometimes characterizes Levinas's description of the level of the Third. Hence if each discourse partner is equal in that his or her unique needs and unique sufferings are to be taken seriously, then it would be most probable that in a well-conducted discourse the differences between discourse partners would emerge *all the more* into prominence and one would more readily realize the differences in treatment required. Discourse thus provides a framework of equality that, in a sense, loosens up one's understanding of equality by compelling one to take cognizance of the diverse needs of those partaking in the discourse. As such, transcendental pragmatics would support the notion of equality through which Dworkin justifies the differences in treatment that affirmative action authorizes, namely, that persons ought to be treated not equally but as equals, that is, by having their unique needs and circumstances taken seriously and treated accordingly.

Although the dynamics of transcendental pragmatics spurs one to enter sympathetically into the experience of the Other, the affirmative action debate itself reveals the supplementation that a phenomenology of alterity offers for argumentation as such. For the debate itself illustrates dangers endemic to rationality: how easy it is to wrap oneself in one's rational and ethical principles, to highlight aggressively the seeming inconsistencies of counterpositions, and to use one's rationality as a weapon to deflect any criticisms, all the while, as Nietzsche would add, convinced of one's rationality and virtue. Rationality, then, depends upon an affective-ethical context, and it will do better when that context is characterized by the generosity and vulnerability which the Other invites rather than by indifference or aggression. Indeed, Apel's own description of dialogical versus monological rationality seems to draw on, without explicitly acknowledging, the need for such an affective-ethical context (e.g., "allowing the Other to make an incursion on one's life"). Suggesting that one overcome one's self-enclosure within rational defenses by striving to be more rational might end up reinforcing the very tendencies one needs to escape. By contrast, openness to what lies beyond the sphere of rationality, to the Other whose suffering calls upon one to rethink one's rational processes and universals, would enable one to proceed with the kind of flexibility and creativity to be found in rationality at its best. Levinas's emphasis on the Other's height is precisely the antidote correlative to the self-immurement and impregnability that rationality can easily foster. Of course, it is still true that some kind of rational appropriation of the insights the Other provokes is required, as the interactionist model between the Third and the face as well as the arguments of Rosenfeld, Fiss, and Dworkin all suggest. In fact, the appeal of the Other from outside rationality enhances rationality, sharpens its sensitivity to context, and thus, as it were, rises to meet the self-transcending trajectory that Apel finds internal to rationality itself.

To be sure, many questions remain. There is still the question of whether the unique sufferings minorities have undergone, which ought to be taken with equal seriousness, would call for the remedy of affirmative action. In other words, having discarded the old definition of equality (as equal treatment) for the new one (treatment as equals), how can one show positively that affirmative action is warranted? The first stage of that argument, developed in the next section, requires showing how the argument for compensation mediates between this new understanding of equality and affirmative action.

3. COMPENSATION

In his own discussion of compensation, Alan Goldman, as stated above, supports the competent individual's right to be hired against arbitrary denials of equal opportunity. However, when this distributive rule has been unjustly violated and when one's right to a position has been overridden by arbitrary factors (as discrimination did in the past), rational contractors would agree that one should be restored to the position one would have occupied, had the injustice not occurred. Goldman here articulates the common intuition that one deserves restitution when injured or robbed in proportion to that injury or theft. When one undertakes to treat African-Americans not equally but "as equals," that is, to take seriously their unique circumstances and sufferings, including the unique injustices they have suffered, one becomes aware of centuries of "pervasive and deeply rooted prejudice, negative stereotypes, demeaning treatment, and a constant stream of indignities experienced on a daily basis," and even state-supported discrimination that has deprived African-Americans of the equal opportunities available to others. In taking such systemically inflicted sufferings seriously, it seems entirely in accord with common intuition that African-Americans deserve to be compensated for what they have suffered, even if this implies that they will not be treated the same (equally) as others. The courts in their legal justifications have repeatedly conceived affirmative action as a mode of compensating this past injury. Thus, the concept of compensation serves as the bridge between the definition of equals (treating others as equals, i.e., in accord with what they have suffered) and affirmative action (which is intended to redress past injury). However, one cannot yet conclude that affirmative action affords *adequate* or *appropriate* compensation, and to determine whether it does so—the topic of the next chapter—requires facing a nest of questions that cast doubt upon the legitimacy of a compensation justification of affirmative action as a whole. Before turning to these questions, it is worthwhile to tarry a bit more over the significance of compensation itself.[18]

As Goldman continues his reflection upon the compensation due for job discrimination, he recommends a series of additional conditions delimiting such compensation. For instance, ideally the perpetrator of the injury, rather than others unrelated to his act of discrimination, is responsible for such restoration. Furthermore, since such preferential treatment to compensate for past injustice entails overriding the prima facie rights of others to compete for such positions, it remains of utmost importance to decide precisely who deserves to be compensated. This "backward-looking" scrutiny, associating as exactly as possible present remedies with past damages, makes compensation appear like punishment, even though, Goldman reminds us, legal practice generally distinguishes the two since the focus of compensation is the restoration of the victim and not the penalization of the perpetrator.[19]

The deontological rather than teleological grounds of Goldman's view emerge clearly when he insists that the positive intent of a policy is irrelevant if that policy violates rights to equal opportunity for a job. Since the rights of those competent for positions would trump any plan meant to achieve beneficial effects and utilities by means of a program of reverse discrimination, Goldman would doubtlessly prefer a compensation justification of affirmative action to present-day teleological justifications of affirmative action, such as that it increases the diversity of the work force. Moreover, Goldman would probably be wary of whether affirmative action directed toward groups might inevitably involve a teleological suspension of individual rights. In order to respond to Goldman's cautiousness on this point, the next chapter will turn to Michel Rosenfeld's explanation of group-regarding preferential treatment as a prerequisite for achieving deontologically based rights to equal opportunity for individuals. Rosenfeld's approach, as will be seen, provides a careful approach that by no means warrants the sacrifice of individual rights so that one race can better its position at the expense of another.[20]

There are various meanings of compensation and diverse exemplifications of it. For instance, Goldman frequently refers to the case of someone unfairly excluded from a labor position, and he also distinguishes other types of compensation depending on whether the harms involved were distributive or nondistributive in character. Rosenfeld, in turn, argues that the specific harms experienced by African-Americans warrant a kind of compensation irreducible to these other types. In order to account for the cross-generational aspects of affirmative action compensation arguments, Gross compares affirmative action to the situation of a son who would deserve compensation for his father's bicycle if another person has stolen that bicycle from his father in order to give that bicycle to that other person's child. These various examples suggest that compensation is first and foremost a *metaphor* capturing the common intuition that someone injured deserves rectification. But this metaphorical ideal of restitution, with which all the different positions might concur on an abstract level, needs to be rationally applied to the concrete case of the long history of institutionalized discrimination, and it needs to be shown that affirmative action constitutes a proper compensation for that history. This will be the theme of the next chapter.[21]

However, instead of applying compensation in the concrete, one can inquire into the ultimate justification of the metaphor of compensation. The abstract ideal that one ought to be paid back exactly in proportion to what one deserves also underlies retributivist theories of punishment, although one must constantly recall that compensation is not punishment. This abstract, metaphorical standard of restitution, underlying arguments for compensation and retributivist views of punishment, is usually associated with deontological theories such as Kant's. Such theories, out of respect for rational agency and the rational order of law and not for any utilitarian purpose, such as producing a happier society or deterring crimes, demand that any infringement of rights or law be restored to an equilibrium by compensatory action as proportional as possible (and hence rational) to the harm inflicted. Indeed, this respect for rational agency, which would refuse to allow that agency to be damaged without restoration, as if it were merely a thing or pawn at the service of the utilitarian pleasure of a transgressor, is the kind of respect called for between autonomous discourse partners according to transcendental pragmatics. Indeed the very discourse in which compensation is discussed furnishes the ultimate presuppositions of respect for rational agency to which any final justification of compensation could make its appeal.

While the transcendental tier of the two-tiered ethics developed in the last two chapters can serve to justify the ideal of compensation underpinning affirmative action, the notion of compensation can also be checked critically from the other end of the ethical spectrum, the phenomenology of alterity. From the perspective of alterity, compensation can often to be appear to result from a rigid, grudging, and ungenerous mode of thinking: one is not entitled to anything unless one can prove that one deserves it. An example of the illiberal extreme to which the compensation framework can be steered appears in the Supreme Court's decision in *Wygant* v. *Jackson Board of Education* (1986), in which the Court utilized the compensation framework to restrict the scope of affirmative action. In that case, the Court employed the most stringent standard, the "strict scrutiny" test, to ensure that classifications of race or sex were necessary to achieving the state's purposes. However, unlike earlier usages of strict scrutiny aimed at preventing discrimination against *minorities*, in *Wygant* the Court was concerned about discrimination against *whites*. In its decision, the Court ruled unconstitutional a voluntarily adopted plan that resulted in the layoffs of senior, tenured, nonminority teachers. That plan, in whose formation even those laid off had enjoyed full participation, was directed toward preserving the present balance of minority and nonminority teachers. Justice Powell's plurality opinion, in its first argument, which did not win majority assent and which was separate from a second argument that disputed the appropriateness of layoffs for achieving the school board's end, contended that in spite of past prejudices, insufficiently proven, the school board was not sufficiently responsible for past discrimination to justify its assumption of a duty of compensation. According to Powell, the board could not be singled out as the origin of past discrimination any more than other institutions and so should not be allowed to remedy the effects of societal discrimination through an affirmative action plan. *Where there was no evidence of wrong-doing, one could not even voluntarily assume responsibility for righting the effects of societal discrimination apparently because only the perpetrator should compensate.* The principle of compensation here leads to the paradoxical conclusion that if one has done no wrong, one is not even permitted to be responsible.[22]

The approach to the Other underlying such a position is utterly at odds with the Levinasian conception of human solidarity, which *Otherwise Than Being* presents as a contrast to a view beginning with one's self in which one "is only for-himself, and washes his hands of the faults and misfortunes that do not begin in his own freedom or in his present." Such a refusal of responsibility for the Other finds an echo in the frequently heard commonsense argument against affirmative action that because in one's *present* lifetime one never participated in the institution of slavery one owes nothing to its present or past victims. It is as if one were to say, "If I have done nothing against you, I owe you nothing; and conversely if there is anything in you that deserves my response it is only because of something wrong that I have done to you in the first place." How similar is such a view to that of Job's false friends who believe that "in a meaningful world one cannot be held to answer when one has not done anything" and how distant is this view from Levinas's "I have not done anything and I have always been under accusation."[23]

But how has the compensatory framework come to such a position of nonsolidarity? Could such an outcome be the result of its starting point, at least as articulated by Goldman, that is, in a conception of rights, particularly the negative right not to be interfered with by extraneous, arbitrary forces as one pursues the employment for which one is qualified? Does not a theory of negative rights quintessentially commence with oneself and not the Other, who is perceived as a threat to oneself? It is perhaps no wonder that a theory of the state correlative to such a theory of negative rights generally traces its origin to Hobbes's portrayal of the war of all against all or to Locke's mistrust of arbitrary, absolute monarchs, rather than to a Levinasian irreducible responsibility of the one for all? In the first argument in the plurality opinion in *Wygant*, does not Justice Powell's view lack solidarity, as if it were the precipitate of an underlying notion of intersubjectivity based upon allergy toward the Other instead of responsibility for the Other?

And yet in Goldman's contractarian-deontological solicitude, which has its roots in the procupations of Hobbes and Locke, one can glimpse at the same time a possible vigilance on behalf of the excluded Other, whom Levinas describes as offering ethical resistance to the totality threatening to engulf him or her. In Goldman's liberal-contractarian defense of the competent person who could be rejected from a job on capricious grounds or for utilitarian goals, he manifests a concern for the Other who can be cast aside for the purposes of a more encompassing statist totality, in some ways not all that different from the socialist's preoccupation for the poor on the fringes of the capitalist totality. Whether one proposes a contractarian, negative rights-based liberal theory or a socialist theory, it is possible that these theories at the level of the Third can proceed from an underlying solidarity on behalf of the Other, concerned at their origin more for the Other than the self. Furthermore, even the compensation metaphor itself functions ambiguously since at the level of the Third, the level of principles, it can be used, on the one hand, to include those injured by societal discrimination (without arbitrarily running over the nonpreferred) or, on the other hand, to excuse oneself from responsibility for the Other because one has done nothing wrong. Thus it would seem that Levinas's ethics provides one with a diagnostic perspective for assessing theories as either being in solidarity or lacking it.

The danger to solidarity may lie, though, in the nature of theorizing activity itself. For the very pursuit of theory involves a prescinding from the face to face, a turning from a first-person "I" facing the Other and receptive to the Other's prescriptives to a third-person attitude—taking the other's "prescriptive" as a "denotative," as an imperative to be commented upon or reasoned about and thereby depriving such an imperative of all its executive force. In theorizing, one shifts from being the addressee of a prescriptive to being an addresser directing the claims one elaborates to others. In spite of the benefits of theorizing that Levinas acknowledges, such as correcting asymmetry, developing universal norms, and prescribing duties to self, the theoretical stance inevitably withdraws one from the face to face and sets one on a track where it becomes more possible to forget the Other. The very act of theorizing opens up a space where, unless one is vigilant, an orientation lacking in solidarity and beginning with oneself can subtly slip into one's discourse and replace the Other-orientation from which the theoretician, seeking to respond to a query, must have already embarked. Theorizers who have forgotten the Other and who make themselves their theoretical point of departure place an even greater distance between themselves and the Other since theory by itself is already once removed from the face, although it is still neutral enough to be put itself at the service of the Other, as the writings of Fiss, Rosenfeld, and Dworkin show. Thus, Levinas's thought suggests that notions of equality and rights hammered out within neutral theoretical frameworks depend upon more fundamental orientations commencing either with the I or the Other. The impartiality and impersonality that one supposes to characterize one's discursive activity at the level of the third can actually conceal from oneself and others the underlying personal orientation that one has in fact adopted. Beneath the third person, there is a first person who is or is not responsive to the Other.[24]

Below the theoretical stratum, on which the affirmative action debate occurs, on which justifications are offered, and on which competing rights are weighed, one finds oneself at the primordial level of the face to face to be no longer an anonymous "anyone" or "everyone," but an "I," facing an Other and invited into responsibility for that Other. There, I, the author, find myself, a white male, facing women and minorities, who summon me to responsibility. As a white male favoring carefully delineated affirmative action, I also find myself facing the non-preferred white male, who, due to affirmative action, will be at least temporarily left out of the totality to which I belong: those established in an occupation and career. At this first moment, pulled in several directions at once because of responsibilities to diverse constituencies, I must revert to a theoretical level to weigh these conflicting demands that cannot be simultaneously satisfied. On this level of the Third, where one right is pitted against another and one type of otherness against another, one must form one's own judgment. On this plane, one discovers reasons as to why the unique circumstances and affliction of minorities and women deserve compensation, why this compensation can be fittingly achieved through affirmative action, and why the rights of minorities and women to compensation outweigh the right of an equally competent white male to be considered for a position on the basis of his merits alone. But when affirmative action displaces white males, one does not forget the face to face since such displacement ought not to be undertaken lightly, but rather with a sense of regret and concern. The face of the Other that requires one to deliberate in the first place, remains present throughout the course of deliberation and is not to be forgotten even after the final judgments are reached.

At the discursive level, the conflict between competing needs and rights, such as those that surface in the affirmative action debate about compensation, can become so absorbing that one can forget that the very arguments about compensation emerge in an effort to circumscribe the demands issuing from the level of the face to face. Compensation questions break out on a ground where one finds oneself pressed by appeals to distribute goods more fairly—for instance, from those who claim that their competence entitles them to a fair hearing for a job and from those whose past mistreatment entitles them to a recompense, namely, affirmative action hiring in jobs for which they are competent. Hence, one cannot too easily set the compensatory character of affirmative action against its distributive aspects since it represents a mechanism for arbitrating among a surplus of distributive demands that are already there, exerting their influence. The seemingly restrictive character of compensation arguments grows out of the excessive generosity engendered by the face of the Other and several Others. Caught up in the vertigo of discourse, one is liable to overlook that even the discourse itself, the necessity of choosing and adjudicating, grew out of a more primordial and more encompassing atmosphere of responsibility for the Other *and Others.*

Furthermore, when one is impelled to choose between groups and so must theoretically differentiate, weigh, and hierarchize the needs and desires of competitors, one is tempted to fashion air-tight arguments, definitive proofs, that will silence any further contestations from those who will be inevitably excluded—whether white males or women or minorities. In some sense, our very defensiveness about whatever judgments our community reaches reflects how the Other, that is, the one who might "lose" as a result of our community's decision, still has a hold on us, even though our decisions may be perfectly justifiable. The face to face, then, never allows us to forget or close off the Other whom our theoretical choices will consign to second or last place; the Other continually haunts the theoretical and political choices we and our community could not avoid making and challenges any ideological foreclosures of continued discourse. Since the political-theoretical discourse aims at choices which will frequently designate losers, the fact that such discourse arises against the backdrop of the face to face, the responsibility of the one for all, implies that there always ought to be a moment of tragedy and regret accompanying the exercise of such political decisions.[25] Choices have to be made, just as violence may need to be deployed to uphold a social order guaranteeing deontologically founded rights; but in sight of the face to face, neither ought to occur with triumphalism or without the wish that things might have been otherwise, that all needs could have been satisfied, and that violence might have been avoided.

The phenomenological recapturing of the face to face subverts the narrow perspective of theory itself by revealing its presuppositions. Phenomenology in a Levinasian key brings to light the wider horizon of our bonds, duties, and responsibilities to Other to whom we can never do sufficient justice—a horizon of which theorizers striving to make the right distinctions and fair judgments can easily lose sight. Whatever tendencies against solidarity are to be found in theory only spring up in response to the more encompassing solidarity of the face. To view political decision making on the plane of the Third through the prism of the phenomenology of alterity is to affect a kind of Copernican revolution in one's understanding of politics.[26]

NOTES

1. Goldman permits the right to equal opportunity for a position to be overridden where it can be clearly demonstrated that an individual was unjustly excluded due to past discrimination, even though that individual may not be as competent as those presently occupying that position. Alan H. Goldman, *Justice and Reverse Discrimination* (Princeton, N.J.: Princeton University Press, 1979), pp. 24–34, 65-67, 124–27, 207; Thomas Nagel, "Equal Treatment and Compensatory Discrimination," in *Equality and Preferential Treatment: A Philosophy & Public Affairs Reader*, ed. Marshall Cohen, Thomas Nagel, and Thomas Scanlon (Princeton, N.J.: Princeton University

Press, 1977), p. 9; Judith Jarvis Thomson, "Preferential Hiring," in *Equality and Preferential Treatment*, pp. 24–39.

2. Nathan Glazer, *Affirmative Discrimination: Ethnic Inequality and Public Policy* (Cambridge, Mass., and London: Harvard University Press, 1987), pp. 96, 169; Barry R. Gross, *Discrimination in Reverse: Is Turnabout Fair Play?* (New York: New York University Press, 1978), pp. 117–19; Ernest Van den Haag, "Jews and Negroes," in *Racial Preference and Racial Justice: The New Affirmative Action Controversy*, ed. Russell Nieli (Washington, D.C.: Ethics and Public Policy Center, 1991), pp. 388–89; George Sher, "Justifying Reverse Discrimination in Employment," in *Equality and Preferential Treatment*, pp. 53–54; Robert Simon, "Preferential Hiring: A Reply to Judith Jarvis Thomson," in *Equality and Preferential Treatment*, pp. 47–48; Stephen Carter, *Reflections of an Affirmative Action Baby* (New York: Basic Books, 1991), pp. 16, 50–51, 54, 66-67; Thomas Sowell, *Preferential Policies: An International Perspective* (New York: William Morrow and Company, Inc., 1990), pp. 162, 184; Goldman, *Justice and Reverse Discrimination*, pp. 60, 62.

3. Robert Drinan, "Affirmative Action under Attack," in *Racial Preference and Racial Justice*, p. 121; Goldman, *Justice and Reverse Discrimination*, p. 215.

4. Cornel West, *Race Matters* (New York: Vintage Books, 1994), pp. 78–79.

5. Carter, *Reflections of an Affirmative Action Baby*, pp. 83–84, 142–52, 224; Sowell, *Preferential Policies*, p. 182.

6. West, *Race Matters*, p. 79; Derrick Bell, *Faces at the Bottom of the Well: The Permanence of Racism* (New York: Basic Books, 1992), pp. 1–14, 47–64. Bell proposes a racial preference licensing act that would tax those who wish to practice overt discrimination since such discriminators have already devised all kinds of subtleties to evade civil rights legislation, but no benefits for society result from these evasions. It should also be noted that Cornel West himself is by no means uncritical of the African-American community, as is evident in his essay "Nihilism in Black America" in *Race Matters*, pp. 15–31. See Simon, "Preferential Hiring: A Reply to Judith Jarvis Thomson," pp. 41–43, 46–47; Thomson, "Preferential Hiring," pp. 35–37; Goldman, *Justice and Reverse Discrimination*, pp. 6–7; Thomas Sowell, *Civil Rights: Rhetoric or Reality?* (New York: William Morrow and Company, Inc., 1984), pp. 34, 50, 52, 64, 84, 133; Randalll Kennedy, "Persuasion and Distrust," in *Racial Preference and Racial Justice: The New Affirmative Action Controversy*, p. 52; Sowell, *Preferential Policies*, pp. 15, 170; Gross, *Discrimination in Reverse: Is Turnabout Fair Play?* pp. 76, 128, 131; Jonathan Leonard, "The Impact of Affirmative Action on Employment," in *Racial Preference and Racial Justice: The New Affirmative Action Controversy*, p. 498; James P. Smith and Finis R. Welch, "Closing the Gap: Forty Years of Economic Progress for Blacks," in *Racial Preference and Racial Justice: The New Affirmative Action Controversy*, p. 508.

In arguing against the effectiveness of affirmative action, Sowell himself notes that black high school dropouts made 79 percent of what whites made in 1967 and it fell to 69 percent by 1978 during the heyday of affirmative action. However, the income of black workers with college and six years work experience—those at whom affirmative action was targeted as opposed to high school dropouts—rose from 75 percent to 98 percent of that of whites from 1967 to 1978 (Sowell, *Civil Rights: Rhetoric or Reality?* p. 52). Sowell mentions further that the trend of black advancement preceded the Civil Rights Act of 1964, with the number of blacks in professions and technical careers doubling in the decade before 1964. According to Sowell, the Civil Rights Act and quotas did not accelerate this trend; and the disadvantaged retrogressed relative to whites while more advantaged blacks rose absolutely and relative to whites (Sowell, *Civil Rights: Rhetoric or Reality?* pp. 84, 133). To be sure, the large scale movement of industry to the South, where more than 50 percent of the black population lives, and governmentally supplied education played a role in the Southern growth of black status before Civil Rights legislation. These facts may have contributed to improved trends for blacks prior to 1964, as James J. Heckman suggests ("The Impact of Government on the Economic Status of Black Americans," in *The Question of Discrimination: Racial Inequality in the U.S. Labor Market*, ed. by Steven Schulman and William Darity, Jr. [Middletown, Conn.: Wesleyan University Press, 1989], pp. 70–73, 78). But of course trends can rise quite quickly when one's starting point is low. In different settings, at a later time, after movements of industry and increased education have had their effects, when surviving discrimination or simply stubborn inflexible hiring patterns might still inhibit black employment, it is highly plausible that affirmative action plays an important role, too, as the following data will suggest.

Heckman himself is quick to affirm that government activity has not been unimportant, even if it is not the exclusive remedy (ibid., p. 78). According to U.S. Bureau of Labor Statistics cited by John Work in *Race, Economics, and Corporate America*, blacks increased their percentages among managers and administrators at a higher rate during the 1965–1977 period than during the 1959–1965 period (John Work, *Race, Economics, and Corporate America*, [Wilmington, Del.: Scholarly Resources, Inc., 1984], p. 52). Work also cites several articles in the *American Economic Review* and elsewhere supporting the general consensus that Title VII of the 1964 Civil Rights Act and the subsequent Executive Order defining affirmative action have had positive impacts on the general employment status of black Americans (ibid., p. 51). Charles Brown's article, "The Federal Attack on Labor Market Discrimination: The Mouse That Roared?" *Research in Labor Economics* 5 (1982): 33–68, reviewed various studies and supported the view that pressures from the EEOC and President Lyndon Johnson's Revised Order No. 4 to Executive Order 112466 requiring government contractors to take affirmative action helped account for the improvement in black incomes and the movement of young educated blacks into the mainstream of the American economy that characterized the period from the 1965 to the mid-1970s. John Bound and Richard B. Freeman attribute the worsening of the relative economic position of black men from the late 1970s to the mid 1980s in part to slackened governmental affirmative action and antibias efforts in John Bound and Richard B. Freeman, "Black Economic Progress: Erosion of the Post-1965 Gains in the 1980's," in *The Question of Discrimination: Racial Inequality in the U.S. Labor Market*, pp. 32–33; Heidi Hartmann from the Joint Center for Political and Economic Studies argues that the weak enforcement efforts of the federal contract compliance program and Title VII of the Civil Rights Act have had modest effects in helping women and minorities, and she states that finding a significant effect at all should be taken "as a powerful indicator of the value of these laws and regulations" (Heidi Hartmann, "Who Has Benefited from Affirmative Action in Employment?" in *The Affirmative Action Debate*, ed. George E. Curry [Reading, Mass.: Addison-Wesley Publishing Company, Inc., 1996], pp. 91–92).

7. Gross, *Discrimination in Reverse: Is Turnabout Fair Play?* p. 102; see also pp. 127, 130; Goldman, *Justice and Reverse Discrimination*, p. 194.

8. Gross, *Discrimination in Reverse: Is Turnabout Fair Play?* p. 106; Carl Cohen, "Justice Debased," in *Racial Preference and Racial Justice: The New Affirmative Action Controversy*, pp. 329–36; Sowell, *Civil Rights: Rhetoric or Reality?* pp. 40–42; Glazer, *Affirmative Discrimination: Ethnic Inequality and Public Policy*, pp. 43–58; Sowell, *Preferential Policies*, p. 165. A recent *USA Today*/CNN/Gallup poll of March 17–19, 1995, indicated in response to "Do you favor or oppose affirmative action programs?" that 53 percent of whites expressed support with only 36 percent opposed and 72 percent of African-Americans were in favor with only 21 percent against. See Manning Marable, "Staying on the Path to Racial Equality," in *The Affirmative Action Debate*, p. 8. Renowned professional pollster Louis Harris discusses the kinds of questions asked and asserts that every poll that has simply asked whether people favor or oppose affirmative action without strict quotas has favored affirmative action, with the percentages ranging between 55 percent and 60 percent in favor. See "The Future of Affirmative Action," in *The Affirmative Action Debate*, p. 326.

9. Michel Rosenfeld, *Affirmative Action and Justice: A Philosophical and Constitutional Inquiry* (New Haven and London: Yale University Press, 1991), pp. 160–63, 170, 296, 308, 331.

10. Owen M. Fiss, "Groups and the Equal Protection Clause," in *Equality and Preferential Treatment*, pp. 83–94.

11. Ibid., pp. 95–123.

12. Ibid., pp. 124–44, 147–48.

13. Derek Bok, "Admitting Success," in *Racial Preference and Racial Justice: The New Affirmative Action Controversy*, p. 412.

14. Ronald Dworkin, "DeFunis v. Sweatt," in *Equality and Preferential Treatment*, pp. 66–70, 83; Blackmun is cited in Randall Kennedy, "Persuasion and Distrust," in *Racial Preference and Racial Justice: The New Affirmative Action Controversy*, p. 47; Justice Blackmun's actual quotation is to be found

in *University of California* v. *Bakke*, in *West's Supreme Court Reporter* 98A (St. Paul, Minn.: West Publishing Co., 1980), 2807.

15. Emmanuel Levinas, *Otherwise Than Being, or Beyond Essence*, trans. Alphonso Lingis (The Hague, Boston, London: Martinus Nijhoff, 1981), pp. 157, 193, 196; Emmanuel Levinas, *Totality and Infinity: An Essay in Exteriority*, trans. Alphonso Lingis (The Hague, Boston, London: Martinus Nijhoff, 1979), pp. 35–40.

16. Levinas, *Otherwise Than Being*, p. 159; *Totality and Infinity*, pp. 212–14.

17. This idea of an interaction between the levels of the face to face and the Third would require much more elaboration than can be given here. How does one assess one's principles in the light of the face and the demands of the Other in the light of principles? Are there certain mediating principles between these levels? How does one know whether one should revise one's principles or challenge the Other's demands, or engage in apology (self-defense) in Levinas's terms? The problematic itself suggests the existence of the two levels and the two levels explain the kinds of theoretical adjustments that Rosenfeld, Fiss, or Dworkin have made. This does not mean that all the dimensions of this complex problematic have been worked out.

18. Goldman, *Justice and Reverse Discrimination*, pp. 65–70; Rosenfeld, *Affirmative Action and Justice*, p. 291.

19. Goldman, *Justice and Reverse Discrimination*, p. 70–76.

20. Ibid., pp. 119, 169, 207. However, if one requires, as does Cornel West, that affirmative action be set in motion after minority and women candidates have established that their equal competence merits a job, then it would seem that no one's rights to a job would be overridden, as Goldman himself acknowledges. Judith Jarvis Thomson argues that rights can be overridden to attain a greater benefit, even though her own argument in favor of affirmative action seems to be in a deontological vein, weighting the rights of victims of discrimination over the rights of white males to a job. Thomson also supports parity of competence, although she thinks such parity is not so easily established. Thompson, "Preferential Hiring," pp. 20–22, 32–36; Rosenfeld, *Affirmative Action and Justice*, pp. 191–92, 296–304.

21. Goldman, *Justice and Reverse Discrimination*, pp. 76–94; Gross, *Discrimination in Reverse: Is Turnabout Fair Play?* pp. 44–47; Rosenfeld, *Affirmative Action and Justice*, pp. 284–96. Our effort here involves trying to develop an argument that captures the compensatory dimension of affirmative action by avoiding the mistakes in the reconstructions of compensatory argument (Gross, *Discrimination in Reverse: Is Turnabout Fair Play?* pp. 33–49) that Gross produces and criticizes. It is unclear, for instance, why premises of compensation arguments should only be directed to the past and not be able to affect the present (Gross, *Discrimination in Reverse: Is Turnabout Fair Play?* p. 35), merely because Gross's organization of types of arguments separates the past from the present. There is not time here to consider in depth all Gross's arguments against the various kinds of arguments supporting affirmative action. One can find fault with his reconstructed argu-

ments, as he himself does, but the argument sketched here lacks the objectionable features of these reconstructed arguments. Gross's method seems somewhat arbitrary—to reconstruct arguments that one thinks others are making and then demolish those arguments oneself.

22. *West's Supreme Court Recorder*, Vol. 106A (St. Paul, Minn.: West Publishing Company, 1989), 1848–52, 1853–56, 1867; Rosenfeld, *Affirmative Action and Justice*, pp. 116, 151–52, 178–80; Sandra Day O'Connor, "Set-Asides Violate the Equal Protection Clause," in *Racial Preference and Racial Justice: The New Affirmative Action Controversy*, pp. 263–64.

23. Levinas, *Otherwise Than Being*, pp. 114, 116, 122, 157, 159.

24. Ibid., pp. 128, 158; Jean-François Lyotard, "Levinas's Logic," in *Face to Face with Levinas*, ed. Richard Cohen (Albany: State University of New York Press, 1986), pp. 125, 130, 145.

25. Lani Guinier has made a strong case for why political decisions need not be merely win-lose decisions by suggesting, instead, different ways in which election losers might recuperate some benefits in proportion to their numbers. See Lani Guinier, *The Tyranny of the Majority: Fundamental Fairness in Representative Democracy* (New York: The Free Press, 1994).

26. Levinas, *Otherwise Than Being*, pp. 84, 117. In the end, though, even the compensatory framework for determining which distributive needs ought to be met is shadowed by its Other. By distributing goods to victims of past discrimination whose deprivation was *not* their own fault, it could imply that distribution is not due those whose deprivation *is* their own fault. But could one bid adieu to those who are indolent or irresponsible, who do not live up to the moral and cultural standards one holds sacred, such as those of hard work, diligence, and responsibility? If one were do to so, once again one's responsibility would begin with oneself instead of with the Other. In this case, that of those whose deprivation is their own fault, one is responsible not merely for their well-being, but also, as Levinas is accustomed to say, responsible for their responsibility.

8

THE TWO-TIERED ETHICS AND THE AFFIRMATIVE ACTION DEBATE

Over- and Underinclusion, Causality, and the Excluded White Male

The last chapter opted for Cornel West's definition of affirmative action, formed an alternative definition of equality as "treatment as equals," and contended that the taking seriously of the systematic discrimination experienced by African-Americans implies that they are deserving of some compensation, which depends upon a deontological basis that is more appropriate for justifying affirmative action than a teleological one. There are many who might accept the argument up to this point, but who would then contend that affirmative action is not an appropriate compensation for past discrimination. They construct their arguments on three general bases: (1) that it includes either too many or not enough of those deserving compensation, (2) that the presence of statistical disparities between black and white representation in various professions does not prove that these disparities were caused by a discrimination meriting compensation, and (3) that white males who did not discriminate against blacks unfairly bear the brunt of the compensation burden. If the arguments in these three areas succeed, then the defense of affirmative action fails, for one would have to admit that compensation is due, but that some other form is required. Therefore, this final chapter will attempt to take up these three sets of arguments and to argue against those who claim that affirmative action is not an appropriate form of compensation for the systematic discrimination of the past.

1. OVERINCLUSIVENESS AND UNDERINCLUSIVENESS

If, as this book does, one opts for a compensation approach to affirmative action as more likely to respect the rights of all parties involved than a teleological approach, one immediately ventures into a domain where one must strive to ensure that the proportions are preserved between what one receives and what one merits and between what one pays and what one owes. The deontological refusal to slight the dignity of the Other, evident both in discourse and in the phenomenology of alterity, lies at the root of such a balancing, even though one would also hope to avoid the excessive illiberality of the first argument in plurality opinion authored by Justice Powell in *Wygant*. Affirmative action would not live up to its own deontological foundation if it could be shown that it failed in two cases, namely, that affirmative action compensates some who do not deserve it (overinclusion) or fails to compensate some who do (underinclusiveness). The first case would seem to entail taking what belongs to one and giving it to another who is undeserving, thereby using the first person for the sake of the second in way that would not accord with whole deontological underpinning of the argument. In the second case, affirmative action would seem to be inadequate in leaving those deserving uncompensated and thus in failing at the very purpose for which it was established.

In the effort to decide who deserves affirmative action, an important first step in determining whether some who do receive it do not deserve it, the discussants have generally avoided speaking of "group" desert. Indeed, the idea of "group rights," according to Nathan Glazer, conflicts with the explicit wording of the Civil Rights Act of 1964; "historical American legal practice"; and liberalism's focus upon individual welfare, rights, and responsibilities. Owen Fiss, however, has argued that when one follows a recommendation such as Glazer's and moves toward the individual level that mechanistic jurisprudence favors, that is, when one considers individuals on a case-by-case basis, the margins of the overinclusiveness (individuals benefiting from affirmative action who do not deserve it) or the underinclusiveness (individuals deserving it who do not benefit) of affirmative action become more visible. Instead of succumbing to the mandates of mechanistic jurisprudence, Fiss himself founds his commitment to affirmative action on the group-disadvantaging principle. George Sher stakes out a middle position between individualist and group approaches by construing group classifications as constituting racial and sexual boundaries roughly suggesting which individuals are likely to have been disadvantaged by past discrimination, but for Sher it is necessary to establish which group members have been disadvantaged by past discrimination in order to avoid overinclusion. Goldman, because of his concern for those who might be displaced from opportunities for which they are qualified, insists that affirmative action should only be undertaken on behalf of the individuals meriting it and hence should avoid any overinclusion, but like Sher, he would probably concede that group affiliation furnishes at least a starting point for determining whether one merits affirmative action.[1]

Goldman begins by attempting to eliminate any overinclusion by first claiming that women and African-Americans do not deserve compensation *as a group*. He distinguishes two types of harms requiring differing compensations: distributive and nondistributive harms. Distributive harms involve one agency wronging separately to the same degree each member of a group, such as when a landlord's lack of services to a whole building affects all its tenants equally. The proper remedy in such a case, according to Goldman, would involve a "class action suit," by which individuals in the class are compensated as individuals for their equal damages. Although women and African-Americans may have suffered distributive harms in the past, Goldman claims that those in the present do not experience this kind of harm or experience it in quite varied degrees. As a result, one could not justify affirmative action as a kind of class-action compensation to be distributed in accord with damages suffered equally. In contrast, nondistributive harms are done to a group as a whole in such a way that the harm cannot be exhaustively analyzed into specific injuries to each member separately compensable, such as when one athletic team deliberately breaks the arm of one key member of another football team in order that that the entire team might lose a game. In order for a group to suffer a nondistributive harm, there must be actual interaction among group members for a common purpose and the roles occupied by members must be mutually dependent. The proper compensation here would be a lump sum to be given to the whole group, but women and African-Americans would seem to lack this tight-knit group identity with mutually dependent roles as well as any official body that could act as the recipient of payment for all. Even if it could be shown that women and African-Americans have suffered a nondistributive harm, reverse discrimination also seems to be an inappropriate remedy for such a harm because it functions distributively, working differently in favor of different members within a minority group. Goldman's conclusion is that compensation must be awarded case by case since women and African-Americans have not suffered as a group either distributive or nondistributive harms and so do not deserve the remedies properly tailored for such harms.[2]

The linchpin of Goldman's position against the overinclusion that would result from distributive compensation for African-Americans and women as groups is that there are members of such groups who have not suffered the overt and glaring denial experienced by previous generations.

> Even if the middle-class black or woman graduate student may have had to struggle against psychological handicaps, although always accepted to the best schools, we cannot be true to the compensatory principle by creating a policy that benefits such individuals while leaving unaided those who have suffered more overt injustice and deprivation . . . if injustices in the educational system have led to real compensable harms and decreased opportunities, we would expect injustice to be generally proportionate to present disabilities of different individuals.[3]

Goldman admits that victims may have suffered wrongs, such as insults, due to discriminatory attitudes, but only wrongful harms require compensation, that is, those harms that are "clear and measurable" and resulting from a violation of rights as opposed to wrongs that are "remote, indirect or speculative." He sums up the problem of overinclusiveness besetting the practice of affirmative action: "those who are now most qualified will tend to be those who have been discriminated against least in the past" and preferential policies "invert the ratio of past harm to present benefit."[4]

In contrast to Goldman's willingness to salvage affirmative action by tightening up the requirements its beneficiaries must meet, Thomas Sowell believes that affirmative action's overinclusiveness undermines it. Sowell contends that an enduring policy of group preferences creates incentives for the more successful and less needy (and so undeserving) inside or outside of a preferred group to take advantage of such a policy.

> As the case of untouchables in India and blacks in the United States both illustrate, it is all too easy for a tragically unfortunate group of people to be used simply as an entering wedge to create benefits

going largely to others in much more fortunate circumstances, whether those others are within their own racial or social group or numerous outsiders to whom the preferential principle is successively extended. Clearly, no recitation of the historic oppressions suffered by blacks can justify preferences for white, middle-class women, whom some believe to be the principal beneficiaries of the acceptance of the preferential principle.[5]

Sowell's discussion here further suggests that overinclusiveness is in fact the "overside" of affirmative action policies' underinclusiveness, which often results when more assertive individuals secure positions while the less assertive are left behind. Numerous commentators, including Stephen Carter, Nathan Glazer, Alan Goldman, Barry Gross, Robert Simon, and Thomas Sowell, have emphasized how affirmative action policies also leave out other deserving minority groups as well as the economically disadvantaged within the same minority group and outside of it.[6]

What response might be made to these many criticisms of affirmative action? One response offered is a purely practical one, which bypasses the theoretical level on which most of the discussion in the book has been conducted. According to this argument, it is impractical to proceed case by case, and thus the law needs to operate with racial and group classifications for administrative efficiency, even if some overinclusion results. Goldman counters by denying that case-by-case proceedings are impracticable since an administrative board (like the Equal Employment Opportunity Commission) could process such cases, although one wonders if Goldman underestimates the complexities involved. After all, he at one point claimed that a company which had regular openings for fixed-level competencies but which hired few or no minority-group members *obviously* must have discriminated—an affirmation that oversimplifies the difficulties and that was not accepted by subsequent court decisions. Against this pragmatic defense of overinclusion, Goldman also marshals a moral argument when he states that justifying racial classifications on the basis of administrative efficiency would open the door to discrimination against minorities or women in favor of whites if "administrative efficiency" demanded it. This opposition to justifying overinclusiveness through an appeal to the teleology of efficiency is fully consistent with Goldman's own deontological framework and also with the two-tiered ethics underpinning this study.[7]

The individualistic, case-by-case focus, however, which is favored by Glazer and Goldman and which both derives from and heightens a fastidiousness about avoiding overinclusion, ultimately tends to desocialize and dehistoricize individuals and, as a consequence, to minimize the harm that affirmative action remedies, as shall be shown. Michel Rosenfeld restores this sociohistorical dimension to the discussion when he points out that, in the case of race discrimination, *it was the racist* who, by labeling blacks inferior, transformed a morally neutral predicate, namely, being black, into a mark calling for inferior treatment. The prevalence and pervasiveness of this treatment throughout the history of the United States have deprived African-Americans of material assets, reduced motivation, or effected harmful distortions in their self-image. This history of systematic discrimination, Rosenfeld concludes, makes group affiliation derivatively morally relevant and justifies individual compensation on the basis of group affiliation.[8]

Rosenfeld's understanding of the individual in terms of social and historical factors dovetails perfectly with the social, intersubjective turn that is distinctive of Schutzian phenomenology and both components of the two-tiered ethics, which, as an ethics, has not forfeited its deontological emphasis by including such social dimensions. Rosenfeld, too, preserves deontological features since he seeks to reestablish a disturbed equilibrium for individuals, that is, to reverse policies whereby group classifications were used to deny individuals their dignity by employing these very classifications to restore to individuals a dignity that would have been theirs, absent discrimination. Hence, Rosenfeld's approach to affirmative action need not be conceived as a teleological program trying to promote the well-being of a group at the expense of individuals, as individualistic viewpoints might argue. Furthermore, by properly recognizing the connection between group and individual, as Rosenfeld does, one need not venture into the thorny question of whether groups have rights.

While Goldman might look favorably upon the deontological features of Rosenfeld's group-regarding argument, his objection remains centered on whether all African-Americans have suffered from what Rosenfeld categorizes as a pervasive and prevalent treatment as inferiors or even the "overt and glaring denial" experienced by the previous generation. In making his case that not all African-Americans have suffered such injury, Goldman tends to underestimate the psychological harm that discrimination produces. By classifying present-day prejudicial incidents not as "harms" but as "wrongs" that are "remote, indirect or speculative," he seems to have overlooked how racial slights and insults in the present connect up with a long history of systematic degradation and so carry a "connotative weight" significantly heavier for African-Americans than other types of insults might be for other groups. Perhaps, however, Goldman's distinction between "harms" and "wrongs" is meant to distinguish offenses that might deserve legal prosecution or compensation from those that do not, and certainly not every individual insult deserves legal compensation or prosecution. Nevertheless, the legal system itself, insofar as it has acknowledged the criminal character of certain kinds of insults, for example, in cases of defamation, "hate crimes," or workplace harassment, appears to have recognized that the neat distinction between prosecutable harms and wrongs that are merely insults is not so easily drawn. Even though Goldman is certainly correct that a society ought not legally prosecute every insult, still the cumulative effect of present-day insults and past history might warrant a response that is less prosecutorial (of every individual insult) and yet more comprehensive. The comprehensive harm of systematic racism deserves a more comprehensive response than simply determining case by case whether an individual suffered racial harm, and it would seem that affirmative action on behalf of those equally capable for positions achieves comprehensiveness without being excessively prosecutorial.[9]

In addition, Goldman downplays the *long-range* psychological damage inflicted by centuries of degradation from slavery to Jim Crow laws. For instance, he suggests that such damage disappears upon the passage to a new generation, when in fact any such impairment could not but be transmitted across generations and would dissipate only gradually across several generations. Just because African-Americans are still able to achieve, one cannot assume that they have emerged without harms, unscathed by these centuries of degradation. Who knows what additional resolution they may have had to master to overcome this history of prejudices? Who knows the psychological sufferings or griefs, within the individual, in the family or neighborhood, that they may have endured and that would be expected among a people whom the majority of society have ostracized? Sometimes even the desire to achieve itself, when pursued to perilous extremes, can be symptomatic of psychic wounds, a desire to compensate for a sense of inferiority produced and continually reinforced by surrounding society. Being middle class is not necessarily a sign that one has not suffered from the evils of racism. Lastly, Goldman displays more psychological perspicacity when, cognizant of the encompassing effects of economic deprivation, he refuses to call for case-by-case determination of whether the low motivation of poor children versus rich children may be their own freely chosen fault. Instead, he grants the socially induced character of this motivation and calls for compensation. Given his appreciation for the powerful effect of history upon the chronically poor, it would seem that if Goldman had entered more deeply into the African-American experience, he would have acknowledged that the harms of systematic, centuries-old discrimination *likewise* merit compensation.[10]

Goldman's sympathetic understanding of the *global* significance of the consequences of poverty in the case of the low motivation of chronically poor children contrasts with the stringent, individualistic framework governing his approach to affirmative action for women and minorities and underlying his requirement that harms be measurable. In the case of the candidates for affirmative action, Goldman requires that they prove their harm one by one in order to protect those not preferred by affirmative action. This procedure, though, diminishes the significance of the society-wide injustice of systemic racial discrimination by subordinating it to an individualistic framework and thus placing it on a par with other arbitrary means of denying individuals jobs for which they are competent, such as nepotism, political spoils systems, or preferences for good looks over ability. Furthermore, this individualistic approach has the effect of shifting the burden of proof onto the individual discriminated against and exculpates society since its own past monstrous deeds would seem to fade from sight, except insofar as their traces are demonstrable in individual cases. However, when it comes to the case of the children of the chronically poor, the pressure of ethical considerations seems to outstrip the epistemic question regarding whether damage deserving compensation is present. In this case, Goldman states without hesitation, "we must give the underdog the benefit of the doubt and assume that the difference [between rich and poor children's motivation] is socially caused." In Levinas's terminology, it is as if a moment of gratuity interrupts the strict bookkeeping, the balancing of accounts that typify the strict reciprocity endemic to what Levinas calls "essence-thinking." While Goldman bends his theory in response to the Other, destitute because of chronic poverty, that same theory seems strangely less accountable to the Other ravaged by centuries of systematic discrimination; in fact, his proposed solution to discrimination has the effect of concealing those ravages.[11]

Because the harm inflicted upon African-Americans is neither that of tenants equally neglected by a landlord all at the same time and so deserving equal distributive compensation nor that of a football team with an injured member deserving nondistributive compensation, Goldman assumes that the only other recourse is to portray it diffusely, only in terms of individual harms. But these theoretical suppositions about the types of harms possible keep Goldman from recognizing the *sui generis character* of the group harm inflicted upon African-Americans, centuries of systemic discrimination whose effects perdure through generations, entitling them to a group-regarding remedy aimed at uplifting individuals.

Goldman's oversights here perhaps can be traced to the fact that he never escapes his *ethical* starting point, however deserving of praise this starting point might be. He begins with the individual whose rights are liable to be trampled by the overzealous implementation of affirmative action, and this starting point shapes his entire theoretical framework. This ethical commitment prompts Goldman's preoccupation with overinclusion and his individualistic approach, but it blinds him to the uniqueness of African-American suffering which must be understood as globally as that of the chronically poor. The view in this book secures Goldman's deontological concerns for the displaced, competent, white male not by an individualistic focus that neglects the unique type of group harm done to African-Americans, but by firmly emphasizing that equal competence must be exhibited as a prerequisite to affirmative action and that thus the competence of the displaced person is recognized. This discussion of Goldman's position illustrates how the adjudication between competing claims at the level of the Third requires a prior careful entrance into the experience of the excluded Other, whose suffering ought to be properly understood and weighted and to find its expression and defense at the level of theory and political decision making.

The tone of Goldman's emphasis on individual, case-by-case scrutiny, formed out of his concern for the right to equal opportunity of the nonpreferred, contrasts with Sowell's rejection of affirmative action because of his suspicions of avaricious individuals whom he sees to be all too willing to advance their own interests at the expense of others in a highly competitive society. Although Sowell's mention of "a tragically unfortunate group of people" lends an initial altruistic ring to his argument, his portrayal of more fortunate blacks, white middle-class women, or other minorities as willing to use the less fortunate as an entering wedge to gain benefits for themselves projects on to them the lack of solidarity characteristic of the war of all against all, in which every person is a wolf to every other. Any bonds of solidarity that might exist at the level of the face to face between blacks of different economic standing and between blacks and white middle-class women are written off by Sowell's account, which tends to atomize groups and to pit one against the other. Middle-class blacks and white women make use of their own (lesser) suffering to secure their private advancement according to Sowell, who does not entertain the possibility that they might envision their advancement as something achieved on behalf of their whole race or sex. Sowell never conjectures that those who advance through affirmative action might interpret their advantages as "for the Other," that is, as a benefit that heightens their sympathy for those who have suffered more, as, therefore, an incentive to return to promote the advancement of their Other (e.g., the poor), as a call to responsibility for those left behind. Similarly, Sowell's argument hints that lower-class African-Americans, upon seeing other African-Americans meeting prerequisites that they could not satisfy and therefore advancing beyond them, would begrudge them their progress because no program has been targeted at their particular needs.

Sowell's pure strategic, economic reading of preferential policies as providing "incentives" to be capitalized upon at the expense of the needier may capture the cutthroat market attitudes influencing some beneficiaries of affirmative action who might be willing to dispossess others without the least concern for them. But this interpretation occludes from sight the moral purposes intended by affirmative action and the sense of solidarity between many of its beneficiaries and those not yet helped by it or other suitable programs. Sowell's argument here seems to draw its force from and reveal an underlying allergic conception of human intersubjectivity at odds with the Levinasian view. From that Levinasian perspective, Goldman appears magnanimous in his fear *for* the Other, even as Sowell advocates a view of society in which it is best to be cynically fearful *of* the Other.[12]

The argument of underinclusiveness, that others, such as poor African-American and other minorities, are left out by present affirmative action policies, is often used to oppose affirmative action even though the logic of the argument seems rather to call for its extension. Some have asserted, however, that the underinclusiveness indicates an arbitrariness in determining which groups are to be preferred that ren-

ders unjustifiable any preference at all. However, it is important to recollect the history, since affirmative action commenced in the United
States at a time when little had been done to diminish large disparities
between whites and blacks, the largest minority, and so it at first was
warranted to redress the evident ravages of past discrimination. Randall Kennedy recalls that affirmative action took its start when other
more encompassing and expensive solutions were not available, that it
originally targeted strategically important sectors of the black community in order to desegregate the professions and to stimulate
broader hope, and that it was not designed to resolve a vast expanse of
social problems. The idea of reversing and redressing the past anticipated the thoeretico-legal compensation arguments later developed to
justify affirmative action.

Its original justifiability, however, does not rule out the possibilities that there are now other groups more or equally deserving or that
other, new social programs are needed. While such new programs may
be desirable, were one to abolish affirmative action or to substitute for
it programs not based on race (e.g., university admission for the top 10
percent of an entire state's graduating high school classes, regardless
of race), one would seem to be overlooking that past damages with all
their continuing effects were inflicted on the basis of race and that it is
fitting that race be taken into account as part of a just compensation.
In addition, there is a question whether one should abandon affirmative action because it does not compensate *all* who are victims of discrimination or whether it would be better to retain a program
redressing *some* past injustices and achieving *some* good, even if much
more needs to be done. Moreover, one must be suspicious of those
who oppose affirmative action on behalf of minorities and recommend
as replacements expensive social and educational programs that they
have generally not supported or that are unlikely to be approved in a
cost-conscious era. If anything, the question of underinclusiveness precisely discloses that in the arbitration of competing claims, one stands
on an island in the midst of a sea of needs that continually exceed
one's capacity to respond—with infinite responsibilities, Levinas
would say. One ought not despair of doing any good, though, because
so much remains to be done, any more than one is exonerated from
responsibility because the responsibility is infinite.[13]

2. CAUSAL ARGUMENTS

Several authors, such as Morris Abram, Robert Bork, Nathan Glazer, Harvey Mansfield, and Thomas Sowell, argue that statistical imbalances in employment and academic settings do not prove discrimination warranting compensatory adjustments. Imbalanced racial proportions in schools result from residential racial concentrations that depend not upon prejudice against other groups but upon economics and cultural preferences, according to Glazer. Similarly, Sowell argues that since cultural groups are inclined to certain professions, such as the Irish toward police groups, low representations of minorities or women in certain professions does not prove the existence of discrimination. Sowell further contends that the causal factors affecting representation, such as cultural patterns, age, habits, discipline, sobriety, and innumerable demographic and geographical differences, are much more complex than the proponents of affirmative action have recognized in their rush to interpret employment discrepancies as the result of discrimination, often to prevent others from attributing such differences to "innate inferiority." Hence, Sowell calls for a more careful analysis of the statistics that are supposed to indicate discrimination. For instance, the statistical evidence that black academics earn less than whites has not been broken down university by university, and such a breakdown might well indicate that blacks and whites within the same universities earn comparable wages. Similarly, if one claims that Asians make more money than whites, one needs to consider the states and cities where Asians work since wages may be higher in those areas. As an instance of a confused, generalized causal argument, Sowell cites the claims repeated for years that the high rate of single-parent, teenage pregnancy among blacks was "a legacy of slavery." Research suggests, on the contrary, that the vast majority of black children grew up in two-parent homes, even under slavery itself and for generations afterward, and that current levels of single-parent teenage pregnancy have appeared among blacks and other groups only in the last half of the twentieth century.[14]

But if the causal factors underlying disproportionalities in minority representation in various domains are as complex as Sowell claims, then one could easily doubt whether social science and statistical analyses could *ever* be employed in favor of affirmative action. Sowell criticizes judges who, attributing racial groups' performance differentials to discrimination, attempt to restore particular individuals to where they would have been but for the offending discrimination—as if anyone could ever possess such a range of knowledge. Indeed, affirmative action arguments capitalize precisely—and, in Sowell's view, unjustifiably—on what cannot be known, as Sowell notes:

> But virtually no statistical study can control for all the relevant variables simultaneously, because the in-depth data, especially among qualitative dimensions, are often simply not available. By controlling for the available variables and implicitly assuming that the unaccounted-for variables do not differ significantly between groups, one can generate considerable residual "unexplained" statistical disparity and equate that with discrimination—or with genes, if one's thinking runs in that direction.[15]

The fact that numerous groups have suffered discrimination and yet succeeded quite well without compensatory measures (e.g., the Japanese in Canada and the United States, the Chinese in Malaysia and Indonesia, the Jews in the face of anti-Semitism) illustrates how the differences between groups do not result so much from "discrimination" as from a vast aggregate of cultural and motivational factors that science cannot easily master. "To pretend to disentangle the innumerable sources of intergroup differences is an exercise in hubris rather than morality," Sowell insists. Discrimination may be there as a cause underlying present inequities, but one wonders how it could ever be proven, given the myriad alternative causal factors of which one could never take sufficient account.[16]

The Supreme Court in a similar fashion appealed to the complexity of causal factors in order to limit the scope of affirmative action in the 1989 case of *City of Richmond* v. *J. A. Croson Co.* In that decision, the Court ruled unconstitutional a minority business set-aside program ordered by the city of Richmond, Virginia. In spite of its 1975 outlawing of discrimination in public contracts, from the years 1978 to 1983 Richmond found that although its population was 50 percent African-American, only .67 percent of its prime construction contracts had been awarded to minority businesses. The program Richmond enacted required that those given contracts for city construction subcontract a minimum of 30 percent of the total dollar amount of each contract to minority businesses for a five-year period. In rejecting this program, the Court required that race-based preferences under the equal protection clause meet strict scrutiny tests. Justice Sandra Day O'Connor, writing for the plurality (four) of the majority (six) position, stated that a remedial race-based affirmative action plan must be circumscribed to compensate only actual victims of discrimination and that, therefore, a causal nexus between present injury or disadvantage and past or ongoing racial discrimination must be shown. In spite of "the sorry history of both private and public discrimination," O'Connor claimed that it could not be positively shown that anyone in the Richmond construction industry engaged in discrimination. Furthermore, where specific qualifications are required (construction expertise), one needed to consider how many minority business enterprises have been awarded contracts not with reference to the entire black population of Richmond, but instead with regard to the relevant statistical pool (e.g., the total number of qualified minority business enterprises available). In brief, the dearth of minority business participation in the construction industry did not prove discrimination in the local construction industry. She continued:

> There are numerous explanations for this dearth of minority participation, including past societal discrimination in education and economic opportunities as well as both black and white career and entrepreneurial choices. Blacks may be disproportionately attracted to industries other than construction. The mere fact that black membership in these trade organizations is low, standing alone, cannot establish a prima facie case of discrimination.[17]

The merely hypothetical character of O'Connor's suggestion about alternative causal explanations ("Blacks *may* be . . . ") indicates clearly that she did not feel that she had to provide evidence that discrimination *was not* involved and that instead the burden of proof had been placed squarely on those who would claim that discrimination *was* involved. O'Connor finished up by affirming that to accept Richmond's claim that past societal discrimination justified racial preferences would open the door for claims by every disadvantaged group based on "inherently unmeasurable claims of past wrongs." As a result, the dream of a nation of equal citizens in a society where race would be irrelevant to personal opportunity and achievement would dissipate.[18]

In considering the statistical data and causal correlations employed within the affirmative action debate, it is important first of all to recognize that however neutrally they may appear to be presented, such data are developed, shaped, and interpreted in the light of one's overall commitments. For instance, Sowell argues that second-generation black West Indians who have lost their accent still tend to do better than United States blacks. For Sowell this suggests that it is not the case that prejudice against blacks causes the disadvantaged status of United States blacks since employers are generally willing to employ blacks (on the basis of their competence) and not only those blacks whose special accents indicate that they are distinct from United States blacks. But Sowell's interpretation of the statistics showing the undeniable success of West Indian blacks draws out far more than those statistics warrant. Those statistics do not show that unbiased white employers are responsible for this success, since it could well be that expanding West Indian businesses hire their immigrant compatriots. There are good grounds for such an interpretation since Sowell and his sources indicate that West Indians have owned a number of United States businesses disproportional to their population from as early as 1901; that West Indians tend to form tight-knit, self-enclosed communities among themselves; and that it would thus be plausible that West Indians would tend to hire incoming West Indians. Furthermore, the confidence and energy that Sowell finds exhibited among West Indians in contrast to United States blacks may not at all be due to the lack of paternalism and the rugged market competition that West Indians experienced under slavery, as Sowell believes. A more promising explanation lies in what David Lowenthal, one of Sowell's own sources, designates as the fact from which "the whole flavor of affairs derives": that blacks in the West Indies constitute a numerical majority since whites almost everywhere make up less than 5 percent of the population. Although the physical aspects of slavery may have been more brutal in the West Indies, it is entirely plausible that the psychological impact for United States blacks of living under centuries of discrimination as a minority population may in the long term have been more devastating to them. If this were so, then the West Indian example would serve a purpose exactly opposite to that for which Sowell cites it: it would highlight the importance of discrimination and the need for compensatory measures. Finally, Sowell ignores the distinctive experience of United States blacks here, when, for instance, he assimilates their experience with that of the Japanese (who were not enslaved) or Jews (who are not visibly "marked" for discrimination the way blacks are by their racial features except during the brutal, systematized anti-Semitism of National Socialism).[19]

Sowell also molds statistical data when he refuses to attribute differences in income between men and women to employer discrimination, but explains the disparities by the lack of educational attainment by women, the economic disadvantages caused by marriage and child-bearing, and the tendencies of women to quit voluntarily more frequently than men. These causal explanations overlook how the pervasive prejudicial pressures presented by Simone de Beauvoir and others retard the confidence of women to pursue an education and even to hope for a career beyond motherhood in the first place. By assigning the origins of disparities to the free choice of individual women, Sowell also conceals how societal and business resistance to maternity leaves and child care provisions presents women with such limited options that the choice to "quit voluntarily" is the best available option. Sowell thus engages in a kind of reverse bad faith, attributing to freedom of choice outcomes that are actually circumscribed heavily by socioeconomic disincentives and thereby hiding from sight these very disincentives. The deeper reason for Sowell's opposition to interventions on behalf of such progressive policies lies in his confidence in the free market whose mechanisms, if not interfered with, he believes, will induce employers to make jobs attractive, will achieve equal pay for women over the long run, and will produce self-corrections such that workers passed over by some will be hired by others. Of course, the human solidarity mandated by both the face to face and the structures of communication prevalent in the life-world would never countenance uncritical trust in impersonal market mechanisms, which Habermas groups under the rubric of "system," when it comes to providing people's livelihood, and would, instead, call for perpetual vigilance for those who might be left out by these blind processes.[20]

Finally, Sowell cites the fact that large northern cities had less residential segregation in the late nineteenth century than today, but without the presently existing fair housing laws, prohibitions against restrictive covenants, or court advocacy on behalf of African-Americans. Just as one is about to object that these correlations, which seem to discredit concerted efforts to desegregate, ignore that only a small number of African-Americans populated northern cities prior to the turn of the century and that massive migrations of African-Americans from the South to the North soon followed, Sowell mentions these migrations. But he then counters with the ambiguous statement that what changed were not the perceptions, but the realities. If by this statement, he intends to assert that there were no discriminatory perceptions either prior to the migrations or after them, but that only the realities of the massive influx of migrants accounts for the present segregated neighborhoods, such a conclusion would appear naive. Furthermore, anti-discriminatory housing measures did function effectively insofar as they enabled African-Americans to move into white neighborhoods, although they did not achieve integration—which was not their purpose or within their power—because of white flight, a phenomenon that no one could claim was free from discriminatory influences. All these examples suggest that Sowell imposes interpretations upon factual data to suit his own purpose, that is, to impugn anti-discriminatory policies.[21]

Just as Dworkin and Blackmun elaborated an alternative account of equality on behalf of disadvantaged groups, Rosenfeld develops an alternative account of causality than that used by those interested in restricting affirmative action. Rosenfeld characterizes his opponents' account of causality as an "atomistic mode of interpretation" that disconnects facts from their context and recombines them in mechanistic, causal chains of direct and linear links. Hence Justice O'Connor, faced with a shocking lack of minority representation in Richmond's construction industry (what Thurgood Marshall referred to as a "gross statistical disparity") and acknowledging the "sorry history" of discrimination, nevertheless suggests that one cannot appeal to "amorphous" societal discrimination as a cause. Rather, she insists that one must show direct linear links between discrimination and minority underrepresentation, and until one demonstrates such specific links, one cannot claim that discrimination is or has been operative.[22]

In contrast, Rosenfeld develops an "ecological" mode of interpretation which is more holistic and systematic in character, approaching social facts and events in terms of the interaction between individuals, groups, and their social, political, and historical environments. This ecological interpretation of causality favors the influence of indirect and multifaceted factors. In *Croson*, for instance, while O'Connor admits the history of discrimination and its impact upon black educational and economic opportunities, she wonders whether black career choices or attractions to different industries might help explain the paucity of contracts awarded to minority businesses. Such choices or attractions are detached, however, from the systematic exclusion that has deterred and would deter minorities from choosing to enter or to explore the construction industry. By neglecting the institutional underpinnings of what are presented as private career choices and attractions, O'Connor engages in a bit of the reverse bad faith that Sowell exhibits when he attributes women's lesser wages to their tendency "to quit voluntarily more frequently than men," as if the tendency to quit occurred in an institutional vacuum. Furthermore, while O'Connor grants that blacks might be affected by "deficiencies in working capital, inability to meet bonding requirements, unfamiliarity with bidding procedures," she classifies these factors as "non-racial" factors, which plague *any* racial group seeking to set up a new business. By extending such factors to other groups, she gives the impression that there is nothing unique about the handicaps affecting blacks, and, one supposes, no race-specific compensation is called for.[23]

In contrast, a more ecological approach would understand that, though such causal factors are "race-neutral" to the extent that they can also afflict nonminorities, insofar as they are found to be at work among minority entrepreneurs, it is difficult to separate them from the long history of discrimination and exclusion to which blacks have been uniquely subjected. Thus, an ecological understanding of causality would tend neither to dehistoricize such causal factors nor to dilute the impact of centuries of discrimination upon blacks by emphasizing the commonality of their handicaps with others. Utlimately, the entrepreneurial "choices" and "attractions" of minority businesspersons to withdraw and the supposedly race-neutral handicaps they face conjoin with the extremely low representation of minorities—which, contrary to O'Connor's view, does not "stand alone"—as traces of a "sorry history." That, as a result, this sorry history does not figure very prominently in O'Connor's analysis comes as no surprise since she, like Goldman and Glazer, tends to desocialize and dehistoricize the victims of discrimination. To offset this "infinite regress," in which discrimination seems absent in the pattern of awarding contracts because other causes are given for this pattern, causes from which discrimination itself seems absent, an ecological interpretation of causality is required.

Just as the atomized interpretation of causality does not sweep the field clean of competing interpretations, so Sowell's skepticism, which leads him to question whether one can ever prove the presence of discrimination at all, can cut the other way. One might equally ask whether it is possible to know with any certainty that discrimination has *not* been at work, especially since it is much more comforting (to give a Nietzschean twist to this discussion) to conceal its ugly presence by referring instead to such factors as the "unfamiliarity with bidding procedures" or "black preferences for other industries." Also, of course, those who discriminate, recognizing that discrimination is either immoral or publicly frowned upon, are usually reluctant to admit to it. Fiss's earlier explanation of how, in the later phases of the civil rights struggle, even the anti-discrimination principle was used to support discrimination and how "facially innocent criteria" concealed discriminatory intents makes one wonder if perhaps Sowell's skepticism about proving the presence of discrimination is but a highly sophisticated version of this kind of camouflaging.

Of course, the question of whether one has to prove whether discrimination has or has not been present depends upon who must shoulder the burden of proof. While early civil rights legislation placed the burden on institutions to prove that they were not discriminating, *Croson* shifts the responsibility of proof to the victim. To some extent this shift can be accounted for by the fact that later cases have been brought forward by *whites* claiming discrimination against themselves and thus calling upon proponents of affirmative action to demonstrate the presence of discrimination justifying affirmative action measures. While arguments must be met by counterarguments, one ought not to neglect how the burden of proof has shifted in favor of the majority members excluded by a policy designed to include minorities.

It is quite conceivable and often the case that institutions with statistical imbalances in the number of minority or women employees are not deliberately discriminating and that they may have even struggled in vain to recruit such employees and so do not deserve blame. There are also legitimate concerns about disadvantaged groups exacting unjustifiable and unfair indemnities; but it is for this reason that this study, out of concern for those displaced by affirmation action, has embraced a deontologically based compensation framework. In addition, Justice O'Connor's worry about "inherently unmeasurable claims of past wrongs" deserves some attention. For instance, in the case of the set-asides in *Croson*, which differ from affirmative action hirings, it could be the case that the demand that subcontractors farm out 30 percent of contracts to minority businesses was excessive given the relevant statistical pool, whereas no action at all would be insufficient in the other direction. There is certainly a place for judicial discretion in such matters.

Still, anyone sincerely concerned about the Other on the periphery of one's totality would be troubled by a case such as *Croson* in which a city with a 50 percent African-American population finds only .67 percent of its prime construction contracts awarded to minority businesses; there are other situations in which minorities or women seem severely underrepresented in proportion to their populations in society in general. One would be troubled even before asking the theoretical question at the level of the Third about why there is such underrepresentation. And one would continue to be troubled if those voices attempting to reassure and pacify one's conscience at the level of the Third appealed to less than convincing conceptualizations and explanations for which there are highly plausible alternatives. For instance, equality could be understood as treating others as equals instead of treating others equally; causality could be ecologically rather than atomistically interpreted; one could wonder more about disguised discrimination or the long-lasting, immeasurable effects of centuries-old discrimination than about the unrecognized variables other than discrimination that might account for inequities; the burden of proof can be shifted in different directions, and statistics read through entirely different interpretive lenses. In the face of such disparities and legitimate explanatory alternatives, it still remains plausible that more minority individuals would be represented than at present had systematic discrimination never occurred, that one ought to strive to include those thus excluded, and that affirmative action programs are appropriate means of inclusion. Of course, one must take continual account of those seriously displaced, of the differences of such programs and their effect upon those for whom they are designed, and of the counterarguments that might call for restrictions on such programs.

Finally, in discussing the domain of causality, it is possible to be so mesmerized by the compulsions and determinisms of what Kant called the kingdom of nature, of that which *is* the case, that one loses sight of the ethical challenge raised by the kingdom of ends, of that which *ought* to be. Sowell falls into just this trap when he cites a study by Donald L. Horowitz, which concludes that few if any societies have ever approximated the ideal according to which groups would be "proportionally represented" at different levels and in different sectors. On the basis of this study, Sowell, who earlier had opposed any ethical attempts to intervene in the value-free market, ends up discrediting this ethical ideal of proportional representation on the basis of facts.

> That what exists widely across the planet is regarded as an anomaly, while what exists virtually nowhere is regarded as a norm, is a tribute to the effectiveness of sheer reiteration in establishing a vision—and of the difficulties of dispelling a prevailing vision by facts.[24]

Paradoxically, Sowell's derogatory comment about the utopian nature of "vision" captures what is the core of Kantian ethics, in which the ethical norms discovered by practical reason place in question whatever is taken to be an immutable, scientifically established fact. While scientific, speculative reason seeks to conform to the facts, ethicopractical rationality can require that the facts conform to its norms and thus be re-formed. Thus, for Kant, one may never have experienced factually a perfect friend, and yet one knows that one ought to be one, and the practical reason which commands one to be such a friend can also go on to justify such a command. Kant's notion of practical reason irreducible to speculative reason, Habermas's separating moral-practical rationality from cognitive-instrumental rationality, and Levinas's face which the totality never silences flow into a common current of philosophical protest in order that ethical ideals might not succumb to the inertia of the factual domain. For all of these figures, ethics forms the context within which causal analyses take their place and play their role.[25]

3. THE EXCLUDED WHITE MALE

An array of arguments has been advanced on behalf of the white males who, while not necessarily culpable, seem to end up paying the price of affirmative action policies in a way that threatens to undermine any compensatory justification of such policies. Nathan Glazer, for example, cannot see why the descendants of white European immigrants after 1880, who were not responsible for black slavery, should bear the burden of redressing a past in which they had no or little part. He further asks why they should be called upon to aid those who presently receive more assistance than either they or their ancestors ever did. Thomas Sowell also insists that guilt is not inherited, and hence even if one's ancestors were complicit in the institution of slavery, their guilt is not transmitted to their descendants. Alan Goldman, too, contends that young white males will disproportionately bear the compensatory burden since they are the ones now applying for jobs, and he bemoans the fact that the rules of the game seem to be changing in midstream for them.[26]

In addition, since the compensatory approach to affirmative action seems to inculpate and unfairly disadvantage innocent young white males, and since it thus engenders hostile reactions, as Glazer, Kennedy, and Sowell have all pointed out, some have argued that these hostile reactions themselves present grounds for rejecting affirmative action. Sowell compares racial preference policies to a "pile of combustible material" about to explode, although the metaphor itself engages in a kind of bad faith insofar as it suggests that future hostile reactions to affirmative action beneficiaries are mechanically produced, without the free agency of those reacting with antagonism. Ironically, authors can accentuate the unfairness of affirmative action, often by misconstruing its meaning, as will be shown, and thus fan the flames of enmity, and then appeal to this increasing enmity *itself* as a further argument against affirmative action.[27]

It is necessary, first of all, to correct misrepresentations of affirmative action which present it as unethical and thus all the more liable to antagonize the white males it displaces. Rosenfeld attempts to correct one important misunderstanding of affirmative action when he notes that although compensation involves certain retributive dimensions, which are usually associated with guilt in the context of criminal transgressions and which are usually unjustifiable unless those doing the recompensing have engaged in culpable conduct, affirmative action is not a matter of punitive retribution. Compensation involves, rather, restitution, using the proceeds of an unjust enrichment to make up for an unjust loss. Goldman, as pointed out above, rightly distinguishes compensation from punishment. Goldman, too, argues that ideally the perpetrator of the injury should be responsible for such restoration; but, since in the case of massive society-wide discrimination it is often difficult to identify any perpetrator and since many perpetrators are long since deceased, this ideal cannot be realized. However, because compensation focuses upon the restoration of the victim and not the penalization of the perpetrator, it is not as necessary for affirmative action to pursue the negative task of ferreting out those who are to be blamed for discrimination as to pursue the positive task of trying to reinstate those trampled upon by discrimination.[28]

Avoiding inculpatory accusations is but one way of lessening the divisive effect that misunderstandings of affirmative action can produce. In addition, affirmative action need not be construed as one person or group exacting its pound of flesh from another person or group, but rather as a policy which society itself has adopted. Judith Jarvis Thomson emphasizes that it is the community who makes amends and not the white male, who only happens to be applying for the very job that the community, in its process of making amends, awards to an equally competent member of a group discriminated against. If one considers affirmative action as a societal action undertaken in the legal forum, it does not seem particularly unjust that such a displacement of white males should occur since society regularly enacts policies that have inconvenient effects for some of its members. Regrettably, for instance, established small businesses fail because new and superior roads are built, the draft discriminates by age, and the placement of toxic waste dumps discriminates by geography. One group or other is often asked to bear special burdens, given society-wide decisions.[29]

Moreover, the concept of affirmative action would demolish the bonds of solidarity to a lesser degree, if it were not perceived as a program undertaken by society for a teleological "greater benefit" for which young white individuals are sacrificed. This teleological framing of the question, which is Thomson's own, permits one to envision young white males as sacrificial pawns in a way that a deontological conception would not. Hence, affirmative action is better comprehended as employing group classifications to restore to individuals affiliated with a group a dignity that was denied to them and their ancestors unfairly precisely on the basis of this group affiliation. Affirmative action consists not in a social-program juggernaut rolling over innocent individuals for a telos, but in adjudication of a conflict between individual needs and rights, each of whose dignity merits upholding and each of whose claims deserves consideration.[30]

Finally, viewing affirmative action as society's deed can help remove any insinuation that whites are being discriminated against "because of their race." The unfortunate exclusion of some whites for some positions needs to be grasped as what Randall Kennedy calls "an incidental consequence of addressing a compelling social need," involving no malice or prejudice against whites. Facile and vague statements to the effect, for instance, that Bakke was kept out of medical school "because of his race," occludes the character of society's attempt to balance claims and restore individuals to dignity and falsely implies that the law is now operating with the same kind of racial prejudice against whites that once directed its treatment of minorities.[31]

But the intergroup tensions over affirmative action cannot be resolved simply by more careful renditions of the meaning of affirmative action, as if better public relations alone could heal profound societal balkanization. However, to call for the abandonment of preferential policies simply because they are likely to stir up animosity pitches the discussion at the merely strategic level of taking whatever means will avoid discomfort and conflict. More importantly, such an argument retreats from the ethical high ground and surrenders the field to the intergroup competitiveness and bias fueling white backlashes; it allows the *is* to swallow up the *ought* completely. Sowell's use of this argument shows the earlier mentioned tendency to be critical of African-Americans and to retreat when it comes to criticizing whites.

There is no doubt that one can interpret affirmative action as part of a comprehensive war of all against all in which each group, suspecting the other of trying to take advantage, rises to a defense of its own rights against the other. Sowell and Nieli portray affirmative action as a tactic within such a war when they claim that a sense of group grievance supports a "now it's our turn" attitude. But it is also possible to elucidate affirmative action *ethically*, as a response to an appeal from those who have been excluded from the totality. In line with the cynical reading of affirmative action, Glazer's white ethnic groups who, along with their ancestors, never received the special protections given to minority groups nowadays, are no doubt tempted to interpret affirmative action as part of intercultural warfare and to react out of a spirit of competition and jealousy. They might well choose to convert the misery of their ancestors into a miserliness by zealously striving to deny to others what was never granted to their ancestors or themselves. Likewise, they might well indulge in an almost sadistic willingness to inflict on others the very pain their ancestors suffered. On the other hand, they could respond *ethically* to their sufferings and those of their predecessors by understanding these sufferings not by beginning with the "I," or with their in-group, but with the Other, with the need of the out-group. That is, they could allow their sufferings and those of their ancestors to augment their sympathy for other disadvantaged groups. Levinas depicts just such an ethical response to suffering when he comments on how one's suffering can break through the crust of egoism, decenter the self, engender vulnerability, displace one's center of gravity outside of itself in such a way that one's suffering can be placed at the service of the Other. For Levinas, the defensive posture of "Because I have suffered I will never let anyone take advantage of *me* again" gives way to the generosity of "Because I have suffered, I will try to ensure that *no one else* suffers as I have." The ethical person so transcends self-preocupation in order to center on the Other that even the prospects of her own death open her outward to the Other, with the result that, as Levinas expresses it, she fears the murder of the Other more than her own death.[32]

One can feel a certain discomfort, though, demanding such high generosity to which one perhaps at best may only be able to inspire another. Levinas locates the hesitancy one might feel about demanding generosity from the Other at the level of the face to face, at a point before one can require reciprocity or ask anything of another.

> The ego involved in responsibility is me and no one else, me with whom one would have liked to pair up a sister soul, from whom one would require substitution and sacrifice. But to say that the other has to sacrifice himself to the others would be to preach human sacrifice.[33]

Even though one is convinced that affirmative action as public policy is not particularly unethical, in asking white males as a group to bear the burden of a societal decision, as other groups are asked to do at other moments, the unease one experiences at exacting moral behavior from another reflects the fundamental discrepancies between the level of the face to face and the Third; indeed it confirms the fact that there are two such distinctive levels. To be sure, one cannot dispense with the level of the Third on which one is impelled to provide ethical justifications for universal norms and institutional policies. However, such norms and policies, by subsuming or intending to subsume individuals under their prerogatives, inevitably exert a kind of coercion upon others who may not concur with these norms or policies. It is such coercion that might engender a sense of alienation or resentment among those to whom these policies extend, and the opposition of some white males to affirmative action is but one instance of this more comprehensive situation, in spite of the fact that affirmative action itself is a justifiable public policy. Utilizing coercive power to rectify injustices, law has difficulty producing the generosity of heart that would make the reforms it introduces lasting. As a result, the level of the Third, as necessary and indispensable as it is, always represents a falling away from the perfect nonviolence of the face to face, in which one faces up to what is required only of oneself, without daring to exact anything from an Other.

Just as the victims of discrimination invite Glazer's white ethnics to an exalted form of generosity, so white males, banned from positions by the ethically legitimate societal intervention of affirmative action, issue a similar summons to those who might favor affirmative action. Thomson rightly raises this concern when she points out that well-entrenched older white males, who might recommend affirmative action, are precisely those who have benefited from the exclusion of blacks and women more than the young males who now bear the brunt of affirmative action policies. Consistency would, at the least, not permit indifference to these younger males. These young white males, in fact, correspond to Dworkin's child who did not receive the serum given to the dying child and so deserve sympathy and support in order that both might receive treatment as equals even if they cannot be treated equally. In order that they receive treatment as equals, this study has insisted upon a deontological rather than a teleological approach, upon a compensation argument rather than a diversity argument, and it has called for affirmative action hirings only after equal competence has been demonstrated so that the competence of the white male is not disregarded. It would also seem appropriate that structures be established to assist those whites turned away because of affirmative action to find alternative educational or employment opportunities. Once again, the level of the face to face will not allow those in favor of affirmative action for those excluded by past discrimination to pursue their agenda without any regard for the white males displaced by affirmative action.[34]

4. CONCLUSION: DIVERSITY AND THE NATURE OF LAW

In the *Bakke, Weber,* and *Paradise* cases, the Supreme Court maintained that government interventions to increase equality of opportunity among minorities must be shown to compensate for effects causally produced by past discrimination. Similarly, after surveying constitutional justifications of affirmative action, Rosenfeld concludes that constitutional practice needs to be both forward- and backward-looking, since in its future-oriented attempts to restore victims of discrimination it needs to look backward to distinguish those deprivations the state should rectify from those it should not. Affirmative action thus involves a distributive component (allocating jobs or positions to those previously deprived of them) which has been circumscribed and limited by the compensatory component (only those deprived due to past discrimination deserve such an allocation). In my view, it is the sense of ethical responsibility to those who experience exclusion from a system of goods (the distributive factor) that forms the founding context for all "higher" level adjudication regarding who deserves distribution and on what basis. Compensatory arguments are located at this higher level.[35]

The restoration of individuals to jobs from which they have been previously excluded due to group affiliation on compensatory grounds produces a secondary utilitarian effect because other individuals within such previously excluded groups can acquire an enhanced sense of their own dignity precisely by seeing other members of their group represented. Goldman, Glazer, and others who tend to minimize the importance of group affiliation overlook these secondary benefits of affirmative action. Goldman even insinuates that seriously harmed African-Americans would experience jealousy if a "less harmed" representative of their race were to receive compensation on their behalf. But a mere consultation of popular African-American magazines and a consideration of community and national celebrations of African-American achievements indicate, to the contrary, that first and foremost African-Americans take pride in the diverse achievements of other members of their race. In fact, there is rarely, if ever, even a question raised as to whether those achievements have resulted from the less harmed benefiting at the expense of those more seriously harmed.[36]

Hiring preferences for equally competent minority and women candidates not only provides affirmation and inspiration for members of their own groups, it also produces the salutary byproduct of diversifying the workplace. In such cases, the race or sex of a person so hired, of course, does not constitute a qualification for a job since the criteria of equal qualification must be met before an employer considers tipping the scales in favor of an affirmative action hiring. Although the justification offered here for affirmative action depends upon compensation instead of upon augmenting diversity, diversity still constitutes an *additional* valuable outcome of affirmative action justified on compensatory grounds.

Finally, by placing an emphasis upon a compensation justification of affirmative action instead of a diversity approach, one will be less prone to the homogenization of the viewpoints of minorities or women that is a distinct danger in the diversity justification according to Stephen Carter. Carter complains that employers at times seem to be hiring minorities or women in order that they represent "the black's" or "the woman's" point of view, as if there were one black or female point of view. Ironically, a policy aimed at diversity in a university or business might effectively de-diversify those hired under affirmative action insofar as the university or business might convey expectations that there is a single ideological position with which those hired must agree. Even if diversity is subordinated to compensation, there is still a danger of expecting a certain conformism among affirmative action hirees and thus of installing a new totality in the very effort to break out of another. While Carter has strongly opposed such demands for conformity, he has also attempted to explain what is distinctive about African-Americans: their collective history or experience, their common past of woeful oppression, their gloriously triumphant present, and their sense of ethical responsibility and love for each other. Indeed, commonalities such as these create a loose perspective diverse from that of the majority without translating into "loyalty tests," "shibboleths," an "identity of perspective," or an "isomorphic mapping of one person's experience and personality onto another."[37]

In spite of these subsidiary benefits of group affirmation and diversification, a growing number still wish to do away with affirmative action without inquiring whether there are any alternatives which might be put in its place. Once again, Thomas Sowell adopts an extreme position that views affirmative action as only destructive and needing no replacement. "No one who extinguishes a forest fire or removes a cancer has to 'replace' it with anything. We are well rid of evils," Sowell writes. However, Sowell does suggest a substitute later, when he recommends an educational program improving the skills and work habits of less fortunate people. In Sowell's view, such a program may cost more money, may take more time, and will be ignored by the media, which prefers to applaud politically symbolic policies such as affirmative action. In addition, Justice Antonin Scalia, for instance, urges, as a replacement for affirmative action, programs for the poor and disadvantaged as long as the selection criteria for admission are not racial. Similarly Justice O'Connor recommends training and financial aid for disadvantaged entrepreneurs of all races, and even a race-neutral program of city financing for small firms. While such recommendations for increased social responsibility have their merit, they do relinquish the effort to compensate those who were unfairly targeted and excluded because of their race. Such recommendations seem willing to forget the past in the way that some post-Holocaust Germans seek to "get over the past" and "put it behind us."[38]

This study has attempted to show that the legal policy of affirmative action is ethically justifiable. However, the debate over affirmative action raises deeper questions about the role of law and jurisprudence. On the one hand, a formalized notion of law, which supports the anti-discrimination principle that tends to rule out affirmative action, according to Fiss, excludes features such as race from the legal decision. It strives for a kind of value-neutrality since one need only exercise a mechanical jurisprudence, determining whether a program (e.g., requiring a passing grade on a test for civil service) fits its goal (hiring competent civil servants). Its rules are clear, and its individual focus eliminates any need to focus on social groups, as the anti-discrimination principle illustrates. Underlying this appeal of the anti-discrimination principle is a conception of law that is focused on the morality of the process, as Robert Bork suggests, rather than the moral results of the process.[39]

But there are those who consider this mechanistic, means-end focus of law to be opting for legal formalism at the expense of substantive justice, to be neglecting society-wide injustice, and to be maintaining intact present exclusions. Fiss, for one, argues that such formalism already implies a substantive notion of justice when, for instance, he challenges the value-neutrality of the anti-discrimination principle since it must determine, among other things, whether the state end is legitimate, which classifications are suspect, which rights are fundamental, and which legitimate state interests are compelling. While pretending not to take a stand on broader questions of justice, such a conception of law actually does favor a minimal formalized notion of justice. Fiss himself, for instance, states that one must argue why the ideals of mechanical jurisprudence and its institutional advantages ought to outweigh the substantive results deemed just. In his view, the "redistributed aims served by the group-disadvantaging principle—the elevation of at least one group that has spent two centuries in this country in a position of subordination—may simply override these supposed institutional advantages." Similarly, Derek Bell recalls the legal realist movement of the 1930s which challenged the classical, formalistic structure of the law exemplified in the Supreme Court's rejection of New Deal legislation in spite of the prevalent starvation and desperate need for state intervention during the Great Depression. Randall Kennedy likewise points out how the Supreme Court was reluctant to invalidate segregation statutes since they seemed to function race-neutrally, excluding white children from black schools and black children from white schools, until finally the Court decided in *Brown* that segregation laws actually entailed racial subjugation. Furthermore, in Kennedy's opinion, it was really blindness to contemporary social realities that helped produce *Plessy* v. *Ferguson* which institutionalized the "lie" that segregation of blacks had nothing to do with racial oppression. Clearly, a formalized, mechanical conception of law out of touch with human suffering would exemplify the Levinasian level of the Third at its worst, deaf to and detached from the face to face of which it is a moment.[40]

To be sure, many would oppose the idea that such substantive notions of justice ought to determine law. Morris Abram argues that the American system ensures only civil political rights and not social and economic rights since enforcement of the latter might interfere with the market system and fail to produce high standards of living. Ernest Van den Haag believes that the law is only meant to produce justice (in the sense of formal legal fairness) and that charity and benevolence pertain to the private sector. While Abram and Van den Haag might seem to some to be defining justice, their definition vastly restricts its scope to others.[41]

Recent writing in the philosophy of law by Ronald Dworkin has attacked the positivistic foundations of law and articulated a comprehensive theory of political and economic rights in opposition to viewpoints such as those of Abram and Van den Haag and more in accord with the viewpoint advanced in this book. Dworkin criticizes H. L. A. Hart's positivistic view of law that reduces it to extent rules (as did J. Austin). Dworkin illustrates, to the contrary, that judges and lawyers often appeal in their argumentation beyond existing rules to "principles," that is, standards to be observed because they are requirements of justice, fairness, or some other dimension of morality (e.g., the standard that no one ought to profit by his or her own wrong in the famous case of *Riggs* v. *Palmer*). In Dworkin's account, law becomes a complex, interpretive process in which one must take account of diverse principles and their weighting and appropriateness, one's moral and political convictions, and the history of legal practice and precedents.[42]

Dworkin is right, there are certain moral principles implicit in the practices of law and more specifically in the defenses of affirmative action and even in the criticism of affirmative action by those who fear for the rights of those who will be displaced by its hirings. Such principles are implicit in Sartre's criticism of anti-Semitic reification, in Beauvoir's outrage over the inequities to which women are subjected, and in Schutz's endeavor to ensure that the viewpoint of the racially oppressed be taken into account. These principles converge in a desire to uphold the dignity of individuals, to protect the equality of free agents, and to prevent individuals from being subordinated to teleological processes in which they count for nothing. If we look to make those principles explicit and to provide them with justification, we have only to turn to the presuppositions of the very discourse in which we attempt to justify and in which opponents combat our justifications. In the very give and take of reasoning, in which we replace violence with an appeal to the sovereignty of the each to assent or dissent, a version of Kant's categorical imperative to treat people as ends in themselves still holds sway, and whoever would argue against it must presuppose it.

But ethics is more than this principle, even though we dare not attempt to argue it away. Ethical principles, though, are dangerous, for in their name we can demand conformity, inflict violence on ourselves or others all the while thinking we are moral, immunize ourselves against others' input, or harden our hearts or blind our eyes in the face of our neighbor's suffering and destitution. In the other person lies our hope that our ethics will be authentic and our principles well applied. But our principles also help us to discern what is really for the other's good, as long, of course, as our discernment also is vulnerable to the other with whom we are discerning. Two poles of ethics in dialectical tension, neither one able to do without the other, and both discoverable to a restless phenomenology, soaring to transcendental heights and plunging to the soil of the life-world.

NOTES

1. Nathan Glazer, *Affirmative Discrimination: Ethnic Inequality and Public Policy* (Cambridge, Mass., and London: Harvard University Press, 1987), pp. 44, 197, 204, 221; Lee Nisbet, "Affirmative Action: A Liberal Program?" in *Racial Preference and Racial Justice: The New Affirmative Action Controversy*, ed. Russell Nieli (Washington, D.C.: Ethics and Public Policy Center, 1991), p. 115; George Sher "Justifying Reverse Discrimination in Employment," in *Equality and Preferential Treatment: A Philosophy and Public Affairs Reader*, ed. Marshall Cohen, Thomas Nagel, and Thomas Scanlon (Princeton, N.J.: Princeton University Press, 1977), pp. 59–60; Owen Fiss, "Groups and the Equal Protection Clause," in *Equality and Preferential Treatment*, p. 107; Alan Goldman, *Justice and Reverse Discrimination* (Princeton, N.J.: Princeton University Press, 1979), pp. 77, 93.

2. Goldman, *Justice and Reverse Discrimination*, pp. 76–94.

3. Ibid., p. 92.

4. Ibid., pp. 6–7, 67–69, 77, 80–81, 90, 92, 202–203.

5. Thomas Sowell, *Preferential Policies: An International Perspective* (New York: William Morrow and Company, Inc., 1990), p. 170; see also pp. 15, 169, 171.

6. Stephen Carter, *Reflections of an Affirmative Action Baby* (New York: Basic Books, 1991), pp. 71–95, 174–81; Glazer, *Affirmative Discrimination, Ethnic Inequality and Public Policy*, pp. 72–73; Goldman, *Justice and Reverse Discrimination*, p. 191; Barry R. Gross, *Discrimination in Reverse: Is Turnabout Fair Play?* (New York: New York University Press, 1978), p. 112; Robert Simon, "Preferential Hiring: A Reply to Judith Jarvis Thomson," in *Equality and Preferential Treatment*, pp. 41–44; Thomas Sowell, *Civil Rights: Rhetoric or Reality?* (New York: William Morrow and Company, Inc., 1984), pp. 52, 133–34.

7. Goldman, *Justice and Reverse Discrimination*, pp. 94–102.

8. Michel Rosenfeld, *Affirmative Action and Justice: A Philosophical and Constitutional Inquiry* (New Haven and London: Yale University Press, 1991), pp. 7, 239, 258–75, 296–304.

9. Catharine A. MacKinnon, *Only Words* (Cambridge, Mass.: Harvard University Press, 1993), pp. 30, 45, 48, 53, 99–100, 109; Mari J. Matsuda, "Public Response to Racist Speech: Considering the Victim's Story," in Mari J. Matsuda, et al., *Words that Wound: Critical Race Theory, Assaultive Speech and the First Amendment* (Boulder, San Francisco, Oxford: Westview Press, 1993), pp. 34–35, 36, 43, 46, 47, 133; Charles R. Lawrence III, "If He Hollers Let Him Go: Regulating Racist Speech on Campus," in *Words That Wound*, pp. 62, 67, 72–73, 81; Richard Delgado, "Words That Wound: A Tort Action for Racial Insults, Epithets, and Name Calling," in *Words That Wound*, pp. 96ff., 107, 110. The authors of *Words That Wound* make a strong case in the passages cited that racial and sexual insults have been at certain levels of the court system in

the United States prohibited by law and that they ought to be. These authors represent a movement called "critical race theory," one of whose major premises comes close to a theme of this book, namely, that it is quite possible to uphold an abstract concept (e.g., "freedom of speech") that one would not hold to so absolutely if one took account of the viewpoint of those who suffer racial or sexual insults.

10. Goldman, *Justice and Reverse Discrimination*, pp. 182, 191–92; Rosenfeld, *Affirmative Action and Justice: A Philosophical and Constitutional Inquiry*, pp. 82–83, 92, 298. The difficulty of providing psychological measurements of harm is something that Goldman himself admits. For a discussion of the harms caused by racist insults even to those of high socioeconomic status see Delgado, "Words That Wound: A Tort Action for Racial Insults, Epithets, and Name Calling," p. 91.

11. Goldman, *Justice and Reverse Discrimination*, p. 182; Emmanuel Levinas, *Otherwise Than Being, or Beyond Essence*, trans. Alphonso Lingis (The Hague, Boston, London: Martinus Nijhoff, 1981), p. 125; *supra*, chapter 5, p. 26.

12. An interesting book critical of the philosophical presuppositions that underlie a work like Sowell's is Axel Honneth's *The Struggle for Recognition: The Moral Grammar of Social Conflicts*, trans. Joel Anderson (Cambridge: Polity Press, 1995). Honneth argues from a critical theory perspective that conflicts between human beings can be traced back not to motives of self-preservation but to moral impulses. In Honneth's view Hegel sought to bring these impulses to light to reverse the tradition that began with Machiavelli and Hobbes. Honneth's identification of the "moral infrastructure" of interactions resembles Levinas's move beneath the Third, although Honneth envisions these interactions as reversible, from a third-person perspective, as opposed to the Levinasian face to face. See pp. 5, 10, 143, 161.

13. Randall Kennedy, "Persuasion and Distrust," in *Racial Preference and Racial Justice: The New Affirmative Action Controversy*, p. 52; Fiss, "Groups and the Equal Protection Clause," p. 139; Rosenfeld, *Affirmative Action and Justice: A Philosophical and Constitutional Inquiry*, p. 303; John Edwards, *When Race Counts: The Morality of Racial Preference in Britain and America* (London and New York: Routledge, 1995), pp. 20–21; see Stephan Thernstrom and Abigail Thernstrom, *American in Black and White: One Nation, Indivisible* (New York: Simon and Schuster, 1997), p. 11. It is somewhat ironic that opponents of affirmative action such as Justices Scalia and O'Connor recommend as replacements for affirmative action expensive social and educational programs directed toward the poor and disadvantaged while those of similar political persuasions in Congress seek to limit the scope of such programs.

14. Morris B. Abram, "Fair Shakers and Social Engineers," in *Racial Preference and Racial Justice: The New Affirmative Action Controversy*, p. 35; Robert H. Bork, "The Supreme Court and Civil Rights," in *Racial Preference and Racial Justice: The New Affirmative Action Controversy*, p. 273; Glazer,

Affirmative Discrimination, Ethnic Inequality and Public Policy, pp. 63, 69, 96, 155, 203; Harvey C. Mansfield Jr., "The Underhandedness of Affirmative Action," in *Racial Preference and Racial Justice: The New Affirmative Action Controversy*, p. 132; Thomas Sowell, "Are Quotas Good for Blacks?" in *Racial Preference and Racial Justice: The New Affirmative Action Controversy*, p. 417; Sowell, *Civil Rights: Rhetoric or Reality?* pp. 16, 23, 43, 45, 48, 57, 59, 94, 114; Sowell, *Preferential Policies, An International Perspective*, pp. 105, 131, 140, 149–50.

15. Sowell, *Preferential Policies: An International Perspective*, p. 140.

16. Ibid., p. 149, see also pp. 129, 140; Sowell, *Civil Rights: Rhetoric or Reality?* pp. 130, 132.

17. Sandra Day O'Connor, "Set-Asides Violate the Equal Protection Clause," in *Racial Preference and Racial Justice: The New Affirmative Action Controversy*, p. 242.

18. Ibid., pp. 239–44; Rosenfeld, *Affirmative Action and Justice: A Philosophical and Constitutional Inquiry*, pp. 204–15; *City of Richmond* v. *J. A. Croson Company, West's Supreme Court Reporter* (St. Paul, Minn.: West Publishing Company, 1993), 109:713–31.

19. Sowell, *Civil Rights: Rhetoric or Reality?* p. 78; Thomas Sowell, *Ethnic America, A History* (New York: Basic Books, 1981), pp. 216, 218, 219; Thomas Sowell, "Three Black Histories," in *Essays and Data on American Ethnic Groups*, ed. by Thomas Sowell (Washington, D.C.: The Urban Institute, 1978), pp. 41–49; David Lowenthal, "Race and Color in the West Indies," *Daedalus* 96 (Spring 1967): 585, 587, 610.

20. Sowell, *Civil Rights: Rhetoric or Reality?* pp. 92–107, 116.

21. Ibid., p. 135. Sowell also skews the data when he claims that affirmative action *causes* the disadvantages of suffering, lower-class minorities since it creates a demand for "safe" minorities and thus leaves out the less educated and skilled. This entire argument (cf. Sowell, *Civil Rights: Rhetoric or Reality?* p. 53; *Preferential Policies, An International Perspective*, pp. 158, 172) neglects that better educated minorities—those who would benefit more from affirmative action—are not competing for the same type of job as less educated lower-class minorities. Affirmative action, as we have already mentioned, targeted specific strategic groups in order to redress past injustices, to improve the status of minorities as a whole, and to open up the possibilities that had been denied to those minorities, without necessarily intending to elevate every single member of those minorities. It is difficult to see how the hiring of professionally qualified minorities *causes* the sufferings of those who are not qualified to compete for such positions. Those sufferings, in fact, would seem to call for some type of effort, parallel to affirmative action, to improve the lot of those less educated.

22. Rosenfeld, *Affirmative Action and Justice: A Philosophical and Constitutional Inquiry*, pp. 211–14, 292; *City of Richmond* v. *J. A. Croson Company*, pp. 713–31, 747.

23. *City of Richmond* v. *J. A. Croson Company*, pp. 713–31.

24. Sowell, *Preferential Policies: An International Perspective*, p. 134, see pp. 132–34; Immanuel Kant, *Grounding for the Metaphysics of Morals*, trans. James W. Ellington (Indianapolis and Cambridge: Hackett Publishing Company, 1981), p. 43.

25. Kant, *Grounding for the Metaphysics of Morals*, p. 20; see *supra*, chapter 5, p. 15.

26. Glazer, *Affirmative Discrimination, Ethnic Inequality and Public Policy*, p. 201; Sowell, *Preferential Policies: An International Perspective*, p. 148; Goldman, *Justice and Reverse Discrimination*, pp. 115–16.

27. Glazer, *Affirmative Discrimination, Ethnic Inequality and Public Policy*, pp. 194–98; Kennedy, "Persuasion and Distrust," p. 49; Sowell, *Civil Rights: Rhetoric or Reality?* pp. 90, 118, 122.

28. *Affirmative Action and Justice: A Philosophical and Constitutional Inquiry*, p. 87; Goldman, *Justice and Reverse Discrimination*, p. 72; *supra*, chapter 7, p. 9.

29. Judith Jarvis Thomson, "Preferential Hiring," in *Equality and Preferential Treatment*, p. 38; Ronald Dworkin, "Are Quotas Unfair?" *Racial Preference and Racial Justice: The New Affirmative Action Controversy*, p. 189; Charles Krauthammer, "Why We Need Race Consciousness," in *Racial Preference and Racial Justice: The New Affirmative Action Controversy*, p. 147.

30. Judith Jarvis Thomson, "Preferential Hiring: A Reply to Judith Jarvis Thomson," in *Equality and Preferential Treatment*, p. 33.

31. Kennedy, "Persuasion and Distrust," p. 54; Dworkin, "Are Quotas Unfair?" p. 187.

32. Sowell, *Preferential Policies: An International Perspective*, p. 153; Russell Nieli, "Ethnic Tribalism and Human Personhood," in *Racial Preference and Racial Justice: The New Affirmative Action Controversy*, p. 82; Emmanuel Levinas, *Totality and Infinity: An Essay on Exteriority*, trans. Alphonso Lingis (The Hague, Boston, London: Martinus Nijhoff, 1979), pp. 21–22, 239, 244–46; Levinas, *Otherwise Than Being*, p. 126.

33. Levinas, *Otherwise Than Being*, p. 126.

34. Thomson, "Preferential Hiring," p. 39.

35. Goldman, *Affirmative Action and Justice*, pp. 171–74, 186–87, 195, 293, 328–29; Abram, "Fair Shakers and Social Engineers," p. 44; Gross, *Discrimination in Reverse: Is Turnabout Fair Play?* p. 94; Goldman, *Justice and Reverse Discrimination*, pp. 64, 121.

36. Goldman, *Justice and Reverse Discrimination*, p. 85. The value that seeing members of one's race or sex in important positions, the resultant enhancement of one's own identity, cannot be underestimated. This is especially so in the light of research by Claude M. Steele which shows the negative impact of pervasive stereotypes on even the most successful black students when they take tests. Steele comments, "This threat [of self-fulfilling broadly disseminated negative stereotypes] can befall anyone with a group identity about which some negative stereotype exists, and for the person to be threat-

ened in this way, he need not even believe the stereotype. He need only know that it stands as a hypothesis about him in situations where the stereotype is relevant." Claude M. Steele and Joshua Aronson, "Stereotype Threat and the Intellectual Test Performance of African Americans," *Journal of Personality and Social Psychology* 69, no. 5 (1995): 798.

37. Carter, *Reflections of an Affirmative Action Baby*, pp. 34, 38, 40, 42, 44–45, 99–102, 199, 237–53; Kwame Anthony Appiah, *In My Father's House: Africa in the Philosophy of Culture* (New York and Oxford: Oxford University Press, 1992), pp. 28–46; Goldman, *Justice and Reverse Discrimination*, pp. 57, 148, 167–68, 226–27.

38. Sowell, *Preferential Policies: An International Perspective*, pp. 168, 182; Antonin Scalia, "The Disease as Cure," in *Racial Preference and Racial Justice: The New Affirmative Action Controversy*, p. 221; O'Connor, "Set-Asides Violate the Equal Protection Clause," pp. 243–44. The question arises whether that compensation might ever reach a point where it is completed. It is difficult to spell out criteria for such a moment, which may indeed be possible. Certainly proportions of representation ought to be more in line with proportions of population, and certainly the viewpoint of all affected ought to be considered.

39. Fiss, "Groups and the Equal Protection Clause," pp. 95–106, 152; Bork, "The Supreme Court and Civil Rights," p. 275.

40. Derrick Bell, *Faces at the Bottom of the Well: The Permanence of Racism* (New York: Basic Books, 1992), pp. 100–101; Kennedy, "Persuasion and Distrust," pp. 55–57.

41. Abram, "Fair Shakers and Social Engineers," p. 44; Ernest Van den Haag, "Jews and Negroes," in *Racial Preference and Racial Justice: The New Affirmative Action Controversy*, p. 392.

42. Ronald Dworkin, *Taking Rights Seriously* (Cambridge, Mass.: Harvard University Press, 1977), pp. 18–19, 22, 112, 147, 149; Ronald Dworkin, *Law's Empire* (Cambridge, Mass., and London: The Belknap Press of Harvard University Press, 1986), pp. 123, 190, 215, 243, 263, 321, 358, 369, 371, 413.

Dworkin's revelation of how moral principles inevitably shape the formation of law opens the door to an ethicotheoretical position such as that of Alan Gewirth's *The Community of Rights*, which argues for positive and negative rights on the basis of the conditions universally requisite for anyone to engage in purposive activity. By upholding positive rights, including rights to having basic economic necessities met, Gewirth avoids the adversarial relationship between rights and community typical of those who conceive rights only negatively and whose view of society is often antagonistic to values of community and solidarity. By complementing rights with community and community with rights, Gewirth avoids the extremes and includes the advantages of libertarianism and communitarianism in a way that resembles our earlier account of how Levinas's description of the Other underpins both libertarian and socialist, although Gewirth's account proceeds on the plane of the Third. See

Alan Gewirth, *The Community of Rights* (Chicago and London: University of Chicago Press, 1996), pp. 31–32, 39, 73, 75, 87–88, 319–26. The Case of *Riggs* v. *Palmer* (1889) had to do with whether someone could inherit under a will naming him a beneficiary when he had murdered the testator, his grandfather, presented before the New York Court of Appeals. The court was divided in the issue; see *West's Encyclopedia of American Law* (St. Paul, Minn.: West Group, 1998): 6:426.

BIBLIOGRAPHY

Abram, Morris B. "Fair Shakers and Social Engineers." In *Racial Preference and Racial Justice: The New Affirmative Action Controversy*, edited by Russell Nieli, pp. 29–44. Washington, D.C.: Ethics and Public Policy Center, 1991.

Alcoff, Linda Martin, and Merold Westphal, eds. *Conflicts and Convergences*, vol. 16 of *Selected Studies in Phenomenology and Existential Philosophy*. Chicago: DePaul University, 1999.

Allen, Jeffner. "An Introduction to Patriarchal Existentialism: A Proposal for a Way Out of Existential Patriarchy." In *The Thinking Muse: Feminism and Modern French Philosophy*, edited by Jeffner Allen and Iris Marion Young, pp. 71–84. Bloomington and Indianapolis: Indiana University Press, 1989.

Allen, Jeffner, and Iris Marion Young, eds. *The Thinking Muse: Feminism and Modern French Philosophy*. Bloomington and Indianapolis: Indiana University Press, 1989.

Anderson, Thomas C. *Sartre's Two Ethics: From Authenticity to Integral Humanity*. Chicago and LaSalle, Ill.: Open Court, 1993.

Apel, Karl-Otto. *Diskurs und Verantwortung: Das Problem des Übergangs zur postkonventionellen Moral*. Frankfurt am Main: Suhrkamp Verlag, 1988.

———. "Fallibilismus, Konsenstheorie der Wahrheit, und Letztbegründung." In *Philosophie und Begründung*, edited by Wolfgang R. Köhler, Wolfgang Kuhlmann, and Peter Rohs, pp. 116–211. Frankfurt am Main: Suhrkamp Verlag, 1987.

———. "Die Herausforderung der totalen Vernunftkritik und das Programm einer philosophischen Theorie der Rationalitätstypen." *Concordia* (Frankfurt) 11 (1987): 2–23.

————. "Normatively Grounding 'Critical Theory' through a Recourse to the Life-world? A Transcendental Pragmatic Attempt to Think with Habermas against Habermas." In *Philosophical Interventions in the Unfinished Project of Enlightenment*, edited by Axel Honneth, Thomas McCarthy, Claus Offe, and Albrecht Wellmer, translated by William Rehg, pp. 125–70. Cambridge, Mass., and London: MIT Press, 1992.

————. "Pragmatic Philosophy of Language Based on Transcendental Semiotics." In *Selected Essays*, vol. 1: *Toward a Transcendental Semiotics*, edited by Eduardo Mendieta, pp. 231–53. Atlantic Highlands, N.J.: Humanities Press, 1994.

————. "The Problem of Philosophical Foundations in Light of a Transcendental Pragmatics of Language." In *After Philosophy, End or Transformation?* edited by Kenneth Baynes, James Bohman, and Thomas McCarthy, pp. 250–90. Cambridge, Mass., and London: MIT Press, 1987.

————. "Scientistics, Hermeneutics and the Critique of Ideology: Outline of a Theory of Science from a Cognitivie-Anthropological Standpoint." In *Toward a Transformation of Philosophy*, translated by Glyn Adey and David Frisby, pp. 46–76. London, Boston, Henley: Routledge and Kegan Paul, 1980.

————. *Selected Essays*, Vol. 1: *Toward a Transcendental Semiotics*. Edited by Eduardo Mendieta. Atlantic Highlands, N.J.: Humanities Press, 1994.

————. *Toward a Transformation of Philosophy*. Translated by Glyn Adey and David Frisby. London and Boston: Routledge and Kegan Paul, 1980.

————. "Towards a Reconstruction of Critical Theory." In *Philosophical Disputes in the Social Sciences*, edited by S. C. Brown, pp. 127–39. Sussex: Harvester Press and Atlantic Highlands, N.J.: Humanities Press, 1979.

————. *Transformation der Philosophie*, vol. 1: *Sprachanalytik, Semiotik, Hermeneutik*. Frankfurt am Main: Suhrkamp Verlag, 1973.

————. *Transformation der Philosophie*, vol. 2: *Das Apriori der Kommunikationsgemeinschaft*. Frankfurt am Main: Suhrkamp Verlag, 1973.

————. *Understanding and Explanation, A Transcendental-Pragmatic Perspective*. Translated by Georgia Warnke. Cambridge, Mass., and London: MIT Press, 1984.

Apel, Karl-Otto, Dietrich Böhler, Alfred Berlich, and Gerhard Plumpe, eds. *(Funk-Kolleg) Praktische Philosophie/Ethik*. Weinheim-Basel: Fischer Verlag, 1984.

Appiah, Kwame Anthony. *In My Father's House: Africa in the Philosophy of Culture*. New York and Oxford: Oxford University Press, 1992.

Aronson, Ronald, and Adrian van den Hoven, eds. *Sartre Alive*. Detroit: Wayne State University Press, 1991.

Arp, Kristiana. "Beauvoir's Concept of Bodily Alienation." In *Feminist Interpretations of Simone de Beauvoir*, edited by Margaret A. Simons, pp. 161–77. University Park: Pennsylvania State University Press, 1995.

Azzi, Marie-Denise Boros. "Representation of Character in Sartre's Drama, Fiction, and Biography." In *The Philosophy of Jean-Paul Sartre*, vol.16 of *The*

Library of Living Philosophers, edited by Paul Arthur Schilpp, pp. 438–76. Lasalle, Ill.: Open Court, 1981.

Bair, Deirdre. *Simone de Beauvoir: A Biography*. New York: Summit Books, 1990.

Barnes, Hazel. "Response to Margaret Simons." In *Conflicts and Convergences*, vol. 24 of *Selected Studies in Phenomenology and Existential Philosophy*, edited by Linda Martin Alcoff and Merold Westphal, pp. 29–34. Chicago: DePaul University, 1999.

———. "Sartre and Sexism." *Philosophy and Literature* 14, no. 2 (1990): 340–47.

Barber, Michael D., S.J. "Constitution and the Sedimentation of the Social in Alfred Schutz's Theory of Typification." *The Modern Schoolman* 64 (1987): 111–20.

———. *Ethical Hermeneutics: Rationality in Enrique Dussel's Philosophy of Liberation*. New York: Fordham University Press, 1998.

———. "The Ethics behind the Absence of Ethics in Alfred Schutz's Thought." *Human Studies* 14 (1991): 129–40.

———. *Guardian of Dialogue: Max Scheler's Phenomenology, Sociology of Knowledge, and Philosophy of Love*. Lewisburg, Penn.: Bucknell University Press and London and Toronto: Associated University Presses, 1993.

———. "Phenomenology and the Ethical Bases of Pluralism: Arendt's and Beauvoir's Treatment of Race in America." In *The Existential Phenomenology of Simone de Beauvoir*, edited by Lester Embree. Dordrecht, Boston, London: Kluwer Academic Press, forthcoming.

———. "The Vulnerability of Reason: The Philosophical Foundations of Emmanuel Levinas and K. O. Apel." In *The Prism of the Self, Philosophical Essays in Honor of Maurice Natanson*, edited by Steven Galt Crowell, pp. 93–106. Dordrecht, Boston, London: Kluwer Academic Publishers, 1995.

Baynes, Kenneth, James Bohman, and Thomas McCarthy, eds. *After Philosophy: End or Transformation?* Cambridge, Mass., and London: MIT Press, 1987.

Beauvoir, Simone de. *All Said and Done*. Translated by Patrick O'Brian. New York: Warner Books, 1974.

———. *America Day by Day*. Translated by Carol Cosman (Berkeley, Los Angeles, London: University of California Press, 1999). A translation of *L'Amérique au jour le jour*. Paris: Gallimard, 1947.

———. *The Ethics of Ambiguity*. Translated by Bernard Frechtman. New York: The Citadel Press, 1948.

———. *Force of Circumstance*, vol. 1: *After the War*. Translated by Richard Howard. New York: Paragon House, 1992.

———. *Force of Circumstance*, vol. 2: *Hard Times*. Translated by Richard Howard. New York: Paragon House, 1992.

———. *Memoirs of a Dutiful Daughter*. Translated by James Kirkup. New York: Harper & Row, 1959.

———. "Merleau-Ponty and Pseudo-Sartreanism." *International Studies in Philosophy* 21 (1989): 3–48.

————. "Must We Burn Sade?" In *The Marquis de Sade*, translated by Annette Michelson, edited by Paul Dinnage. London: John Calder, 1962.

————. *The Prime of Life*. Translated by Peter Green. Cleveland and New York: The World Publishing Company, 1962.

————. *Pyrrhus et Cinéas*. In *Pour une morale de l-ambiguïté suivi de Pyrrhus et Cinéas*. Paris: Gallimard, 1944.

————. "Review of *La phénoménologie de la perception*." *Les Temps Modernes* 1 (1945): 363–67.

————. *The Second Sex*. Translated by H. M. Parshley. New York: Vintage Books, 1989. English translation of *Le deuxième sexe*, vol. 1: *Les faits et les mythes*. Paris: Gallimard, 1976, and vol. 2: *L'expérience vécue*. Paris: Gallimard, 1976.

————. *She Came to Stay*. Cleveland, Ohio, and New York: The World Publishing Company, 1954.

Bell, Derek. *Faces at the Bottom of the Well: The Permanence of Racism*. New York: Basic Books, 1992.

Bergoffen, Debra. *The Philosophy of Simone de Beauvoir: Gendered Phenomenologies, Erotic Generosities*. Albany: State University of New York Press, 1997.

Bernasconi, Robert. "Sartre's Gaze Returned: The Transformation of the Phenomenology of Racism." *Graduate Faculty Philosophy Journal* 18 (1995): 201–21.

————. "The Trace of Levinas in Derrida." In *Derrida and Differance*, edited by David Wood and Robert Bernasconi, pp. 13–29. Evanston: Northwestern University Press, 1988.

Bork, Robert H. "The Supreme Court and Civil Rights." In *Racial Preference and Racial Justice: The New Affirmative Action Controversy*, edited by Russell Nieli, pp. 269–75. Washington, D.C.: Ethics and Public Policy Center, 1991.

Bok, Derek. "Admitting Success." In *Racial Preference and Racial Justice: The New Affirmative Action Controversy*, edited by Russell Nieli, pp. 409–16. Washington, D.C.: Ethics and Public Policy Center, 1991.

Bound, John, and Richard B. Freeman. "Black Economic Progress: Erosion of the Post-1965 Gains in the 1980s." In *The Question of Discrimination: Racial Inequality in the U.S. Labor Market*, edited by Steven Shulman and William Darity Jr., pp. 32–49. Middletown, Conn.: Wesleyan University Press, 1989.

Brown, Charles. "The Federal Attack on Labor Market Discrimination: The Mouse That Roared?" *Research in Labor Economics* 5 (1982): 33–68.

Brown, S. C., ed. *Philosophical Disputes in the Social Sciences*. Sussex: Harvester Press and Atlantic Highlands, N.J.: Humanities Press, 1979.

Butler, Judith. "Sex and Gender in Simone de Beauvoir's *Second Sex*." In *Yale French Studies*, no. 72, pp. 00–00. New Haven, Conn.: Yale University Press, 1986. *Simone de Beauvoir: Witness to a Century*, edited by Helene V. Wenzel, pp. 35–49. New Haven, Conn.t: Yale University Press, 1986.

————. "Sexual Ideology and Phenomenological Deception: A Feminist Critique of Merleau-Ponty's Phenomenology of Perception." In *The Thinking*

Muse: Feminism and Modern French Philosophy, edited by Jeffner Allen and Iris Marion Young, pp. 85–100. Bloomington and Indianapolis: Indiana University Press, 1989.

Carter, Stephen. *Reflections of an Affirmative Action Baby*. New York: Basic Books, 1991.

Casey, Edward. "Sartre on Imagination." In *The Philosophy of Jean-Paul Sartre*, vol. 16 of *The Library of Living Philosophers*, edited by Paul Arthur Schilpp, pp. 138–66. Lasalle, Ill.: Open Court, 1981.

Cohen, Carl. "Justice Debased." In *Racial Preference and Racial Justice: The New Affirmative Action Controversy*, edited by Russell Nieli, pp. 329–52. Washington, D.C.: Ethics and Public Policy Center, 1991.

Cohen, Richard, ed. *Face to Face with Levinas*. Albany: State University of New York Press, 1986.

———. "Levinas, Rosenzweig and the Phenomenologies of Husserl and Heidegger." *Philosophy Today* 36 (1992): 165–78.

Collins, Margery L., and Christine Pierce. "Holes and Slime: Sexism in Sartre's Psychoanalysis." *The Philosophical Forum* 5, nos. 1–2 (1973–1974): 112–27.

Crowell, Steven Galt, ed. *The Prism of the Self: Philosophical Essays in Honor of Maurice Natanson*. Dordrecht, Boston, London: Kluwer Academic Publishers, 1995.

Curry, George E., ed. *The Affirmative Action Debate*. Reading, Mass.: Addison-Wesley Publishing Company, 1996.

Delgado, Richard. "Words That Wound: A Tort Action for Racial Insults, Epithets, and Name Calling." In *Words That Wound: Critical Race Theory, Assaultive Speech and the First Amendment*, pp. 89–110. Boulder, San Francisco, Oxford: Westview Press, 1993.

Derrida, Jacques. "Violence and Metaphysics, An Essay on the Thought of Emmanuel Levinas." *In Writing and Difference*, translated by Alan Bass, pp. 79–153. Chicago: University of Chicago Press, 1978.

Drinan, Robert. "Affirmative Action under Attack." In *Racial Preference and Racial Justice: The New Affirmative Action Controversy*, edited by Russell Nieli, pp. 117–25. Washington, D.C.: Ethics and Public Policy Center, 1991.

Dworkin, Ronald. "Are Quotas Unfair?" In *Racial Preference and Racial Justice: The New Affirmative Action Controversy*, edited by Russell Nieli, pp. 175–89. Washington, D.C.: Ethics and Public Policy Center, 1991.

———. "DeFunis v. Sweatt." In *Equality and Preferential Treatment: A Philosophy & Public Affairs Reader*, edited by Marshall Cohen, Thomas Nagel, and Thomas Scanlon, pp. 63–83. Princeton, N.J.: Princeton University Press, 1977.

———. *Law's Empire*. Cambridge, Mass., and London: Belknap Press of Harvard University Press, 1986.

———. *Taking Rights Seriously*. Cambridge, Mass.: Harvard University Press, 1977.

Edwards, John. *When Race Counts: The Morality of Racial Preference in Britain and America*. London and New York, Routledge: 1995.

Embree, Lester, ed. *Essays in Memory of Aron Gurwitsch*. Washington, D.C.: Center for Advanced Research in Phenomenology and University Press of America, 1984.

———. "The Ethical-Political Side of Schutz: His Contributions at the 1956 Institute on Ethics concerned with Barrier to Equality of Opportunity." In *Schutzian Social Science*, edited by Lester Embree, pp. 227–307. Dordrecht, Boston, London: Kluwer Academic Publishers, 1998.

———. "Schutz on Science." In *Worldly Phenomenology: The Continuing Influence of Alfred Schutz on North American Human Science*, edited by Lester Embree, pp. 251–73. Washington, D.C.: Center for Advanced Research in Phenomenology and the University Press of America, 1988.

———. "Schutz's Phenomenology of the Practical World." In *Alfred Schutz: Neue Beiträge zur Rezeption seines Werkes*, edited by Elisabeth List and Ilja Srubar, pp. 121–44. Amsterdam: Rodolpi, 1988.

_____, ed. *Schutzian Social Science*. Dordrecht, Boston, London: Kluwer Academic Publishers, 1998.

_____. *Worldly Phenomenology: The Continuing Influence of Alfred Schutz on North American Human Science*. Washington, D.C.: Center for Advanced Research in Phenomenology and the University Press of America, 1988.

Fanon, Frantz. *Black Skin, White Masks*. Translated by Charles Lam Markmann. New York: Grove Weidenfeld, 1967.

———. *The Wretched of the Earth*. Preface by Jean-Paul Sartre. Translated by Constance Farington. New York: Grove Press, Inc. 1963.

Ferguson, Margaret, and Jennifer Wicke, eds. *Feminism and Postmodernism*. Durham, N.C., and London: Duke University Press, 1994.

Fiss, Owen. "Groups and the Equal Protection Clause. In *Equality and Preferential Treatment: A Philosophy & Public Affairs Reader*, edited by Marshall Cohen, Thomas Nagel, and Thomas Scanlon, pp. 84–154. Princeton, N.J.: Princeton University Press, 1977.

Flynn, Thomas R. *Sartre and Marxist Existentialism: The Test Case of Collective Responsibility*. Chicago and London: University of Chicago Press, 1984.

Fullbrook, Kate, and Edward Fullbrook. *Simone de Beauvoir and Jean-Paul Sartre: The Remaking of a Twentieth Century Legend*. New York: Basic Books, 1994.

Gewirth, Alan. *The Community of Rights*. Chicago and London: University of Chicago Press, 1996.

Glazer, Nathan. *Affirmative Discrimination: Ethnic Inequality and Public Policy*. Cambridge, Mass., and London: Harvard University Press, 1987.

Goldman, Alan H. *Justice and Reverse Discrimination*. Princeton, N.J.: Princeton University Press, 1979.

Gordon, Lewis R. *Bad Faith and Antiblack Racism*. Atlantic Highlands, N.J.: Humanities Press, 1995.

Gross, Barry R. *Discrimination in Reverse: Is Turnabout Fair Play?* New York: New York University Press, 1978.

Guinier, Lani. *The Tyranny of the Majority: Fundamental Fairness in Representative Democracy.* New York: The Free Press, 1994.

Günther, Klaus. *The Sense of Appropriateness: Application Discourses in Morality and Law.* Translated by John Farrell. Albany: State University of New York Press, 1993.

Haag, Ernest Van den. "Jews and Negroes." In *Racial Preference and Racial Justice: The New Affirmative Action Controversy,* edited by Russell Nieli, pp. 383–92. Washington, D.C.: Ethics and Public Policy Center, 1991.

Habermas, Jürgen. "Discourse Ethics: Notes on a Program of Philosophical Justification." In *Moral Consciousness and Communicative Action,* translated by Christian Lenhardt and Shierry Weber Nicholsen, pp. 43–115. Cambridge, Mass.: MIT Press, 1990.

———. "Entgegnung." In *Kommunikatives Handeln: Beiträge zu Jürgen Habermas' "Theorie des kommunikativen Handelns,"* edited by Axel Honneth and Hans Joas, pp. 327–405. Frankfurt am Main: Suhrkamp Verlag, 1986.

———. *Justifications and Applications: Remarks on Discourse Ethics.* Translated by Ciaran Cronin. Cambridge, Mass., and London: MIT Press, 1993.

———. *Moral Consciousness and Communicative Action.* Translated by Christian Lenhardt and Shierry Weber Nicholsen. Cambridge, Mass.: MIT Press, 1990.

———. "Philosophy as Stand-In and Interpreter." In *Moral Consciousness and Communicative Action,* translated by Christian Lenhardt and Shierry Weber Nicholsen, pp. 1–20. Cambridge, Mass.: MIT Press, 1990.

———. *The Theory of Communicative Action,* vol. 1: *Reason and the Rationalization of Society.* Translated by Thomas McCarthy. Boston: Beacon Press, 1984.

———. *The Theory of Communicative Action,* vol. 2: *Life-world and System: A Critique of Functionalist Reason.* Translated by Thomas McCarthy. Boston: Beacon Press, 1987.

———. *Zur Logik der Sozialwissenschaften.* Tubingen: J.C.B. Mohr (Paul Siebeck), 1967.

Harris, Louis. "The Future of Affirmative Action." In *The Affirmative Action Debate,* edited by George E. Curry, pp. 326–35. Reading, Mass.: Addison-Wesley Publishing Company, Inc., 1996.

Hartmann, Heidi. "Who Has Benefited from Affirmative Action in Employment?" In *The Affirmative Action Debate,* edited by George E. Curry, pp. 77–96. Reading, Mass.: Addison-Wesley Publishing Company, Inc., 1996.

Heckman, James J. "The Impact of Government on the Economic Status of Black Americans." In *The Question of Discrimination: Racial Inequality in the U.S. Labor Market,* edited by Steven Schulman and William Darity Jr., pp. 50–80. Middletown, Conn.: Wesleyan University Press, 1989.

Holveck, Eleanore. "Can a Woman Be a Philosopher? Reflections of a Beau-voirian Housemaid." In *Feminist Interpretations of Simone de Beauvoir*, edited by Margaret A. Simons, pp. 67–78. University Park: Pennsylvania State University Press, 1995.

Honneth, Axel. *The Struggle for Recognition: The Moral Grammar of Social Conflicts*. Translated by Joel Anderson. Cambridge: Polity Press, 1995.

Honneth, Axel, and Hans Joas, eds. *Kommunikatives Handeln: Beiträge zu Jürgen Habermas' "Theorie des kommunikativen Handelns."* Frankfurt am Main: Suhrkamp Verlag, 1986.

Honneth, Axel, Thomas McCarthy, Claus Offe, and Albrecht Wellmer, eds. *Philosophical Interventions in the Unfinished Project of Enlightenment*. Translated by William Rehg. Cambridge, Mass., and London: MIT Press, 1992.

hooks, bell. *Yearning: Race, Gender, and Cultural Politics*. Boston: South End Press, 1990.

Husserl, Edmund. *Analysen zur passiven Synthesis, aus Vorlesung- und Forschungsmanuskripten 1918–1926*. Edited by Margot Fleischer. The Hague: Martinus Nijhoff, 1966.

———. *Cartesian Meditations: An Introduction to Phenomenology*. Translated by Dorian Cairns. The Hague, Boston, London: Martinus Nijhoff, 1960.

———. *The Crisis of European Sciences and Transcendental Phenomenology: An Introduction to Phenomenological Philosophy*. Translated by David Carr. Evanston, Ill.: Northwestern University Press, 1970.

———. *Erste Philosophie (1923/24)*. Part Two: *Theorie der phänomenologische Reduktion*. Edited by Rudolf Boehm. The Hague: Martinus Nijhoff, 1959.

———. *Ideas Pertaining to a Pure Phenomenology and to a Phenomenological Philosophy*. Book 1: *General Introduction to a Pure Phenomenology*. Translated by F. Kersten. The Hague, Boston, London: Martinus Nijhoff, 1982.

———. *Ideas Pertaining to a Pure Phenomenology and to a Phenomenological Philosophy*. Book 2: *Studies in the Phenomenology of Constitution*, translated by Richard Rojcewicz and Andre Schuwer. Dordrecht, Boston, London: Kluwer Academic Publishers, 1989.

———. "The Vienna Lecture." In *The Crisis of European Sciences and Transcendental Phenomenology: An Introduction to Phenomenological Philosophy*. Translated by David Carr. Evanston, Ill.: Northwestern University Press, 1970.

———. *Vorlesungen uber Ethik und Wertlehre 1908–1914*. Edited by Ullrich Melle. Dordrecht, Boston, London: Kluwer Academic Publishers, 1988.

Jehenson, Roger. "Critical Phenomenology of Domination." In *Worldly Phenomenology: The Continuing Influence of Alfred Schutz on North American Human Science*, edited by Lester Embree, pp. 1–23. Washington, D.C.: Center for Advanced Research in Phenomenolgy and the University Press of America, 1988.

Kant, Immanuel. *Critique of Practical Reason*. Translated by Lewis White Beck. Indianapolis and New York: The Bobbs-Merrill Company, Inc., 1956.

———. *Grounding for the Metaphysics of Morals*. Translated by James W. Ellington. Indianapolis and Cambridge: Hackett Publishing Company, 1981.

Kennedy, Randall. "Persuasion and Distrust." In *Racial Preference and Racial Justice: The New Affirmative Action Controversy*, edited by Russell Nieli, pp. 45–60. Washington, D.C.: Ethics and Public Policy Center, 1991.

Klaw, Barbara. "Sexuality in Beauvoir's *Les Mandarins*." In *Feminist Interpretations of Simone de Beauvoir*, edited by Margaret A. Simons, pp. 193–221. University Park: University of Pennsylvania Press, 1995.

Kockelmans, Joseph J. *Edmund Husserl's Phenomenology*. West Lafayette, Ind.: Purdue University Press, 1994.

Köhler, Wolfgang R. "Zur Debatte um reflexive Argumente in der neueren deutschen Philosophie." In *Philosophie und Begründung*, edited by Wolfgang R. Köhler, Wolfgang Kuhlmann, and Peter Rohs, pp. 303–33. Frankfurt am Main: Suhrkamp Verlag, 1987.

Köhler, Wolfgang, R., Wolfgang Kuhlmann, and Peter Rohs, eds. *Philosophie und Begründung*. Frankfurt am Main: Suhrkamp Verlag, 1987.

Krauthammer, Charles. "Why We Need Race Consciousness." In *Racial Preference and Racial Justice: The New Affirmative Action Controversy*, edited by Russell Nieli, pp. 141–48. Washington, D.C.: Ethics and Public Policy Center, 1991.

Kruks, Sonia. "Simone de Beauvoir: Teaching Sartre about Freedom." In *Sartre Alive*, edited by Ronald Aronson and Adrian van den Hoven, pp. 285–300. Detroit: Wayne State University Press, 1991.

Kuhlmann, Wolfgang. "Ethik der Kommunikation." In *(Funk-Kolleg) Praktische Philosophie/Ethik*, edited by Karl-Otto Apel, Dietrich Böhler, Alfred Berlich, and Gerhard Plumpe, pp. 292–308. Weinheim-Basel: Fischer Verlag, 1984.

Lawrence, Charles R., III. "If He Hollers Let Him Go: Regulating Racist Speech on Campus." In *Words That Wound: Critical Race Theory, Assaultive Speech and the First Amendment*, pp. 53–88. Boulder, San Francisco, Oxford: Westview Press, 1993.

Le Doeuff, Michèle. "Simone de Beauvoir and Existentialism." *Feminist Studies* 6, no. 2 (1980): 277–89.

———. "Simone de Beauvoir: Falling into (Ambiguous) Line." In *Feminist Interpretations of Simone de Beauvoir*, edited by Margaret A. Simons, pp. 59–65. University Park: University of Pennsylvania Press, 1995.

Leon, Celine T. "Beauvoir's Woman: Eunuch or Male?" In *Feminist Interpretations of Simone de Beauvoir*, edited by Margaret A. Simons, pp. 137–59. University Park: University of Pennsylvania Press, 1995.

Leonard, Jonathan. "The Impact of Affirmative Action on Employment." In *Racial Preference and Racial Justice: The New Affirmative Action Controversy*, edited by Russell Nieli, pp. 493–508. Washington, D.C.: Ethics and Public Policy Center, 1991.

Levinas, Emmanuel. *Otherwise Than Being, or Beyond Essence*. Translated by Alphonso Lingis. The Hague, Boston, London: Martinus Nijhoff, 1981.

———. *The Theory of Intuition in Husserl's Phenomenology*. Translated by Andre Orianne. Evanston, Ill.: Northwestern University Press, 1973.

———. *Totality and Infinity: An Essay in Exteriority*. Translated by Alphonso Lingis. The Hague, Boston, London: Martinus Nijhoff, 1979.

Lingis, Alphonso. *The Community of Those Who Have Nothing in Common*. Bloomington and Indianapolis: Indiana University Press, 1994.

———. *Sensation: Intelligibility in Sensibility*. Atlantic Highlands, N.J.: Humanities Press, 1996.

List, Elisabeth, and Ilja Srubar, eds. *Alfred Schutz: Neue Beiträge zur Rezeption seines Werkes*. Amsterdam: Rodolpi, 1988.

Lowenthal, David. "Race and Color in the West Indies." *Daedalus* 96 (1967): 580–626.

Lyotard, Jean François. "Levinas's Logic." In *Face to Face with Levinas*, edited by Richard Cohen, pp. 117–58. Albany: State University of New York Press, 1986.

MacKinnon, Catherine. *Only Words*. Cambridge, Mass.: Harvard University Press, 1993.

Mansfield, Harvey C., Jr. "The Underhandedness of Affirmative Action." In *Racial Preference and Racial Justice: The New Affirmative Action Controversy*, edited by Russell Nieli, pp. 127–40. Washington, D.C.: Ethics and Public Policy Center, 1991.

Marable, Manning. "Staying on the Path to Racial Equality." In *The Affirmative Action Debate*, edited by George E. Curry, pp. 1–15. Reading, Mass.: Addison-Wesley Publishing Company, Inc., 1996.

Marsh, James. *Critique, Action, and Liberation*. Albany: State University of New York Press, 1995.

Matsuda, Mari J. "Public Response to Racist Speech: Considering the Victim's Story." In *Words that Wound: Critical Race Theory, Assaultive Speech and the First Amendment*, pp. 17–51. Boulder, San Francisco, Oxford: Westview Press, 1993.

Matsuda, Mari J., Charles R. Lawrence III, Richard Delgado, and Kimberle Williams Crenshaw. *Words That Wound: Critical Race Theory, Assaultive Speech and the First Amendment*. Boulder, San Francisco, Oxford: Westview Press, 1993.

McBride, William Leon. "Sartre and Marxism." In *The Philosophy of Jean-Paul Sartre*, vol. 16 of *The Library of Living Philosophers*, edited by Paul Arthur Schilpp, pp. 605–30. Lasalle, Ill.: Open Court, 1981.

Merleau-Ponty, Maurice. *Phenomenology of Perception*. Translated by Colin Smith. London: Routlege and Atlantic Highlands, N.J.: Humanities Press, 1962.

———. "The Philosopher and His Shadow." In *Signs*, translated by Richard C. McCleary. Evanston, Ill.: Northwestern University Press, 1964.

———. *Signs*. Translated by Richard C. McCleary. Evanston, Ill.: Northwestern University Press, 1964.

————. *The Visible and the Invisible.* Edited by Claude Lefort. Translated by Alphonso Lingis. Evanston, Ill.: Northwestern University Press, 1968.

Mohanty, J. N. *The Possibility of Transcendental Philosophy.* Dordrecht, Boston, Lancaster: Martinus Nijhoff, 1985.

Moi, Toril. "Ambiguity and Alienation in *The Second Sex.*" In *Feminism and Postmodernism,* edited by Margaret Ferguson and Jennifer Wicke, pp. 86–102. Durham, N.C., and London: Duke University Press, 1994.

Murphy, Julien S. "The Look in Sartre and Rich." In *The Thinking Muse: Feminism and Modern French Philosophy,* edited by Jeffner Allen and Iris Marion Young, pp. 101–12. Bloomington and Indianapolis: Indiana University Press, 1989.

Nagel, Thomas. "Equal Treatment and Compensatory Discrimination." In *Equality and Preferential Treatment: A Philosophy & Public Affairs Reader,* edited by Marshall Cohen, Thomas Nagel, and Thomas Scanlon, pp. 3–18. Princeton, N.J.: Princeton University Press, 1977.

Natanson, Maurice. *A Critique of Jean-Paul Sartre's Ontology.* Lincoln: University of Nebraska Press, 1951.

————. "Descriptive Phenomenology." In *Essays in Memory of Aron Gurwitsch,* edited by Lester Embree. Washington, D.C.: Center for Advanced Research in Phenomenology and University Press of America, 1984.

————. *The Journeying Self: A Study in Philosophy and Social Role.* Reading, Mass.: Addison-Wesley, 1970.

————. "The Problem of Others in *Being and Nothingness.*" In *The Philosophy of Jean-Paul Sartre,* vol. 16 of *The Library of Living Philosophers,* edited by Paul Arthur Schilpp, pp. 326–44. Lasalle, Ill.: Open Court, 1981.

Nieli, Russell. "Ethnic Tribalism and Human Personhood." In *Racial Preference and Racial Justice: The New Affirmative Action Controversy,* edited by Russell Nieli, pp. 61–103. Washington, D.C.: Ethics and Public Policy Center, 1991.

————, ed. *Racial Preference and Racial Justice: The New Affirmative Action Controversy.* Washington, D.C.: Ethics and Public Policy Center, 1991.

Nietzsche, Friedrich. *On the Genealogy of Morals and Ecce Homo.* Translated by Walter Kaufmann. New York: Random House, 1967.

Nisbet, Lee. "Affirmative Action: A Liberal Program?" In *Racial Preference and Racial Justice: The New Affirmative Action Controversy,* edited by Russell Nieli, pp. 111–16. Washington, D.C.: Ethics and Public Policy Center, 1991.

O'Connor, Sandra Day. "Set-Asides Violate the Equal Protection Clause." In *Racial Preference and Racial Justice: The New Affirmative Action Controversy,* edited by Russell Nieli, pp. 237–44. Washington, D.C.: Ethics and Public Policy Center, 1991.

Olafson, Frederick. "Freedom and Choice." In *Phenomenology and Existentialism,* edited by Robert C. Solomon, pp. 474–86. Boston, and London: University Press of America, Inc., 1980.

Outlaw, Lucius. *On Race and Philosophy*. New York and London: Routledge, 1996.

Pellauer, David. "Translator's Introduction." *Notebooks for an Ethics*, pp. vii–xxi. Translated by David Pellauer. Chicago and London: University of Chicago Press, 1992.

Pilardi, Jo-Ann. "The Changing Critical Fortunes of *The Second Sex*." In History and *Theory, Studies in the Philosophy of History* 32 (1993): 51–73.

———. "Philosophy Becomes Autobiography: The Development of the Self in the Writings of Simone de Beauvoir." In *Writing the Politics of Difference*, edited by Hugh J. Silverman, pp. 145–62. Albany: State University of New York Press, 1991.

Rosenfeld, Michel. *Affirmative Action and Justice: A Philosophical and Constitutional Inquiry*. New Haven and London: Yale University Press, 1991.

Rois, Alois. *Edmund Husserls ethische Untersuchungen*. The Hague: Martinus Nijhoff, 1960.

Sartre, Jean Paul. *Anti-Semite and Jew*. Translated by George J. Becker. New York: Schocken Books, 1976.

———. *Baudelaire*. Translated by Martin Turnell. New York: New Directions, 1950.

———. *Being and Nothingness: An Essay on Phenomenological Ontology*. Translated by Hazel Barnes. New York: Washington Square Press, 1953.

———. *Between Existentialism and Marxism*. Translated by John Mathews. New York: Pantheon Books, 1974.

———. *Black Orpheus*. Translated by S. W. Allen. Paris: Presence Africaine, 1963.

———. *Critique of Dialectical Reason*, vol. 1: *Theory of Practical Ensembles*. Translated by Alan Sheridan-Smith. London: NLB, 1976.

———. *The Communists and Peace, with a Reply to Claude Lefort*. Translated by Martha H. Fletcher with the assistance of John R. Kleinschmidt. New York: George Braziller, 1968.

———. *The Emotions: Outline of a Theory*. Translated by Bernard Frechtman. New York: Philosophical Library, 1948.

———. *Essays in Existentialism*. Edited by Wade Baskin. New York: The Citadel Press, 1965.

———. *The Family Idiot: Gustave Flaubert, 1821–1857*. Translated by Carol Cosman. 5 vols. Chicago and London: University of Chicago Press, 1981–1993.

———. *The Freud Scenario*. Edited by J. B. Pontalis. Translated by Quintin Hoare. Chicago: University of Chicago Press, 1985.

———. *Imagination: A Psychological Critique*. Translated by Forrest Williams. Ann Arbor: University of Michigan Press, 1962.

———. "An Interview with Jean-Paul Sartre." In *The Philosophy of Jean-Paul Sartre*, vol. 16 of *The Library of Living Philosophers*, edited by Paul Arthur Schilpp, pp. 50–51. Lasalle, Ill.: Open Court, 1981.

———. *No Exit and Three Other Plays*. New York: Vintage, 1955.

———. *Notebooks for an Ethics*. Translated by David Pellauer. Chicago and London: University of Chicago Press, 1992. English translation of *Cahiers pour une morale*. Paris: Gallimard, 1983.

———. *Plaidoyer pour les intellectuels*. Paris: Editions Gallimard, 1972.

———. "A Plea for Intellectuals." In *Between Existentialism and Marxism*, translated by John Mathews, pp. 228–85. New York: Pantheon Books, 1974.

———. "Portrait du Colonisé." In *Situations*, vol. 5: *Colonialisme et neocolonialisme*, pp. 49–56. Paris: Gallimard, 1964.

———. *The Psychology of Imagination*. Translated by Bernard Frechtman. New York: Philosophical Library, 1948.

———. *The Respectful Prostitute*. In *No Exit and Three Other Plays*, pp. 249–81. New York: Vintage, 1955.

———. *Saint Genet: Actor and Martyr*. Translated by Bernard Frechtman. New York: George Braziller, 1963.

———. *Search for a Method*. Translated by Hazel E. Barnes. New York: Alfred A. Knopf, 1963.

———. *Situations*, vol. 5: *Colonialisme et Neocolonialisme*. Paris: Gallimard, 1964.

———. *The Transcendence of the Ego: An Existentialist Theory of Consciousness*. Translated by Forrest Williams and Robert Kirkpatrick. New York: The Noonday Press, 1957.

———. *Truth and Existence*. Translated by Adrian van den Hoven. Chicago and London: University of Chicago Press, 1992.

Sartre, Jean-Paul, Ph. Gavi, and P. Victor. *On a raison de se revolter: Discussions*. Paris: Gallimard, 1974.

Sartre, Jean-Paul, and Benny Levy. *L'Espoir Maintenant: Les Entretiens de 1980*. Lagrasse, France: Verdier, 1991.

Scalia, Antonin. "The Disease as Cure." In *Racial Preference and Racial Justice: The New Affirmative Action Controversy*, edited by Russell Nieli, pp. 209–21. Washington, D.C.: Ethics and Public Policy Center, 1991.

Scheler, Max. *Formalism in Ethics and Non-Formal Ethics of Value: A New Attempt toward the Foundation of an Ethical Personalism*. Translated by Manfred S. Frings and Roger L. Funk. Evanston, Ill.: Northwestern University Press, 1973.

———. "Phenomenology and the Theory of Cognition." In *Selected Philosophical Essays*, translated by David R. Lachertman, pp. 136–201. Evanston, Ill.: Northwestern University Press, 1973.

Schilpp, Paul Arthur, ed. *The Philosophy of Jean-Paul Sartre*. Vol. 16 of *The Library of Living Philosophers*. Lasalle, Ill.: Open Court, 1981.

Schnädelbach, Herbert. "Transformation der kritischen Theorie." In *Kommunikatives Handeln: Beiträge zu Jürgen Habermas' "Theorie des kommunikativen Handelns,"* edited by Axel Honneth and Hans Joas, pp. 15–34. Frankfurt am Main: Suhrkamp Verlag, 1986.

Schutte, Ofelia. "Origins and Tendencies of the Philosophy of Liberation in

Latin American Thought: A Critique of Dussel's Ethics." *Philosophical Forum* 22 (1991): 270–95.

Schutz, Alfred. "Concept and Theory Formation in the Social Sciences." In *The Problem of Social Reality*, vol. 1 of *Collected Papers*, edited by Maurice Natanson, pp. 48–66. The Hague, Boston, London: Martinus Nijhoff, 1962.

———. "Equality and the Meaning Structure of the Social World." In *Studies in Social Theory*, vol. 2 of *Collected Papers*, edited by Arvid Brodersen, pp. 226–73. The Hague: Martinus Nijhoff, 1964.

———. "Making Music Together, A Study in Social Relationship." In *Studies in Social Theory*, vol. 2 of *Collected Papers*, edited by Arvid Brodersen, pp. 159–78. The Hague: Martinus Nijhoff, 1964.

———. "On Multiple Realities." In *The Problem of Social Reality*, vol. 1 of *Collected Papers*, edited by Maurice Natanson, pp. 207–59. The Hague, Boston, London: Martinus Nijhoff, 1962.

———. "Phenomenology and the Social Sciences." In *The Problem of Social Reality*, vol. 1 of *Collected Papers*, edited by Maurice Natanson, pp. 118–39. The Hague, Boston, London: Martinus Nijhoff, 1962.

———. *The Phenomenology of the Social World*. Translated by George Walsh and Frederick Lehnert. Evanston, Ill.: Northwestern University Press, 1967.

———. "The Problem of Rationality in the Social World." In *Studies in Social Theory*, vol. 2 of *Collected Papers*, edited by Arvid Brodersen, pp. 64–88. The Hague: Martinus Nijhoff, 1964.

———. *The Problem of Social Reality*, vol. 1 of *Collected Papers*. Edited by Maurice Natanson. The Hague, Boston, London: Martinus Nijhoff, 1962.

———. "The Problem of Transcendental Intersubjectivity in Husserl." In *Studies in Phenomenological Philosophy*, vol. 3 of *Collected Papers*, edited by Ilse Schutz, pp. 51–91. The Hague: Martinus Nijhoff, 1966.

———. Review of *Formal and transzendentale Logik*. *Deutsche Literaturzeitung* 54 (1933): 773–84.

———. "Sartre's Theory of the Alter Ego." In *The Problem of Social Reality*, vol. 1 of *Collected Papers*, edited by Maurice Natanson, pp. 180–203. The Hague, Boston, London: Martinus Nijhoff, 1962.

———. "Some Leading Concepts of Phenomenology." In *The Problem of Social Reality*, vol. 1 of *Collected Papers*, edited by Maurice Natanson, pp. 99–117. The Hague, Boston, London: Martinus Nijhoff, 1962.

———. "The Stranger, An Essay in Social Psychology." In *Studies in Social Theory*, vol. 2 of *Collected Papers*, edited by Arvid Brodersen, pp. 91–105. The Hague: Martinus Nijhoff, 1964.

———. *Studies in Phenomenological Philosophy*. Vol. 3 of *Collected Papers*. Edited by Ilse Schutz. The Hague: Martinus Nijhoff, 1966.

———. *Studies in Social Theory*. Vol. 2 of *Collected Papers*. Edited by Arvid Brodersen. The Hague: Martinus Nijhoff, 1964.

———. "Type and Eidos in Husserl's Late Philosophy." In *Studies in Phenom-

enological Philosophy, vol. 3 of *Collected Papers*, edited by Ilse Schutz, pp. 92–115. The Hague: Martinus Nijhoff, 1966.

Sher, George. "Justifying Reverse Discrimination in Employment." In *Equality and Preferential Treatment: A Philosophy & Public Affairs Reader*, edited by Marshall Cohen, Thomas Nagel, and Thomas Scanlon, pp. 49–60. Princeton, N.J.: Princeton University Press, 1977.

Shulman, Steven, and William Darity, Jr., eds. *The Question of Discrimination: Racial Inequality in the U.S. Labor Market*. Middletown, Conn.: Wesleyan University Press, 1989.

Silverman, Hugh J., ed. *Writing the Politics of Difference*. Albany: State University of New York Press, 1991.

Simon, Robert. "Preferential Hiring: A Reply to Judith Jarvis Thomson." In *Equality and Preferential Treatment: A Philosophy & Public Affairs Reader*, edited by Marshall Cohen, Thomas Nagel, and Thomas Scanlon, pp. 40–48. Princeton, N.J.: Princeton University Press, 1977.

Simons, Margaret A. "An Appeal to Reopen the Question of Influence." In *Conflicts and Convergences*, vol. 16 of *Selected Studies in Phenomenology and Existential Philosophy*, edited by Linda Martin Alcoff and Merold Westphal, pp. 17–24. Chicago: DePaul University, 1999.

———. "Beauvoir and Sartre: The Philosophical Relationship." In *Yale French Studies*, no. 72; pp. 00–00. New Haven, Conn.: Yale University Press, 1986, *Simone de Beauvoir: Witness to a Century*, edited by Helene V. Wenzel, pp. 165–79. New Haven, Conn.: Yale University Press, 1986.

———. *Beauvoir and The Second Sex: Feminism, Race, and the Origins of Existentialism*. Lanham, Md., Boulder, New York, Oxford: Rowman & Littlefield, 1999.

———. "*The Second Sex*: From Marxism to Radical Feminism." In *Feminist Interpretations of Simone de Beauvoir*, edited by Margaret A. Simons, pp. 243–62. University Park: Pennsylvania State University Press, 1995.

_____, ed. *Feminist Interpretations of Simone de Beauvoir*. University Park: Pennsylvania State University Press, 1995.

Smith, James P., and Finis R. Welch. "Closing the Gap: Forty Years of Economic Progress for Blacks." In *Racial Preference and Racial Justice: The New Affirmative Action Controversy*, edited by Russell Nieli, pp. 499–510. Washington, D.C.: Ethics and Public Policy Center, 1991.

Solomon, Robert C., ed. *Phenomenology and Existentialism*. Boston and London: University Press of America, Inc., 1980.

Sowell, Thomas. "Are Quotas Good for Blacks?" In *Racial Preference and Racial Justice: The New Affirmative Action Controversy*, edited by Russell Nieli, pp. 415–28. Washington, D.C.: Ethics and Public Policy Center, 1991.

———. *Ethnic America, A History*. New York: Basic Books, 1981.

———. *Civil Rights, Rhetoric or Reality?* New York: William Morrow and Company, Inc., 1984.

————. *Preferential Policies: An International Perspective*. New York: William Morrow and Company, Inc., 1990.

————. "Three Black Histories." In *Essays and Data on American Ethnic Groups*, pp. 7–64. Washington, D.C.: The Urban Institute, 1978.

————, ed. *Essays and Data on American Ethnic Groups*. Washington, D.C.: The Urban Institute, 1978.

Steele, Claude M., and Joshua Aronson. "Stereotype Threat and the Intellectual Test Performance of African Americans." *Journal of Personality and Social Psychology* 69 (1995): 797–811.

Thernstrom, Stephan, and Abigail Thernstrom. *America in Black and White: One Nation, Indivisible*. New York: Simon and Schuster, 1997.

Thomson, Judith Jarvis. "Preferential Hiring." In *Equality and Preferential Treatment: A Philosophy & Public Affairs Reader*, edited by Marshall Cohen, Thomas Nagel, and Thomas Scanlon, pp. 19–39. Princeton, N.J.: Princeton University Press, 1977.

Vintges, Karen. "*The Second Sex* and Philosophy." In *Feminist Interpretations of Simone de Beauvoir*, edited by Margaret A. Simons, pp. 45–58. University Park: Pennsylvania State University Press, 1995.

Ward, Julie. "Beauvoir's Two Senses of 'Body' in *The Second Sex*." In *Feminist Interpretations of Simone de Beauvoir*, edited by Margaret A. Simons, pp. 223–42. University Park: University of Pennsylvania Press, 1995.

Wenzel, Helene, ed. *Yale French Studies*, no. 72: *Simone de Beauvoir: Witness to a Century*. New Haven: Yale University Press, 1986.

West, Cornel. *Race Matters*. New York: Vintage Books, 1994.

West's Encyclopedia of American Law. St. Paul, Minn.: West Group, 1998.

West's Supreme Court Recorder. Vols. 1–112A. St. Paul, Minn.: West Publishing Company: 1882–1991.

Wiggins, Osbourne P., and Michael Alan Schwartz. "Psychiatric Diagnosis and the Phenomenology of Typification." In *Worldly Phenomenology: The Continuing Influence of Alfred Schutz on North American Human Science*, edited by Lester Embree, pp. 203–30. Washington, D.C.: Center for Advanced Research in Phenomenolgy and the University Press of America, 1988.

Work, John. *Race, Economics, and Corporate America*. Wilmington, Del.: Scholarly Resources, Inc., 1984.

INDEX